QMW Library
23 0903210 X

ESSAYS IN BRITISH HISTORY

Lafayette

KEITH GRAHAME FEILING

ESSAYS IN BRITISH HISTORY

Presented to Sir Keith Feiling

EDITED BY

H. R. TREVOR-ROPER

WITH A FOREWORD BY

LORD DAVID CECIL

LONDON

MACMILLAN & CO LTD

NEW YORK · ST MARTIN'S PRESS

1964

MACMILLAN AND COMPANY LIMITED
St Martin's Street London WC 2
also Bombay Calcutta Madras Melbourne

THE MACMILLAN COMPANY OF CANADA LIMITED
70 Bond Street Toronto 2

ST MARTIN'S PRESS INC
175 Fifth Avenue New York 10 NY

PRINTED IN GREAT BRITAIN

FOREWORD

I WRITE this foreword because I am not qualified to contribute to this book in any other way. It is a volume of pieces offered to Sir Keith Feiling on his eightieth birthday by some of his colleagues and former pupils. Since both he and they are historians, these take the form of essays on history. I am not an historian, so that I am unable to contribute such an essay. All I can do is to introduce others.

However, I am very glad to do this, because it gives me a chance to express my admiration and gratitude to Keith. For though I am not now an historian, I was once his pupil ; and I owe more to him than to any other teacher I ever had. His mind and spirit were such as to enable him to interest and inspire pupils of very different kinds, including many who could never become successful professional historians. I was one of these. Such higher education as I ever acquired came mainly from him. For me he was the ideal tutor.

His mode of teaching was individual. The pupil would 'discover' him sitting in a big chair at a table in his room in Tom Quad of Christ Church, and looking, with his delicate features, domed forehead, and shy, sensitive glance, very like one of those Caroline worthies about whom he knew so much. His manner with his pupils was unlike that of the conventional effective tutor. He was not voluble or authoritative, he did not impose himself. Diffidently he would ask the pupil to read his essay. After it was finished, he ventured a few comments. Though apparently tentative, these did in fact clearly indicate any fault or omission in the essay. They would also open the subject, revealing it in a wider perspective than the essay had disclosed. Now it was the pupil's turn to take the initiative and to ask questions. Keith's answers were seldom very long. But they completed the process that his first comments had started. Furthermore, they made the subject spring to life. For he knew it so intimately and apprehended it with so strong an historical imagination that he was able to act as a sort of time-machine in reverse, carrying the pupil back into the living past. Dead controversies became live controversies. I remember how, after an essay I had written about the Elizabethan Church Settlement, he was able to make me suddenly realize why Englishmen in the sixteenth century felt so intensely about the disputes over ecclesiastical vestments. He did this partly by his gift for apt quotation. He would pull down a book from his shelves and read some extract from letter or speech peculiarly empowered to illuminate the subject at issue and make it seem contemporary. He was assisted in his task by another gift, his faculty for realizing the characters of the past. Real to him, they became real to the pupil. Sometimes they became real in an unexpected fashion. Keith's reactions to the mighty dead were too intimate and immediate to be orthodox. I, like most young men of my age, had been taught my idea of them by those Whig historians who dominated the subject in the nineteenth century. I took for granted, for instance, that the leaders of the parliamentary party in the Civil War period were noble and disinterested figures, even if personally they struck me as unattractive. It was refreshing to hear my tutor remark with a delicate contemptuous hesitation, 'I don't care much for Pym and Hampden, do you? Surely they are typical examples of the sharp politician type.'

The tutorial seldom extended to the full hour. But it always made its mark. I came away from it dizzy from my journey in the time-machine and with the influence of all that I had seen thence still working in my mind. Tom Quad was astir with spectral figures from the seventeenth century — or the sixteenth or the twelfth or from any other period which had come under discussion. My hour with my tutor had been an exhilarating experience; and an improving one as well. For I never went back to my room without regretting that I did not do more work since the subject was so absorbing.

I had also learnt how much work I should have to do to reach the standard embodied for me by my tutor. Keith's tutorials were a discipline as well as a stimulus. By his comments on my essay, by his quotations, by the casual asides of his talk, he revealed the extent of his knowledge and his high standard of accuracy. I never had much hope that I would be able to emulate his achievement in these respects. I was in fact often healthily disheartened. But I did come to realize what true learning meant. I have not lost this realization.

I also discovered that learning must be disinterested. History was presented to me as something to be studied for its own sake, never as a means of distinguishing oneself in examination. The last temptation to be overcome by a college tutor is the temptation to care too much about his pupil's place in the class list, and to encourage the pupil to do the same. Keith wholly resisted this temptation. Indeed, I doubt if he was susceptible to it. For so pure and strong was his interest in his subject that it would not have occurred to him to think of it as a means to an end. Certainly I never remember what is called 'examination technique' appearing in our discussions. I do not recall enquiring from him what questions I was likely to be asked. Our interviews were not conducted on a level where such issues were relevant.

As a matter of fact I did, as a result, do better in the examination. Keith had stimulated my individual sense of history so successfully that I was able — so I gathered afterwards from one of my examiners — to communicate this in my papers. If I had thought less about the subject and more about means to success, this could not have happened. The Oxford examination system is sometimes criticized, but it must be said in its favour that it does seek to discriminate between those who have a real interest in their subject and those who are only concerned to get a good degree ; and it distributes its awards accordingly.

Keith was the better able to teach because his interests were so varied. I associate him primarily with the sixteenth and seventeenth centuries because at that time these periods interested me the most. But looking back I remember that he was equally illuminating about Medieval England and Renaissance Italy. In his published works a similar light is shed on the nineteenth and even the twentieth centuries. Indeed, his writings cover an extraordinary range. He has written massively on the origins of the Tory Party, on Warren Hastings, on Neville Chamberlain; he is the author of one of the most compreheusive single-volume histories of England: the list of his reviews and contributions to learned journals shows his knowledge and understanding of a wide variety of periods and persons. But it is not for me to try to estimate his work as a scholar. I must leave this to better qualified judges. Myself I can speak only as a general reader, profoundly impressed by the breadth of the author's learning, by his imaginative capacity intimately to realize the past.

These impressions mean all the more to me personally because they recall those hours — fascinating, disheartening, inspiring hours — spent many years ago in his room in Tom Quad.

DAVID CECIL

CONTENTS

PAGE

FOREWORD — v
By Lord David Cecil, Goldsmith Professor of English Literature in the University of Oxford

1. WANSDYKE AND THE ORIGIN OF WESSEX — 1
By J. N. L. Myres, Bodley's Librarian, Oxford

2. BEFORE WOLSEY — 29
By W. A. Pantin, Fellow of Oriel College, Oxford and Keeper of the University Archives

3. THOMAS BROUNS, BISHOP OF NORWICH 1436–45 — 61
By E. F. Jacob, formerly Chichele Professor of Modern History in the University of Oxford

4. THE FAST SERMONS OF THE LONG PARLIAMENT — 85
By H. R. Trevor-Roper, Regius Professor of Modern History in the University of Oxford

5. ARTHUR ONSLOW AND PARTY POLITICS — 139
By J. Steven Watson, Student of Christ Church, Oxford

6. THE IMPERIAL MACHINERY OF THE YOUNGER PITT — 173
By A. F. McC. Madden, Reader in Commonwealth Government in the University of Oxford

7. LORD BROUGHAM AND THE CONSERVATIVES — 195
By E. G. Collieu, Fellow of Brasenose College, Oxford

8. THE RISE OF DISRAELI — 219
By Robert Blake, Student of Christ Church, Oxford

9. THE PRINCE CONSORT AND MINISTERIAL POLITICS 1856–9 — 247
By C. H. Stuart, Student of Christ Church, Oxford

10. THE WHITE MUTINY — 271
By Michael Maclagan, Fellow of Trinity College, Oxford

11. A BIBLIOGRAPHY OF THE WRITINGS OF Sir Keith FEILING — 303

ILLUSTRATIONS

Keith Grahame Feiling *Frontispiece*

PAGE

General map of Wansdyke 3
The Woden Place-names 10
The Medieval Site of Christ Church, Oxford 28

I

J. N. L. Myres

WANSDYKE AND THE ORIGIN OF WESSEX

WHEN the first volume of the Oxford History of England appeared in 1936[1] both its authors, the late Professor R. G. Collingwood and I, adopted in our respective sections an identical attitude to Wansdyke. We took the same view of the extent, the date, and the purpose of what one of us called 'the most impressive and mysterious of all the monuments of this age'.[2] We described it as 'a huge earthwork',[3] 'a substantial and enigmatic frontier',[4] running 'from the Kennet valley south of Hungerford to the neighbourhood of the Bristol Channel'.[5] We believed that it was 'late Roman or post-Roman in date',[6] and one of us asserted roundly that it 'can be nothing but the work of some British chief organizing the defence of the southwest against invaders, probably West Saxons'.[6]

No serious challenge was made at the time to this diagnosis, which may indeed in broad outline still prove to be as near the truth as it is now possible to go. But between 1955 and 1957 Wansdyke was subjected to a detailed field-study by the penetrating and expert eyes of Sir Cyril and Lady Fox, and about the same time Mr. Anthony Clark carried out some excavations on a crucial section of its presumed course. The

[1] R. G. Collingwood and J. N. L. Myres, *Roman Britain and the English Settlements*. The second edition (1937) is hereafter referred to as C. and M.

[2] C. and M. p. 402. [3] *Ibid*. p. 319. [4] *Ibid*. p. 403. [5] *Ibid*. p. 402.

[6] *Ibid*. pp. 319–20.

publication of their results,[1] which constitute the first major contribution to the understanding of Wansdyke since General Pitt Rivers in 1889–90 proved its date to be no earlier than the late Roman period,[2] makes a reassessment of the extent, date, and purpose of Wansdyke necessary, for new and significant facts have been brought to light. It is the object of this article to consider the new facts and some conclusions that have already been drawn from them, and to examine their meaning for the early history of Wessex. To include such a study in a volume intended as a tribute to Sir Keith Feiling may not be inappropriate: perhaps it may revive for him memories of a splendid stretch of the English country-side, with which he first became familiar when a schoolboy at Marlborough some sixty-five years ago.

The most important of the new facts requiring consideration concern the extent and nature of the earthworks.[3] It has been shown that they comprise not one continuous structure, but two shorter ones that are not necessarily of the same date. East Wansdyke in Wiltshire extends for some twelve miles from Morgan's Hill near Devizes on the west to New Buildings, a little west of Savernake, on the east. West Wansdyke in Somerset extends seven and a half miles from Maes Knoll on the west to the head of the Horsecombe valley which runs into the Avon south-east of Bath. Between the two systems there is a gap, seventeen miles long, where the bank of the Roman road from Mildenhall (*Cunetio*)

[1] Aileen and Cyril Fox, 'Wansdyke reconsidered', *Archaeological Journal*, CXV (1958), 1-48, hereafter referred to as Fox; Anthony Clark, 'The Nature of Wansdyke', *Antiquity*, XXXII. (1958), 89-96, hereafter referred to as Clark. I have made free use not only of the facts but of the ideas in these stimulating papers, although I have not always followed their conclusions. I am also greatly indebted to Professor C. F. C. Hawkes, who has discussed these matters with me in connection with his work on the pagan Saxon period in Wiltshire undertaken for the Victoria County History.

[2] A. Pitt Rivers, *Excavations in Bokerley Dyke and Wansdyke* (1892).

[3] Fox, Fig. 1, here reprinted by permission, shows the general extent of Wansdyke, as indicated by his survey, in relation to the surface geology.

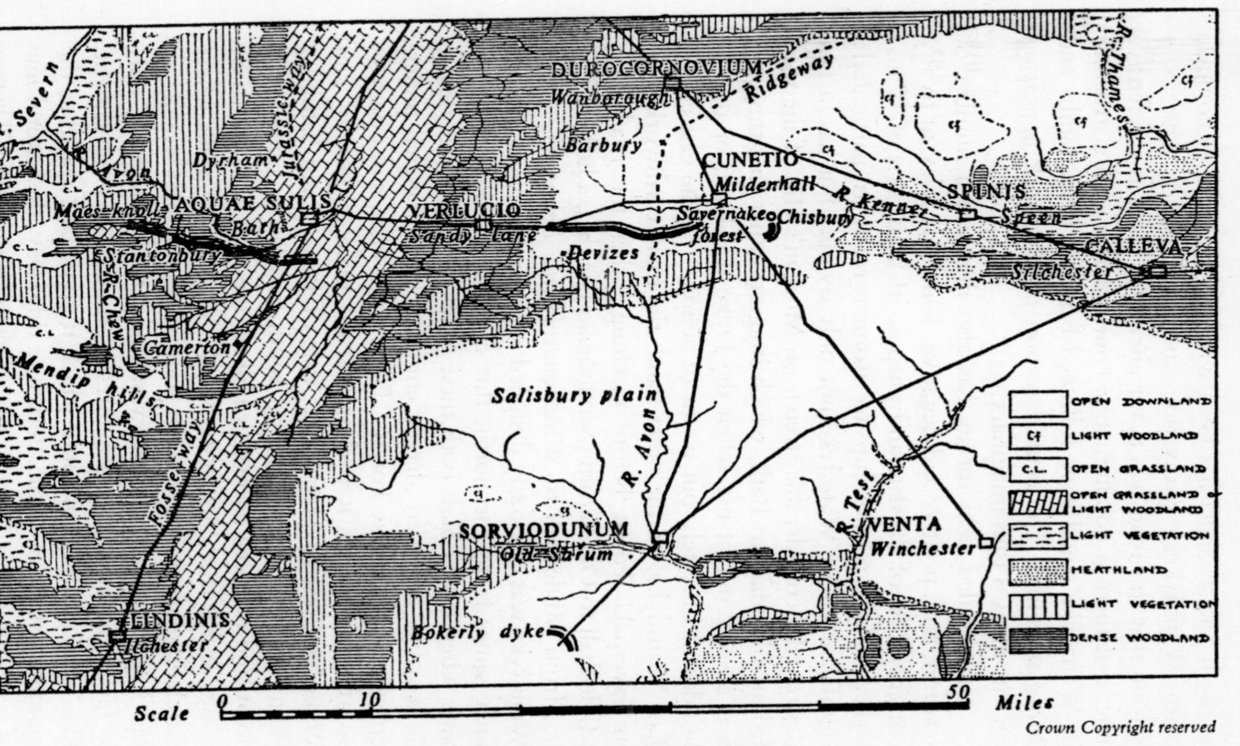

General Map of Wansdyke

to Bath (*Aquæ Sulis*) has been wrongly supposed to coincide with Wansdyke. Excavation and field survey have both shown that this road was never altered to serve as a defensive line, and there is no alternative course which such a structure as Wansdyke could have followed between Horsecombe and Morgan's Hill. The central section of the work appearing on our maps is thus imaginary.

The detailed field survey has also disclosed a number of features, both positive and negative, which are relevant to any consideration of the date and purpose of both parts of Wansdyke. Their relationship to Roman roads is particularly significant. East Wansdyke not only overlies but has in fact destroyed a considerable stretch on Morgan's Hill of the road from Mildenhall to Bath, which suggests either that this road was already out of use when the Dyke was built, or that its builders deliberately put it out of action. At the east end of East Wansdyke, on the other hand, the main earthwork stops in Savernake Forest before reaching either the road from Mildenhall to Old Sarum (*Sorviodunum*) or that, a little farther on, from Mildenhall to Winchester (*Venta Belgarum*). Since Wansdyke was obviously designed to control movement along such routes from the north, this can only mean that at the time when it was built both these roads had already ceased to be passable, and were deeply engulfed in the tangled undergrowth of Savernake Forest. From these facts, and others to be mentioned later, it is clear that the main purpose of East Wansdyke was to protect the Vale of Pewsey and Salisbury Plain from intruders moving south across the open chalk downland between Morgan's Hill on the west and Savernake Forest on the east : its western end is close to the point where the chalk gives way to heavier soils bearing natural woodland, and it penetrates the north-western parts of Savernake only so far as the partially open forest permitted easy movement. The main north-south route which it controlled was thus the southern extension of the Berkshire ridgeway, the natural line of communication in early times between the upper Thames valley and Salisbury Plain. For almost all its course East Wansdyke is so sited as to command extensive views of the country to the north, and it is plain that whoever built it not only anticipated a major threat from that quarter, but enjoyed complete freedom to site his defences on the line best calculated to eliminate the possibility of surprise.

West Wansdyke is similarly related to a major traffic route of early times, the so-called Jurassic Way, which follows the oolite ridge from Gloucestershire into Somerset, and here, immediately south of Bath, is represented also by the Roman road to the south-west known as the Fosse Way. It blocks, or at least controls, this route at Odd Down,[1] now a southern suburb of Bath, and, while it extends only a short distance from this point to the head of the Horsecombe valley on the east, it runs westwards, if intermittently, some seven miles past Stantonbury hill fort to end at another prehistoric earthwork on Maes Knoll. There is no sign that it ever extended farther along the open upland of Dundry Hill towards the Bristol Channel, a fact which clearly indicates that the lower part of the Avon valley was held to present in itself a sufficient obstacle, whether in the form of the Clifton gorge or of the wide tidal marshes between the gorge and Avonmouth, to penetration from the north-east along the coast into Somerset.

The country through which West Wansdyke runs between Maes Knoll and the Fosse Way at Odd Down is wholly unlike the open chalk downland traversed by East Wansdyke, and the difference goes far, though not the whole way, to explain its difference of behaviour. It is for the most part broken country naturally carrying heavy woodland and divided by deep combes, abrupt ridges, and other obstacles to movement in primitive conditions. The gaps in the earthwork, notably the long one at Publow Hill, evidently reflect the persistence of stretches of more or less impenetrable undergrowth through

[1] The Fosse Way at this point is a busy modern thoroughfare, much wider than the original Roman road, so that it is impossible to check its exact relationship to West Wansdyke at the intersection.

which it was not necessary, or perhaps even possible, to carry a continuous barrier of this kind. The fact that the western part of West Wansdyke was built at all shows, first, that this difficult country had for much of the distance been cleared sufficiently to permit some movement through it, and secondly, that a real danger of penetration existed from the country along the Avon valley in the neighbourhood of Bath and for some miles downstream from there. For there is one real difference between the layout of West Wansdyke and that of East Wansdyke which cannot wholly be explained by the difference of terrain. Whoever planned the course of West Wansdyke had no control over Bath and the Avon valley from which the earthwork lies just so far removed as to be forced on to unfavourable positions for commanding either visually or tactically the country beyond its line. No one enjoying political freedom of manœuvre would have chosen to place his frontier voluntarily in this position.

Impressed by these and other considerations which arose from their survey Sir Cyril and Lady Fox put forward suggestions for the origin of both sections of Wansdyke which are wholly different from the doctrine enshrined in the Oxford History of England. Pointing on the one hand to the slighting and ignoring of Roman roads by East Wansdyke, and on the other to the evidence for the extent of forest clearance in the neighbourhood of West Wansdyke, they concluded that both works were more likely to belong to the Saxon than the Sub-Roman age : while the difference in the behaviour of the two systems in relation to forested country and the command of forward areas, coupled with the absence of any physical link between them, led them to propose two different dates and two different sets of historical circumstances for their construction. They suggested in fact that East Wansdyke was most likely the work of Ceawlin of Wessex between 584 and 592, while West Wansdyke could have been related to the settlement between Cynegils of Wessex and Penda of Mercia in 628.

Before we consider further the arguments for and against this twofold historical diagnosis there are a few comments of a general nature to be made on the facts disclosed by the field survey and the excavations. In the first place, as any map will show, East and West Wansdyke follow a general alignment which makes it very natural to consider them part of a single design, even if there is a substantial gap between them. Moreover, it is common ground that the purpose of the two systems is the same, the control of anticipated attempts at penetration into Somerset and south Wiltshire from the north along the natural routes which in any conditions invaders intent on such penetration must follow. East Wansdyke is thus focussed on the control of the Berkshire ridgeway and the open downland on each side of it, while West Wansdyke is focussed on control of the Jurassic ridge and the Fosse Way that ran along it, covering at the same time any attempt to outflank the position on the west.

Now one of the most important facts which Sir Cyril Fox has revealed in his earlier studies of great dyke systems of post-Roman date — the Cambridgeshire dykes, and, in particular, Offa's dyke — is that these great frontiers are often disconcertingly discontinuous. Stretches of massive earthwork alternate with stretches in which nothing of the kind is to be found, or with stretches in which the lines of rivers or other natural obstacles have been followed in linking one piece of earthwork with another. Fox has shown that these apparent irregularities must be understood in the light of the natural conditions prevalent when the frontier was planned, and the purposes it was intended to serve. Where the object was the control of traffic across the line or even the visible demarcation of territory between two rival powers, it was pointless, and often even impossible, to carry the line through dense forest where no traffic ran and where a physical barrier could not in any case be seen.

In his discussion of Wansdyke, Fox does not seem seriously to have applied these doctrines to the gap between East and

West Wansdyke. As can be seen from his map, a substantial part of it on both sides of the little Roman town of *Verlucio*, which, as the name Sandy Lane indicates, is itself on light land, consists of heavy clay soils carrying dense woodland, and even at *Verlucio* there is no north-south traffic route either prehistoric or Roman along which intruders might be expected to infiltrate. The rest of the distance is made up of the eastern slopes of the oolite ridge, and through this passes the river Avon which on its way to Bath receives the tributary valley at the head of which West Wansdyke begins. There is a *prima facie* case therefore for supposing that the line was intended to be continuous with the Avon valley, and it has been urged that the big southward loop of the Avon east of Horsecombe might itself have served the purpose of a visible frontier covering almost half the gap between the man-made earthworks of East and West Wansdyke.[1] Farther east this same visible purpose could still be served by the line of the Roman road between the Avon crossing and Morgan's Hill, even though excavation has now shown that its bank was never modified to form a defensive line and that nothing corresponding to the great ditch of Wansdyke was ever dug. In these wooded areas a defence on the scale of Wansdyke may not have been thought necessary, or its construction in this comparatively unfrequented stretch may have been left for completion at a later opportunity, which never came.

These possibilities all suggest that it may be premature to dismiss the traditional view that both parts of Wansdyke from Savernake to Maes Knoll were conceived as a single defensive frontier in the face of a single military danger, even if it may not have been fully executed throughout its length. It is indeed possible to invoke the doctrine of 'deliberate discontinuity' to prolong the eastern termination of East Wansdyke beyond the limits of Savernake Forest. Various attempts, all rejected by Fox, have been made to see continuations of Wansdyke in several groups of less massive

[1] Clark, Fig. 1A, illustrates this point more clearly than Fox.

earthworks in this area. The most substantial of these is the dyke running south from Chisbury Camp across the valley east of Great Bedwyn, and, once the idea is accepted that Wansdyke can be discontinuous in deep woodland, there seems no reason why this should not be associated with it.[1] Perhaps it was an attempt, contemporary or subsequent, to provide against intruders outflanking the main structure by penetrating Savernake Forest from the east.

There is one further piece of evidence which is relevant to the question whether Wansdyke should be considered as a single whole or as two separate works. That is the evidence of its name. Both parts were known as *Wodnesdic* in the late Saxon period, and the name, though apparently given to no other earthworks in Britain, is of a kind that is likely to go back to pagan times. Whatever the date and circumstances in which the name was first used, it constitutes at least *prima facie* evidence that the two main sections were considered to be parts of a single system at least as early as the end of the pagan period in the seventh century.

It will be necessary to consider the significance of the name Wansdyke further at a later stage in this enquiry. This is, however, the point to draw attention to a fact whose significance Fox has been the first fully to appreciate. Whereas in the neighbourhood of West Wansdyke there appear to be no other place-names compounded with the name of the god Woden, this is not the case with East Wansdyke. Here the name does not stand alone, for just around its central and strategically most important section, where it intersects the ridgeway from Berkshire to Salisbury Plain, there is a whole group of other Woden place-names.[2] At this point, three-quarters of a mile south of the dyke and conspicuously set on a steep bluff in the chalk escarpment overlooking the Vale of

[1] When Fox prepared his Fig. 1 it would seem that he accepted the Bedwyn Dyke as a detached termination of East Wansdyke, although his text (18-20) rejects the association.

[2] See Fox, Fig. 28 (reprinted by permission overleaf).

Pewsey above Alton Priors, is the neolithic long barrow now known as Adam's Grave, but called *Wodnesbeorg* in Saxon times. Battles at this point are recorded in the Anglo-Saxon Chronicle in 592 and 715 and it was evidently a position of recognized strategic significance, where rival powers centred

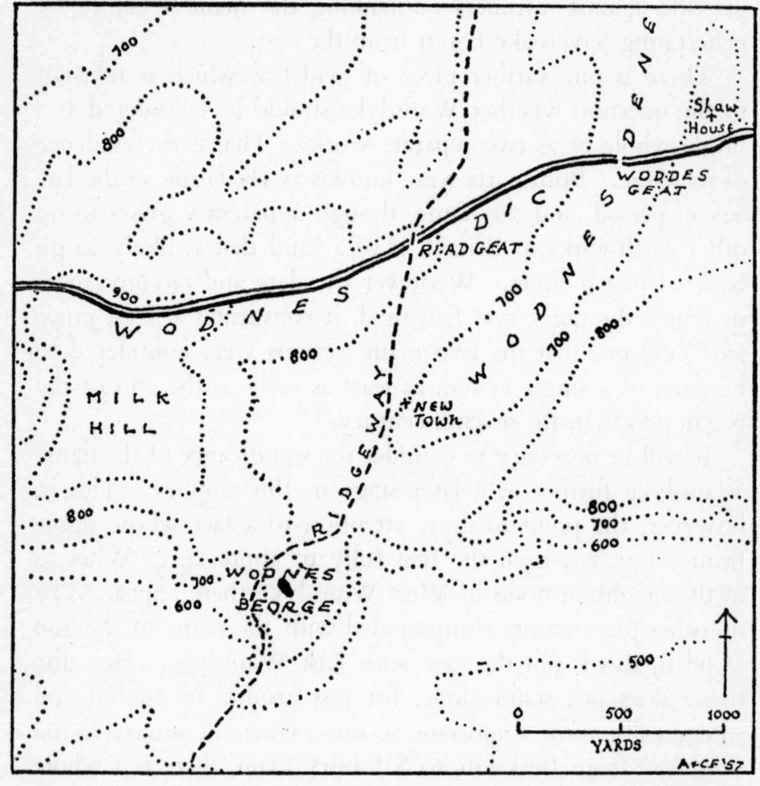

Crown Copyright reserved

The Woden place-names

north and south of the line might be expected to meet in conflict. To the north-east of *Wodnesbeorg* was *Wodnesdene*, a dry valley running from the ridgeway north to the Kennet at Lockeridge; and, somewhere in *Wodnesdene*, near the modern Shaw House, was *Wodnesgeat*, which may well have been an actual gate controlling traffic up the valley at the point where Wansdyke crosses it. There are other *geat* names on East Wansdyke which seem to indicate controlled crossings of this kind.[1] This group of Woden names must clearly be reckoned with in any attempt to explain how Wansdyke came to be so called.

But it is of course not only the name of Wansdyke but its very existence which demands explanation, and the new discoveries outlined above make it the more urgent that a satisfactory historical context should be found for its construction. For, on any interpretation, whether it is to be thought of as one work or two, and whether of fifth century or sixth/seventh century date, Wansdyke is a stupendous achievement. It must represent the answer of some dynamic ruler or rulers to political events that were felt to require action on a truly heroic scale. Moreover, the line taken by these frontier works — at least that of East Wansdyke — virtually bisects from east to west the historic heart of the kingdom of Wessex, leaving to the north the upper Thames valley, the Vale of White Horse, and the chalk uplands of Berkshire and north Wiltshire, and to the south the Vale of Pewsey, Salisbury Plain, and the rest of Hampshire, Wiltshire, and Somerset. The circumstances which gave political significance to a frontier on this line must antedate the consolidation of the historic Wessex ; they could antedate it so long as to be almost irrelevant to it, but they could also be related to some early stage in its formation.

Now it is common ground that the earliest Saxon settlement of the later Wessex did in fact take place in two separate areas, one to the north and the other to the south of the Wansdyke line. The northern settlement was that in the upper Thames valley : the evidence for it is found in riverside cemeteries, mostly on the Berkshire bank of the river but

[1] Readgeat, at the Ridgeway intersection ; Titferth's gate at Hursley Bottom ; Cryppelgeat in North Newnton. Fox, pp. 24-5.

including the little Roman walled town of Dorchester on the Oxfordshire bank, which was, two centuries later, to become the seat of St. Birinus, the first Christian bishop of the West Saxons. At Dorchester itself there is now good evidence, not only from the well-known burials,[1] but from rough buildings and occupation material inside the walls, for the presence, perhaps as early as the end of the fourth century, of Germanic *laeti*, no doubt deliberately settled by some *superbus tyrannus*, of the type described by Gildas, in an effort to maintain his authority both against raiding barbarians and against others of his kind. Pieces of characteristic early equipment not far removed in date from that accompanying the Dorchester *laeti* have been found in several neighbouring Berkshire cemeteries all the way from Frilford, through Abingdon and Long Wittenham to Wallingford. These are all sites where Germanic settlers seem directly to have succeeded to Romano-British communities, and probably before the middle of the fifth century.[2] These four cemeteries just named are also the only ones in northern Wessex to show a substantial proportion of cremations against inhumations : [3] by the time that Saxon settlement had spread farther into Oxfordshire and Gloucestershire, a development that may not have gone far before A.D. 500, this earlier Germanic rite had almost entirely passed out of fashion. Here, perhaps, this may have been partly an effect of the Christian background of the surviving native population.

Most of these cremations are, however, probably due to fresh incursions, arising from that outburst of barbarian violence which Gildas describes as accompanying the breakdown of Vortigern's policy of federate settlement *in orientali parte insulae* soon after the middle of the fifth century. It may be to the eruption of such elements south-westwards from east

[1] Joan R. Kirk and E. T. Leeds in *Oxoniensia*, XVII/XVIII (1954), 63-76.

[2] S. C. Hawkes, 'Soldiers and Settlers in Britain, fourth to fifth century', *Mediaeval Archaeology*, V (1961), 1-70, discusses some of this material.

[3] Joan R. Kirk, 'Anglo-Saxon Cremation and Inhumation in the Upper Thames Valley', *Dark Age Britain* (1956), pp. 123-31.

and middle Anglia that are due the few examples of Saxon *Buckelurnen*,[1] and also of the equal-armed brooches characteristic of the years after 450 in the lower Elbe area in north Germany. They come from Abingdon, Sutton Courtenay, Oseney, and Harwell, the last being a cremation urn that can be claimed as one of the few contributions to archaeological knowledge that are due to the study of atomic energy.[2]

This, briefly, seems to be the historical setting of the earliest Saxon communities in Wessex north of Wansdyke. The settlement in the south was different in date, origin, and character. Its early stages are hinted at in the literary tradition which has left brief entries relating to the doings of Cerdic, Cynric, and their contemporaries in the Anglo-Saxon Chronicle.[3] There is no reason to doubt the essentials of this story which deals with the activities of some invading bands in the region around the Isle of Wight, Portsmouth, and Southampton Water in the first half of the sixth century. Until recently this literary tradition has had little backing from archaeological evidence, but the discovery of a cemetery including a number of early sixth-century cremation urns at Worthy Park just north of Winchester,[4] and some isolated finds, such as the scraps of Saxon pottery above the Roman levels in the Saxon Shore fort at Portchester on Portsmouth Harbour,[5] help to give its early stages substance. There is, however, still good reason to suppose that the story was remembered rather because it preserved the traditions of the royal family than because the events or the personalities were in themselves of much political importance at the time.[6] Indeed, if any credence is to be given to the contemporary

[1] J. N. L. Myres in *Antiq. Journal*, XXXIV (1954), 201-8: XXXVII (1957), 224-5.

[2] Joan R. Kirk and K. Marshall in *Oxoniensia*, XXI (1957), 31-3.

[3] Anglo-Saxon Chronicle, *sub ann.*, 495, 501, 508, 514, 519, 527, 530, 534, 544.

[4] Information from Mrs. Sonia Hawkes.

[5] Information from Mr. J. G. Hurst.

[6] As I suggested in C. and M., p. 402.

evidence of Gildas, no Saxon advance of any memorable kind occurred in the forty years or more that followed the British success at Mount Badon towards the end of the fifth century: and this is precisely the period in which the early part of the Cerdicing story is set.

It was not, in fact, until their establishment in central Wiltshire in the middle of the sixth century, symbolized by the annal recording the victory of *Searoburh* (*Sorviodunum*) in 552, that the leaders of this war-band, though no doubt adding to their numerical following after every victory, gathered the momentum and the authority that gave them status as a political force. It can hardly be a coincidence that the one area of Wiltshire in which from about this time Saxon occupation is archaeologically well-attested is the area within a ten-mile radius of Salisbury. Here is concentrated more than half of all the evidence for pagan Saxon settlement in Wiltshire, the three largest cemeteries, the royal cenotaph on Salisbury racecourse, and the *villa regalis* of Wilton, evidently from early times the administrative centre of the whole folk, those *Wilsaetas*, who might so easily have left their name in a 'Wilset' to match the Somerset and Dorset farther west.[1] It is indeed tempting to see in the Bokerley Dyke which, after serving first as a late Roman estate boundary, and then as a temporary barrier against some late fourth-century disturbances perhaps during the *barbarica conspiratio* of 367, was finally reconstructed to block altogether the Roman road south-west from *Sorviodunum* (*Searoburh*) into Dorset, the reaction of the British *civitates* in those parts to the threat of Cerdicing invasion from the Salisbury area.[2]

If this is the political context for the last phase of Bokerley Dyke, it may be that its builders were for a while successful in diverting the Saxon advance from farther westward penetration into an onslaught northwards towards the Berkshire

[1] *Victoria County History, Wilts*, I, 1 (1957), Map IX.

[2] C. F. C. Hawkes, 'Britons, Romans and Saxons round Salisbury and in Cranborne Chase', *Arch. Journal*, CIV (1948), 27-81.

downs and the Vale of White Horse. The details of this movement, the steps by which the successors of Cerdic forced their way to the conquest of, or perhaps to absorption by, the populous communities already established for well over a century on the gravel spreads of the upper Thames, and extending thence north and west into Oxfordshire and Gloucestershire, remain obstinately obscure. The recorded incidents, beginning with a battle against Britons at *Beranbyrg* (Barbury Hill on the Ridgeway) in 556, are all associated in some way with the dramatic career of Ceawlin, the prince to whom Bede attributes the second Saxon Bretwaldaship : the successor, that is, to the ephemeral overlordship first won by Ælle of the South Saxons in the days before the Saxon disaster of Mount Badon over half a century before.

Ceawlin, who, after fighting the Britons at Barbury in 556, apparently as an ally of Cynric the Cerdicing, is recorded by the Chronicle to have begun 'to reign in Wessex in 560', is the central figure in this story for over a generation until after 'a great slaughter at *Wodnesbeorg*' in 592 he was 'driven out' and perished a year later. But by the time that tragic end had come the Wessex of history had been born : its rulers, still claiming descent from Cerdic, however tortuous the line might be and however distant and tenuous their relationships to one another, were soon to claim a more or less effective supremacy over the whole central section of southern England from Oxfordshire to the Hampshire coast and from the Sussex Weald to the Bristol Avon, even if the British communities of Dorset and the south-west were perhaps still defying conquest behind the nominal and precarious security of Bokerley Dyke. It is plain that the reign of Ceawlin saw the fusion of north and south to form one West Saxon kingdom.

Wansdyke was thus soon to lose for ever what meaning it had once had, or was intended to have, as a political frontier, and it is time to consider in more detail against this historical background the possible moments of time in which it could have made sense. From what has been said it is plain that only three possibilities need to be considered. There is the traditional view that it was a sub-Roman work, built most likely in the later part of the fifth century against the danger presented to the southern British *civitates* by the expanding Saxon communities already well-established on the upper Thames. Secondly, there is the possibility that it belongs to the brief period when the Cerdicings were consolidating their authority on Salisbury plain either before, or even perhaps after, pushing north over the Marlborough downs to Barbury in 556. And there is thirdly the possibility that it is related in some way to the later career of Ceawlin, for its presence is surely implied in the siting upon its line of the battle of Wodnesbeorg which ended that career.

It does not seem possible to exclude, as firmly as Fox now does, the traditional sub-Roman origin and fifth-century date, for, at any rate, East Wansdyke. As he himself pointed out, the technical similarity between this part of Wansdyke and Bokerley Dyke, whose final reconstruction is admittedly sub-Roman, is very close. In layout, scale, and construction the two works are so much alike that Fox, in attributing East Wansdyke to Ceawlin, is forced to suggest that he may have impressed for the purpose a sub-Roman labour force familiar with fortifications in the Bokerley tradition.[1] It is more natural to draw the obvious conclusion that the two works derive from the same need for the Britons to defend their lands against Saxon inroads, even if they are not strictly contemporary. East Wansdyke on this argument would be the earlier, as it is the more extensive, of the two, fitting readily into a situation in which the native rulers of Wiltshire, before the arrival of Cerdic on the south coast, felt in need of protection against attack from the early Saxon settlers on the upper Thames. It could even be suggested that a work of this magnitude might be the creation of Ambrosius Aureli-

[1] Fox, p. 43.

anus, of whom Gildas writes as the principal sub-Roman leader in the temporarily successful period of resistance to the Saxons which culminated at Mount Badon some time between 486 and 516. Now that it is becoming respectable once again to believe that Amesbury, near Stonehenge, contains, in its early form *Ambresbyrig*, the name of Ambrosius, and may therefore have been a centre, or even the centre, of his power, the idea of connecting East Wansdyke with him has a special attraction, for it is precisely the area around Amesbury which East Wansdyke was primarily designed to cover against danger from the north.

Moreover, in spite of what Fox says to the contrary,[1] the name *Wodnesdic* is most naturally to be explained as a name given by pagan Anglo-Saxons to an impressive monument whose origin and purpose they did not know and could not guess, and which was therefore attributed by them to supernatural agency. Woden, like other gods, was presumed to move in a mysterious way, and to suggest his authorship of Wansdyke was at least to proclaim that they could see no human sense in it, and certainly had no recollection of making it themselves. On this argument the name would have arisen in the mid sixth century when the war-bands of Cynric encountered Wansdyke while advancing from the Salisbury area towards Barbury between 552 and 556. By this time the political situation which had faced Ambrosius fifty years before was long forgotten, and no significance was apparent in a derelict and deserted northward-facing frontier, especially when approached, as Cynric's men were now approaching it, from the rear.

In view of these considerations, its nature, its name, and its relevance to a known, or at least reasonably presumed, historic situation, it does not seem proper to deny the possibility that East Wansdyke was built by the sub-Roman Britons of Ambrosius' day in an effort (and a successful effort) to protect the Vale of Pewsey and the Amesbury area from the Thames

[1] *Ibid*. p. 40.

valley Saxons. This was already three-quarters of a century after the end of effective Roman rule, quite long enough for forest undergrowth to have overwhelmed the Roman roads through Savernake in the absence of regular maintenance. It may also be noted as consistent with this view that the early Saxon settlers of the Vale of Pewsey, when they laid out the bounds of their upland pastures on the downs above their townships, ignored the existence of Wansdyke as a living boundary. It is mentioned only where the new bounds intersect it, and is never used as a boundary itslf. Evidently it had no political or military significance whatever at that time.

Nor can the second possibility for the origin of Wansdyke be dismissed, as Fox dismisses it, without consideration. This would make its construction an incident in the advance of the Cerdicings from their strongholds in the Salisbury area to the assault on the Thames valley. The Anglo-Saxon Chronicle mentions only three events of this movement: the battle against Britons at Barbury six miles north of Wansdyke in 556; a battle at the unidentified *Wibbandun* in 568, apparently against the Jutes of Kent, for in the same year their King Æthelbert was driven back to his own territory by Ceawlin and Cutha; and a battle at the equally unidentified *Biedcanford* in 571 which, to judge from the places mentioned as captured after it by Cuthwulf, confirmed the seizure of the Thames valley between Benson and Eynsham as well as the Vale of Aylesbury to the east of it. Although all these campaigns seem to have taken place north of Wansdyke (or, in the case of *Wibbandun*, perhaps too far east to be relevant to our problem), they provide far too little detailed information on nearly twenty eventful years of history to rule out the possibility that an offensive frontier on the Wansdyke line may have played, at some early stage, an essential part in the story.

The third possibility takes us into the later part of Ceawlin's reign and raises questions of much greater complexity than Fox, who believes East Wansdyke to be Ceawlin's work and built between 584 and 592, seems to have appreciated. There are, in fact, a number of different ways in which the incidents of Ceawlin's later career, as recorded in the Anglo-Saxon Chronicle, can be interpreted, and some of the possible situations so suggested could provide historical settings not only for East Wansdyke but for West Wansdyke as well. The incidents recorded in the Chronicle are these :

577 Cuthwine and Ceawlin fought with Britons and slew three Kings . . . at the place called *Deorham*, and they took three 'chesters', Gloucester, Cirencester, and Bath.

584 Ceawlin and Cutha fought with Britons at the place called *Fethanleag* and Cutha was killed, and Ceawlin took many townships and countless spoil and returned in anger to his own.

592 There was a great slaughter at *Wodnesbeorg* and Ceawlin was driven out.

593 Ceawlin and Cwichelm and Crida perished.

It has been generally recognized that the Ceawlin entries in the Chronicle (including probably those of 556, 560, and 568) derive from saga material recalling the deeds of this dramatic figure, and that the poetic phrases included in some of them (584, 592) [1] would stir up familiar memories and associations, conveying to an Anglo-Saxon reader far more information than they do to us. It is a reasonable assumption, however, that the *Deorham* campaign of 577, which brought Ceawlin control of the Roman cities of the west midlands and the lower Avon valley, opened the way, by protecting his western flank against British resistance, for the *Fethanleag* campaign of 584 by which he hoped to extend his conquests northwards not only into British territory but over the 'many townships' of Anglo-Saxon folk already well established in the valleys of the upper Ouse, and Nene, possibly even those on the banks of the Warwickshire Avon. The wording of the entry, especially the note of Cutha's death and Ceawlin's anger and retreat 'to his own', suggests forcibly that the attempt was

[1] K. Sisam in Fox, p. 46.

far from a complete success : it is generally assumed that this heralded a decline in Ceawlin's fortunes which culminated eight years later in the great slaughter at *Wodnesbeorg*, followed by his expulsion and death.

The reference of the final events of 592 and 593 to the problems of East Wansdyke has already been briefly mentioned. The slaughter at *Wodnesbeorg* took place at the very point where the ridgeway giving access to Salisbury plain from the north intersects the Dyke among the significant group of Woden place-names noticed by Fox. If these names are related to that of Wansdyke, as must surely be the case, then not only was the Dyke in existence in 592, but its presence in some sense dictated the location of the conflict. But if we ask what was its occasion and who was denying whom a passage, and in which direction, through *Wodnesgeat*, certainty eludes us. The answer may perhaps depend on a right reading, if we knew how to read it aright, of the ambiguous phrase in which Ceawlin's action after *Fethanleag* is described. He is said to have 'returned in anger to his own'. Where was 'his own' ?

There are two possibilities, and on the choice between them rests our whole understanding of the significance not only of Ceawlin's part in the unification of Wessex, but of the way that unification came about. One is the answer given by Fox. This is that Ceawlin retreated after *Fethanleag* back to the heart of the Cerdicing kingdom in Wiltshire, leaving the whole of his conquests on the upper Thames in open and dangerous revolt against his authority. To meet this threat from the north, Fox suggests that he proceeded between 584 and 592 to build East Wansdyke as a military barrier on the strongest position he could find against invasion from that quarter. It would then follow that, in spite of the tremendous effort involved in its construction, when the invasion materialized in 592, his people failed to hold the vital crossing of the Ridgeway at *Wodnesbeorg*, and, after a great slaughter at that crucial point, Ceawlin was driven out. On this interpretation

East Wansdyke was both Ceawlin's creation, and, within a very few years, the site of his downfall.

There is one obvious obstacle to the ready acceptance of this attractive hypothesis. If East Wansdyke was designed and built as late as 584–92 by no less a personality than the second Bretwalda, how did it ever come to be looked upon in pagan times (which lasted less than another century) as a supernatural creation, the work of Woden himself? It must surely in these circumstances have been associated from the start with Ceawlin's name, in the same way that Offa's Dyke two centuries later was associated with his. The labour force required to build such a work in the short time that the theory requires must have been so large that every part of the West Saxon people would have been more or less directly acquainted with the way it had been built.

To this objection Fox has a brilliant answer. It is to suggest that Wansdyke may owe its name not to the mystification of a pagan people in the presence of something that seemed inexplicable in human terms, but rather to a solemn dedication by such a people to its supreme divinity of a defensive structure built in a moment of emergency by themselves for their own protection. The fact that the strategic focus of the frontier was marked by a whole group of Woden names thus suggests that it was regarded as in some way especially consecrated to Woden. Perhaps *Wodnesbeorg* itself was used as a kind of high-place from which the priests could invoke supernatural assistance in times of danger against any attempted violation of the sacred soil.[1]

Such a solemn dedication could have served not only to strengthen the morale of Ceawlin's people, whom Bede called *paganissimos*,[2] but also to impress them with the seriousness of the threat to their security. It might indeed imply a

[1] Fox (p. 41) pertinently quotes Eddius' account of the reception of Wilfrid by the pagan South Saxons when the chief priest mounted a barrow (*stans . . . in tumulo excelso*) in order to curse the newcomers. (*Vita Wilfridi*, XIII).

[2] Bede, *Historia Ecclesiastica*, III, 7.

direct reflection upon the mixed religious antecedents of the enemy, for, as has been pointed out above, some of the Thames valley Saxons had been settled originally as *laeti* side by side with continuing Romano-British communities whose traditions will have included a veneer of Christianity on a basis of devotion to Celtic rather than Germanic deities. At Frilford, for example, the Saxon newcomers seem to have taken over and maintained a holy place of Roman, and indeed pre-Roman, worship.[1] Objects of Christian association, such as the cross found with the Brighthampton sword, or the Long Wittenham stoup embossed with scenes from the New Testament, have been found in the Thames valley Saxon cemeteries, several of which occupy sites already used for earlier burials, some of them probably Christian. If Ceawlin was thus deliberately staking his fortunes on the protective power of his own ancestral deity against the mongrel syncretism of the Thames valley people there would be a ready explanation for all the Woden names on the crucial section of Wansdyke. Moreover, the failure of his efforts might well have been a significant factor in the swift decay of German heathenism in Wessex after his time: for less than forty years later it was formally abandoned by the royal house on the baptism of Cynegils by St. Birinus in 634.

But there is another possible answer to the question, and this is not examined by Fox at all. When Ceawlin 'returned in anger to his own' after *Fethanleag* he may have been returning not to Wiltshire but to the upper Thames. It has often been observed that Ceawlin fits awkwardly into the West Saxon annals in the Chronicle, as indeed he fits awkwardly into the pedigree of the Cerdicing house.[2] It has already been noted that the entries which deal with his exploits seem

[1] *Oxoniensia*, IV (1939), 1–70.

[2] As I hinted in C. and M. p. 404, n. 3, following G. M. Young, *Origin of the West Saxon Kingdom* (1954), pp. 33 ff. The case for believing that Ceawlin, Cutha, and some other figures associated with him in the West Saxon annals belong to a different kin from that of Cerdic is fully developed in an article by D. P. Kirby shortly to appear in *English Historical Review*.

to come from a source distinct from the other annals with which they are associated in the Chronicle. Moreover, although his name alliterates well enough with Cerdic and Cynric (whose grandson and son he is claimed to be) as well as with the seventh-century West Saxon kings, nearly all of whose names begin with C, yet his reign is ignored altogether by the early West Saxon source preserved in the preface to the Parker MS. of the Chronicle. This passes direct from the reign of Cynric to that of Ceol who became king after *Wodnesbeorg* in 592, and was therefore presumably Ceawlin's opponent at that engagement. These facts have led to the suggestion that the Ceawlin story has been incorporated at a late stage into Cerdicing annals and that he was not originally a Cerdicing at all, but a prince of the Thames valley Saxons. The brief empire created by the campaigns of *Wibbandun*, *Biedcanford*, *Deorham*, and *Fethanleag* would then have been a south midland affair based essentially upon the upper Thames. It is certainly of interest in this connection that every single event with which Ceawlin is associated in the Chronicle took place far away from the historic focus of Cerdicing authority in southern Wiltshire, and all, with the possible exception of the unidentified *Wibbandun*, to the north of Wansdyke. There is indeed nothing in the sources to suggest that Ceawlin ever operated south of Wansdyke at all, and, though he appears to have been associated at first with Cynric in fighting Britons at Barbury in 556, that campaign could easily be explained as a joint effort of the Wiltshire and Thames valley Saxons in temporary alliance against British opposition threatening both alike from the west.

There is some place-name evidence which is relevant to this suggestion. In the upper Thames valley to this day there are two places, Cutteslowe and Cuddesdon, one a mile or two to the north, and the other some five miles south-east, of Oxford, which contain the personal element Cutha. This is an element which, whether in this shortened form, or in the longer Cuthwulf or Cuthwine, was borne by close relatives of Ceawlin associated with his campaigns by the Chronicle. It is therefore plausible to urge that when, after the death of Cutha in the *Fethanleag* campaign of 584, Ceawlin 'returned in anger to his own', he was in fact returning from north Oxfordshire down the Banbury road towards Oxford.[1] And there at Cutteslowe there still stood until 1261 (when it was destroyed by royal orders as a haunt of robbers on the Banbury Road) the *hoga de Cudeslowe*, the mound under which in all probability the prince killed at *Fethanleag* was buried.[2] It is natural to assume that Ceawlin's home country was not far away. It is at least probable that the Cutteslowe property was in early times a royal possession for it became part of the first known endowment of St. Frideswide's monastery in Oxford, founded in the seventh century, together with the King's tithe of the royal vill of Headington near by.[3]

If Ceawlin's homeland was on the upper Thames, a different explanation must be sought for the events of 592 and their relation to East Wansdyke. The easiest is to suppose that Ceawlin, baulked at *Fethanleag* of his ambition to extend his rule northward, turned south against the Cerdicings in Wiltshire, and met his Waterloo at *Wodnesbeorg*. If East Wansdyke is Saxon, it will then have been built, either, as the second alternative already discussed would indicate, as an offensive frontier in the course of Cynric's advance from Old Sarum to Barbury between 552 and 556, or as a defensive barrier against an anticipated southward drive by Ceawlin at any time between 556 and 592. On either showing it would be necessary to explain the Woden place-names in the way that Fox has explained them, with the difference that, on this

[1] *Fethanleag* was identified by Stenton with a lost *Fethelee* in Stoke Lyne, six miles north of Bicester, Oxon — *Trans. R. Hist. Soc.* 4th Ser. XXII (1940), 19-20. This identification has superseded that with a lost *Faeh halean* near Stratford-on-Avon, originally proposed by C. S. Taylor in *Trans. Bristol. and Gloucs. Arch. Soc.*, XX (1896–7), 271, and quoted by Fox, p. 43, n. 1, from *Antiq. Journal*, XXXVIII (1958), 78, n. 1.

[2] *Antiquity*, IX (1935), 46-8. I suggested that this might be Cutha's burial mound in *The Oxford Region* (1954), p. 100.

[3] *Oxoniensia*, I (1936), 111.

alternative, the frontier and its dedication to Woden will have been planned not by Ceawlin but against him. This interpretation possesses the advantage, for what it is worth, that the building of the frontier does not have to be crammed into a brief eight years : it could have been carried out, perhaps in several stages, at any time between 556 and 592.

It is at this point that it may be worth considering whether West Wansdyke also might be related in some way, like East Wansdyke, to the campaigns of Ceawlin. Although Fox has preferred to seek for it a later date and a different historical situation, perhaps in connection with the peace-making between Cynegils of Wessex and Penda of Mercia in 628, it has been suggested above that there are stronger grounds than he allows for considering it to be part of the same frontier system as East Wansdyke, though not necessarily constructed at exactly the same time or in precisely the same circumstances. An obvious context for West Wansdyke is in fact provided by Ceawlin's *Deorham* campaign of 577 which gave him possession of Gloucester, Cirencester, and Bath, and with them the control of the southern Cotswolds and the lower valleys of the Severn and the Bristol Avon.[1]

Unfortunately nothing whatever is known either of the circumstances leading up to this campaign or of its aftermath : it is therefore impossible to be certain how the building of West Wansdyke may have been related to it. But it is certainly tempting to guess that some such relationship is the reason for the peculiar alignment of the dyke behind Bath. Whoever built West Wansdyke had no command of Bath or of the adjacent stretches of the Avon valley, although only a few miles to the east it would seem possible that the Avon itself was used to continue the line of the dyke beyond Horsecombe. It would certainly seem that West Wansdyke was built against whoever held Bath. And Bath passed from British to Saxon hands in 577.

There are several possibilities about the *Deorham* campaign

[1] As I suggested in C. and M. p. 403, n. 1.

of 577. If Ceawlin was a Cerdicing he may have found that those of his people who were penetrating Somerset from Wiltshire — the people, for example, who buried their dead in the Camerton cemetery or left sixth-century brooches to to be discovered at Ilchester — were threatened by the British principalities centred on Bath, Gloucester, and Cirencester. He may have begun by building West Wansdyke for their protection on the best line the Britons of Bath would tolerate, and he may then have burst out from this defence to battle at *Deorham*, and to a seizure of Bath that made his own defences against it meaningless. If, on the other hand, Fox is right in thinking that after the failure at *Fethanleag* he was forced back on to Salisbury Plain, and sought to protect himself by building East Wansdyke against revolt in the Thames valley, then that revolt might have included also the British kingdoms of the southern Cotswolds and the lower Avon temporarily subdued in 577. This may have compelled him to build West Wansdyke also to protect the Saxon pioneers in Somerset, at a moment when he had lost the freedom to select a satisfactory line.

But if the heart of Ceawlin's power lay on the upper Thames, the prelude to *Deorham* will have been different. He will then have appoached the three sub-Roman principalities through Gloucestershire, and his success in securing Bath after the battle may have forced the Cerdicings to build West Wansdyke against him between 577 and 592, just as they will have built East Wansdyke against the more direct threat from his base in the Thames valley.

This is perhaps as far as one can go at present in the attempt to find an historical context in which Wansdyke makes sense. If the discussion has simply exhibited a bewildering variety of alternatives, none of which can be shown to be nearer the truth than the others, it will have achieved what it set out to do. For the premises on which an historical proof can rest are not at present among the facts before us, and perhaps they never will be. It may be possible one day to obtain by excavation a closer date for both the main sections of Wansdyke than we have now, and in particular to determine whether either part belongs to the fifth or the sixth century. But whatever the date or dates may turn out to be, and however tempting it may then appear to associate these great works with the names and deeds of Ambrosius or Ceawlin, the mystery of Wansdyke is likely to remain unsolved. That it is related in some way to the conflict of forces out of which Wessex was born is certain, but the precise part it played in the process cannot with any certainty be told.

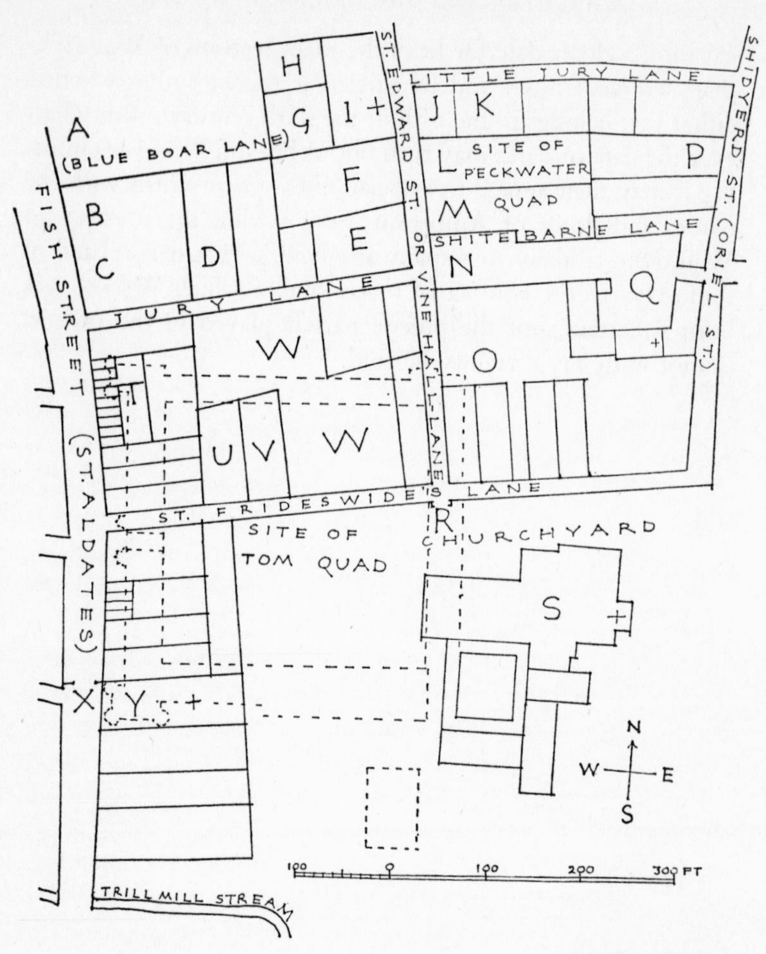

The Medieval Site of Christ Church, Oxford

A, Blue Boar Inn. B–C, First site of Dominican priory ; later B, Unicorn Inn ; C, Bull Inn. D, Civil Law School. E, Ape Hall. F, Eagle Hall. G, St. Edward Hall (in St. Edward's parish). H, Great Canon Law School. I, St. Edward's church. J, Little Canon Law School. K, Solar Hall. L–M, Kepeharm's house ; later L, Glasen Hall ; M, Vine Hall. N, Ship Hall. O, Peckwater Inn. P, St. Edward Hall (in St. Mary's parish). Q, Canterbury College. R, Gate to St. Frideswide's churchyard. S, St. Frideswide's priory. T, Synagogue ; late Pike or Dolphin Inn. U, Leberd Hall. V, Greek Hall. W, Burnell's Inn or London College. X, South Gate. Y, St. Michael's church.

2

W. A. Pantin

BEFORE WOLSEY

THOSE who have lived and worked in an Oxford college must sometimes have wondered what kind of aboriginal inhabitants and institutions existed on the site that they now occupy. This essay is an attempt to answer this question with regard to the site of Christ Church. It is probably easier to answer this kind of question about Oxford than about any other town in England, thanks mainly to the heroic labours of two scholars: the late Dr. H. E. Salter, whose *Survey of Oxford*[1] gives us the history of almost every house in every street of central Oxford from the twelfth to the nineteenth century; and Dr. A. B. Emden, whose *Biographical Register of the University of Oxford*[2] gives us the career of every traceable member of the university down to the sixteenth century.

The site with which we are concerned extended from Fish Street (now St. Aldates) on the west to Shidyerd Street (Oriel Street) on the east; and from the Trill Mill stream on the south to Little Jury Lane (Bear Lane) and Blue Boar Lane on the north, though Blue Boar Lane did not exist as a thoroughfare until the mid sixteenth century. Central Oxford is an interesting medieval example of rectangular or 'chess-board' planning, and the area we are concerned with, like the rest

[1] Volume I of this, covering the north-east and south-east wards of the city, has been published by the Oxford Historical Society (New Series, vol. XIV, 1960); the tenements that correspond to the site of Christ Church are S.E. nos. 99-128, 132-51, 232-51 (pp. 213 ff., 227 ff., 258 ff.).

[2] Three volumes, Oxford, 1957-9; hereafter cited as *B.R.U.O.*

of the city, was divided up into large rectangular islands by a number of comparatively narrow intersecting streets such as Jury Lane, Shitebarne Lane, and St. Frideswide's Lane (running east and west) and St. Edward Street or Vine Hall Lane (running north and south), all of which lanes are now swallowed up in Christ Church. It was in fact to make a substitute for one of the suppressed east-west lanes (Jury Lane) that Christ Church seems to have created Blue Boar Lane along the northern edge of its property in the mid sixteenth century, and this lane was at first known as Tresham's Lane, after an eminent member of Cardinal College and Christ Church, William Tresham (d. 1569). The area we are concerned with measured about 600 feet from east to west and about 750 feet from north to south. Then, as now, the south-east quarter of the area was occupied by the priory church of St. Frideswide (now the cathedral), with its claustral buildings to the south and its churchyard to the north and east. Like so many important buildings in medieval Oxford (New College, for instance) St. Frideswide's lay back, well hidden and screened from the main streets, and approached only by narrow lanes — along St. Frideswide's Lane from St. Aldates or down St. Edward Street from the High Street. St. Frideswide's priory was of course the most important occupant of the area, and its site and buildings and endowments must have been among the main attractions to bring Wolsey to build his college on this site ; but it is obviously not practical to try to give the history of St. Frideswide's priory within the limits of this essay. What I propose to deal with is the other three-quarters of the site, to the west and north of the priory.

This area included two small parish churches, now disappeared, at the northern and southern extremities : St. Edward's to the north, and St. Michael's at the South Gate of the city to the south. St. Michael at Southgate forms an obvious pendant to the other church of St. Michael at Northgate, whose eleventh-century tower is still a landmark in the Cornmarket ; and it reminds us of the curious fact that the four main entrances to medieval Oxford were guarded, as it were, by four churches dedicated to peculiarly appropriate patron saints: St. Peter, the heavenly door-keeper, to the east and west, and St. Michael, the heavenly 'chucker-out', to the north and south. Both St. Edward's and St. Michael's at Southgate seem to have come into existence in the first half of the twelfth century; St. Edward's seems to have disappeared in the late fourteenth century (it stood roughly on the site of the Bear Inn), and St. Michael's was swallowed up by Wolsey (it stood near the south-west corner of Tom Quad). They were thus part of the noticeable expansion and contraction in the number of parishes in medieval Oxford; [1] eight churches existed in 1086, and these had risen to twenty by 1200, but some of these parishes faded out in the course of the later middle ages, as, for instance, St. Mildred's (in the Turl), St. Budoc's (near St. Ebbe's), St. John's (swallowed up in Merton), as well as these two churches of St. Edward and St. Michael at Southgate. This process was no doubt a reflection of the town's commercial prosperity and population, which expanded in the twelfth century but declined after the thirteenth century; but it may also reflect a changing fashion in ecclesiastical organization; instead of the numerous small parishes of the early middle ages, people may have preferred larger, amalgamated parishes, with a larger staff of clergy — a parish priest assisted by stipendiary chaplains and chantry priests — which made the pattern more like the friars' churches or the great town churches of Germany and the low countries, in towns like Nördlingen or Zutphen.

As has been said, the area was divided up by intersecting lanes into rectangular islands; and each island in turn was divided into tenements; there were between 60 and 70 such tenements in the area. On the whole the tenements were large, about 100 or 120 feet long or more by about 30 or 40 feet wide; only a small part at the street end would be occupied by the dwelling house, and the rest would be courtyard

[1] H. E. Salter, *Medieval Oxford* (Oxford Hist. Soc., C, 1936), pp. 113 ff.

or garden. The medieval towns had a persistently rural character, as Lewis Mumford has pointed out.[1] Loggan's bird's-eye view of seventeenth-century Oxford shows how much open ground there was behind the narrow streets.[2] 'Broad gates' (such as one can still see in Holywell) might give on to a miniature farmyard, and the townsman might keep cattle on Port meadow ; in 1605 the inventory of the inn-keeper of the Blue Boar Inn (at the west of the Blue Boar Lane) shows that he kept mares, cows, ducks, and a pig in his yard.[3] It was not till later that people began building rows of cottages or workshops in their backyards.

About two-thirds of these tenements came in the course of the twelfth and thirteenth centuries to belong to corporate landlords : St. Frideswide's Priory naturally owned most, nearly 30, Oseney Abbey owned 9, Godstow 3, Eynsham 1 ; the Hospital of St. John the Baptist (on the site of Magdalen), which owned so much house property in Oxford, only owned one tenement here.

Who lived in these houses ? The majority were of course inhabited by the ordinary tradesmen or craftsmen of the town, as the names in the thirteenth-century deeds show : Geoffrey the Goldsmith, Gunnora le Espicier, John the Tailor, Guy the Armourer, Hugh the Cordwainer.[4] Some of the houses had a more distinguished or specialized use. It is true that we do not find here or anywhere else in Oxford the town houses of noblemen or prelates, like the great houses along the Strand between London and Westminster, or the Courtenays' house in the close at Exeter, or the Norfolks' palace at Norwich. But we do find several examples of what in medieval German towns would be called 'patrician' houses : houses of the leading burgess families, the men who grew rich in the twelfth

[1] Lewis Mumford, *The City in History* (London, 1961), pp. 288 ff.
[2] D. Loggan, *Oxonia Illustrata* (Oxford, 1675), pl. II.
[3] Bodleian, MS. Wills Oxon. 17/2/54 : Inventory of Robert Dawson.
[4] Salter, *Survey*, pp. 223-4, 231, 264. Surnames were beginning to be hereditary in the thirteenth century, but at any rate the fathers or grandfathers would have followed these trades.

and thirteenth centuries and so much resented the growing numbers, privileges, and unruliness of the scholars. A good example of this was the large house of the Kepeharm family, which stood on the east side of St. Edward Street (where staircases 1 and 2 of Peckwater Quad now stand).[1] The Kepeharms had another large house west of St. Aldates, and other tenements scattered about Oxford. About the year 1200 the two leading citizens of Oxford were John Kepeharm and Henry Simeon. John Kepeharm, who seems to have been a fishmonger, died in 1204, leaving a widow, who gave to the king two palfreys and the sum of 100 marks (perhaps something like £10,000 in modern money) that she might marry whom she would and have her legal portion of her late husband's possessions; she married Henry Simeon, who was so rich that when he incurred a fine of £2,000 to the king, he managed to pay off at least half.[2] It was Henry Simeon's son Henry who was outlawed in 1242 for 'the death of scholars at Oxford', and caused a dispersal of the university in 1264;[3] he thus earned the undying hostility of the university, so that every master of arts at his graduation, down to 1827, had to take an oath never to consent to the reconciliation of Henry son of Henry Simeon! John Kepeharm's son, Laurence, who lived in this house, was the first mayor of Oxford. A later owner of the house was Philip the Miller, the second mayor of Oxford, who was deposed for his share in the celebrated episode of the hanging of the scholars in 1209; he gave half the house to Oseney Abbey about 1239.[4] The Kepeharm tenement was very large, about 200 feet by 100 feet; there would have been room for a large dwelling house built round a courtyard, with a garden beyond. Ironically, this home of the scholars' inveterate enemies was later turned into two academic halls, Vine Hall and Glasen Hall. On the other side

[1] *Ibid.* p. 220 (S.E., nos. 117-18).
[2] Salter, *Medieval Oxford*, p. 38.
[3] *English Historical Review*, XXVII (1912), 515-17.
[4] *Oseney Cartulary*, ed. H. E. Salter (Oxford Hist. Soc., LXXXIX, 1929), I, 350-6.

of the street, Ape Hall took its name from a thirteenth-century owner, Thomas son of Thorald le Ape ; however unflattering the sobriquet, the Thoralds were a notable Oxford family. A neighbouring house, Edward Hall, belonged in the 1180s to William son of Sweting, who got into difficulties with the Jews and had to pledge the house to Moses of Bristol for a debt of 14 cows and 12 weights of fat.[1] But of all the Oxford patrician families the one whose name has lasted longest must be the Peckwethers, who lived in Peckwater Inn [2] (just south of the Kepeharm house) and so gave their name to Dean Aldrich's great Palladian quadrangle, where the name is monumentally inscribed : ATRII PECKWATERIENSIS QUOD SPECTAS LATUS. Peckwater Inn was in fact rather to the south of the present quadrangle, roughly on the site of the Deanery and the west end of the library.

Another specialized form of town house, analogous to the 'patrician' houses we have just been considering, were the Jews' houses. The Oxford Jewry existed from probably about the end of the eleventh century until the expulsion of the Jews in 1290 ; the presence of the Jews, like the multiplication of parish churches, thus roughly coincides with the town's maximum expansion and prosperity. The Oxford Jews' houses were mainly concentrated in the area south of Carfax, on both sides of St. Aldates ; and out of some twenty-four identifiable Jews' properties, seven tenements were on the site of Christ Church, on the east side of St. Aldates, including the synagogue, of which more will be said below. The Oxford Jews had ramifications and connections with Jewish families in other English towns, as the names of some of the Oxford inhabitants show : Vives of Gloucester, Copin of

[1] *Oseney Cartulary*, ed. H. E. Salter (Oxford Hist. Soc., LXXXIX, 1929) I, 335.

[2] *Cartulary of the Monastery of St. Frideswide*, ed. S. R. Wigram (Oxford Hist. Soc., XVIII), I, 105-16 ; Peckwater Inn was apparently originally approached by a lane between a row of tenements facing St. Frideswide's churchyard, but by the fifteenth century the Inn had probably swallowed up these tenements and so reached to the churchyard.

Worcester, Moses of Bristol ; all these three owned houses on the site of Christ Church. The Oxford Jews included scholars as well as financiers in the late twelfth and thirteenth centuries, notably Rabbi Yom-tob and his son Moses ; these lived just outside the Christ Church area, the first on the site of the Town Hall, the second near Pembroke Street. Jewish scholars could not of course be members of the university, but their presence meant that if English scholars wanted to learn Hebrew (as some did), there would have been no lack of opportunity in thirteenth-century Oxford.[1]

Just north of the block of Jews' houses was an important group of settlers, namely the Dominican friars, who lived here from their first arrival in Oxford in 1221 until about 1236, and here they constructed their first chapel and school.[2] The friars, like the colleges, were comparatively late-comers to Oxford, and they were lucky to get land where they could. The site they occupied, at the corner of Jury Lane, was a large one, perhaps about 130 feet wide by about 230 feet deep, and may have consisted of several tenements thrown together. Even so the site was not really large enough for their purpose, and the need for expansion, as well as some friction with neighbouring landlords, the canons of St. Frideswide's and of Oseney, led the Dominicans to migrate to a more spacious and permanent home farther out, to the south-west, between the Trill Mill stream and the Thames. The first site of the Dominicans, in St. Aldates, was later two houses, which had both become inns by the seventeenth century ; the northern, at the corner of Blue Boar Lane (No. 6-7 St. Aldates), was the Unicorn, with a racket court behind it ; the southern (No. 8 St. Aldates) was the Bull.

Lastly, there is the most interesting type of house, peculiar to a university town, namely the houses that were used as

[1] Cecil Roth, *The Jews of Medieval Oxford* (Oxford Hist. Soc., New Series, IX, 1951), 83 ff., 112 ff.

[1] W. A. Hinnebusch, 'The Pre-Reformation Sites of the Oxford Blackfriars', *Oxoniensia*, III (1938), 57 ff.

academic halls and as 'schools' (that is to say, lecture rooms).[1] It is important here to remember how different medieval Oxford was from modern Oxford, where everyone belongs to a college, and the town is filled with university and college buildings. In medieval Oxford the colleges did not exist at all until the mid thirteenth century, and until the late fifteenth century the colleges only contained a small fraction of the university, a privileged minority, mostly graduates; in other words, all the colleges were then what All Souls still is. The great mass of graduates and undergraduates lived and worked in hired houses and hired rooms, scattered about the town — in the academic halls and in the schools. An academic hall was simply a reasonably large house, capable of holding a dozen or twenty men (generally crowded two or three or four to a room); it was rented and controlled by a principal, a master of arts recognized by the university. The same building might at one time serve as a private house, at another as a hall. Similarly a 'school' was simply a large room, capable of holding an audience of 30 to 50 persons; such a room might originally have been the hall or solar of a private house, though some of them were specially rebuilt for the purpose. The maximum number of known halls was about 120, and of schools, about 54. The peak period, when there were most halls and schools in existence, was about the year 1300. The number dropped after the Black Death; in the mid fifteenth century there were only 70 halls, by about 1500 this had dropped to about 30, by 1514 to 12, and by 1552 to only 8. Most of the halls and schools were concentrated in the eastern half of the town, especially in the area north and south of St. Mary's; this was the academic centre, just as the commercial centre was round about Carfax and the Cornmarket. The Christ Church area was therefore in the borderland between the academic and the commercial quarters. It contained 3 schools — 2 for canon law and 1 for civil law

[1] *Oxford Studies presented to Daniel Callus* (Oxford Hist. Soc., New Series, XVI, 1694), 31 ff.; and map in *Victoria County History of Oxford*, III, 36-7.

— and at the maximum 12 halls, which thus occupied a little under a quarter of all the tenements in the area. By the early sixteenth century these 12 halls had become reduced to 3 large ones, mostly by amalgamation: Burnell's Inn (with which Greek Hall was amalgamated); St. Edward Hall (with which Eagle Hall and Ape Hall were amalgamated); and Peckwater Inn (with which Vine Hall and Glasen Hall were amalgamated). The Oxford halls were distinguished into three categories, according to the faculties of the scholars who frequented them: grammar halls, halls for arts men, and halls for legists. The grammar halls were few, and they seem to have died out altogether in the late fifteenth century, partly because of the growth of grammar schools like Magdalen College School. In the early fifteenth century Peckwater Inn was occupied by a grammar master who gained some celebrity, John Leland;[1] a verse was quoted in praise of him: '*Ut rosa flos florum, sic Lelande Grammaticorum*'. Like some of the other Oxford grammar masters, but unlike other dons then and for centuries to come, Leland was a married man, and had a son-in-law who kept another grammar hall not far away in Magpie Lane. John Leland's surviving grammatical treatises are rather elementary, but he is interesting as being the common master of a group of grammarians, master John Seward and others, who taught in London and exchanged epigrams and comic invectives; however naïve, this represented one of the things out of which English humanism grew.[2]

Most of the Oxford halls were those of artists or legists, and in the Christ Church area, perhaps because it was on the periphery of the academic area, the legists predominated, occupying more than half the halls; some of these, by a further specialization, were noted as being halls of Welsh or Irish

[1] *B.R.U.O.*, II, 1129; *Oxford Studies presented to Daniel Callus*, pp. 169 f., 181 ff.; for the grammar halls in general, see *Victoria County History of Oxford*, III, 40 ff.

[2] V. H. Galbraith, 'John Seward and his circle', *Medieval and Renaissance Studies*, I (1941), 85 ff.

legists,[1] and indeed there was a strong Welsh and Irish element to the end. The three halls which survived to the end were all law halls — Burnell's Inn, St. Edward Hall, and Peckwater Inn, the latter having turned over from grammar to law. In the early sixteenth century the principals of the law halls seem to have constituted a kind of committee to regulate the law lectures ; and on one occasion, in 1531, when the principals complained to the vice-chancellor of the inutility and negligence of one of the doctors lecturing in canon law, the lecturer produced witnesses from among his students to testify to his diligence, utility, and profit in lecturing.[2]

Of all the academic halls in the Christ Church area, the most important and interesting was Burnell's inn, also known as London College,[3] for at one point it nearly became a college. At the end of the thirteenth century a large block of property, stretching eastwards from St. Aldates, was acquired by one William Burnell (who died in 1304). This consisted of two parts. To the west, abutting directly on St. Aldates, and roughly on the present site of the Junior Common Room in the north-west corner of Tom Quad, was a large tenement, about 80 or 90 feet wide and about 100 feet deep. This was one of the Jews' tenements, having belonged to Moses of Bristol and Copin of Worcester in the early thirteenth century, and from about 1228 to 1290 it was used as a synagogue. After the expulsion of the Jews it was acquired, with other Jewish property, by William Burnell, who had some pull, since he was the nephew of Edward I's chancellor. Almost at once the house was let as an inn, and continued to be so until the sixteenth century ; it was the Pike Inn in 1472, and the Dolphin in 1556. Like some other large houses in Oxford — the Golden Cross, for instance, and Tackley's Inn

[1] Cf. John Rowse's fifteenth-century list of halls, in *Wood's City of Oxford*, ed. A. Clark (Oxford Hist. Soc., XV, 1899), I, 638-41.

[2] Oxford University Archives, Reg. Canc. EEE, fo. 182.

[3] *Oxford Balliol Deeds*, ed. H. E. Salter (Oxford Hist. Soc., LXIV, 1913), 91 ff. and plan.

in the High Street — this house consisted of two distinct parts: the outer part consisted of a row of shops, opening on to the street, with a passage or gateway leading through to the inner part, which was the house proper, looking on to a courtyard or garden. This consisted of a great hall (which no doubt had served as the synagogue), with a cellar and solar (or upper room) at each end; and no doubt there were other upper rooms over the shops.

East of the synagogue was the other and larger part of the property, where William Burnell himself lived; this came to be known as Burnell's Inn. It was on the site of the north range of Tom Quad. It was a large, irregular-shaped tenement, stretching for about 200 feet from Civil School Lane on the north to St. Frideswide's Lane on the south, and about 150 feet wide; it was probably formed by throwing about half a dozen tenements together. We do not know whether William Burnell used existing buildings, or built a new house. The main entrance seems to have been on the south side, from St. Frideswide's Lane; John the Tailor, a neighbour to the south-east, is described as having some shops and a solar 'near the gate of Master William Burnell', and perhaps the house was masked by a fringe of shops on St. Frideswide's Lane. Probably the south half of the property was used as a courtyard and the north half as a garden, with the main range of the house, containing the hall and principal chambers lying between, pleasantly secluded, 'entre cour et jardin' like the great town houses of eighteenth-century France, or (to take a contemporary English example) like the Strangers' Hall at Norwich.

The owner of all this property, the old synagogue and Burnell's Inn, was William Burnell, a Shropshire man who was born about 1268 and died in 1304.[1] William must have owed his rapid success in life to the fact that he was the nephew

[1] *B.R.U.O.*, I, 316 f.

of the great Robert Burnell, Edward I's ablest and most trusted servant and friend, whom the king made his chancellor and bishop of Bath and Wells, and tried to make archbishop of Canterbury. Robert was thus a good example of an important medieval type, the administrator-bishop, a royal servant disguised (for the king's financial convenience) as a bishop. Such powerful churchmen were a sign, not of the church's power but of its subordination to the state, and the system could lead to abuses ; but it must be admitted that such men sometimes made better diocesan bishops than one might have expected, and they could be generous benefactors to learning. A surprisingly large proportion of Oxford and Cambridge colleges—including Christ Church itself — owe their existence to such men, and although Robert Burnell did not found a college, as Wykeham or Wolsey did, his nephew William was a benefactor to one, as we shall see. Although he came of a knightly family, William was thus a sprig of the meritocracy rather than of the aristocracy. From the age of 16 William was loaded with ecclesiastical benefices, which included, at various times, prebends in seven cathedral chapters and two valuable rectories ; and not surprisingly (since his uncle was bishop there) he was provost and dean of Wells and then archdeacon of Taunton. Such an outfit would have been suitable for a rising royal servant, and this may have been what William's uncle intended, but there is no evidence that the nephew entered the royal service. Instead he settled down to an academic life at Oxford. He came up to Oxford perhaps about the age of 16 (*c.* 1284), when he received his first benefices. It would be about seven years later, about 1291, that he graduated as master of arts ; and it so happens that we have a copy of an invitation to his inception, or graduation as master of arts, which would be accompanied by a great feast. This letter is preserved in a letter-roll of the abbey of Thorney, and is worth quoting :

To the religious man, lovable to God, the lord abbot of T[horney] by the grace of God, his W[illiam] B[urnell], provost of Wells, sends greetings and himself prepared to do the good pleasure of his will. Because our lord the bishop of Bath and Wells [Robert Burnell], whom we know for certain cherishes you in the bowels of sincere love, is asking you by letter that you would please to be present at our inception in arts, we add our prayers to his request, in the same way that a little stream joins the sea to swell it ; humbly asking you that on the Monday after the octave of blessed John the Baptist [*c.* 1 July], at Oxford, you would be so good as to decorate our inception with your venerable presence, out of regard for our said lord, and out of consideration for our request. Truly for this cause you will have us the more strictly bound to do anything that you may choose to command us. May the Most High preserve you.[1]

This a neat specimen of the medieval *ars dictandi*, the art of writing in persuasive terms to any person on any subject. Its rather flowery style was simply a contemporary convention, like our own habit of understatement. The writer says what he has to say, and asks what he has to ask, according to the recognized rules. The letter is nicely adapted to the social status of the correspondents. William was the nephew of about the most important man in England next to the king, and was already (at the age of about 23) a dignitary, so he writes with confidence, but also with deference, for the abbot was technically of slightly superior rank. He carefully brings in his uncle the bishop, who was evidently also a friend of the abbot ; one wonders how the Burnells came to be friends of a fenland abbot — unless indeed William was broadcasting invitations to all the abbots and all the bishops of England, which is not impossible.

William Burnell was, in a modest way, a collector of books, as he could well afford to be, and he left seven books to Merton College, and three to Balliol, which still survive.[2] They include commentaries on Aristotle's physics, metaphysics, and ethics ; some patristic works — Augustine's *City of God*, Gregory's *Pastoral care*, some works of Jerome ; and some quite recent theological works — Aquinas, Henry of Ghent,

[1] Cf. Appendix (1) below, p. 57. [2] Listed in *B.R.U.O.*, I, 317.

and Nicholas Gorran (who died *c.* 1295 and was thus a contemporary). The list suggests that William, after graduating in arts, may have gone on to study theology. William Burnell acquired his large Oxford house from the king in 1291 and probably went on living there till his death in 1304 at the age of 36 ; the bishop of Lincoln gave him a licence to have an oratory in his 'inn' at Oxford in 1291 and again in 1304. It is unlikely that Burnell acted as the principal of an academic Hall, which would mean being a kind of lodging-house keeper ; he probably occupied the house as a large private residence, with a staff of servants, though he may have had a few friends or protégés living with him as *commensales*. The rich, well-connected scholar, living in his own large house, was a feature of Oxford in the late thirteenth and early fourteenth centuries — an academic equivalent of the rich burgess households like the Kepeharms ; a number of future bishops lived in this way, like the brothers Anthony and Thomas Bek, and John and Thomas Trillek ; and only a few blocks away from Burnell the large house known as La Oriel (afterwards Oriel College) was occupied in succession by two notable pluralists, Bogo of Clare (son of the earl of Gloucester) and James of Spain (nephew of Queen Eleanor). This kind of arrangement seems to have died out in the late fourteenth and fifteenth centuries, when the well-to-do scholars preferred to hire rooms in one of the colleges, as did Thomas Arundel at Oriel, Henry Beaufort and Richard Courtenay at Queen's, William Gray and George Neville at Balliol ; no doubt this was just as comfortable and less trouble and expense ; it is also a sign of the growing importance and prestige of the colleges.[1]

William Burnell bequeathed his house-property in Oxford to Balliol College, to augment the number of the fellows, and it constituted one of the college's most valuable possessions.[2] For nearly a century and a half the college let the old synagogue

[1] The scholars mentioned above will be found, under their names, in *B.R.U.O.*

[2] *Oxford Balliol Deeds*, pp. 91, 105 ff.

as an inn, and Burnell's Inn as an academic hall. About a hundred years after Burnell's death, in the early fifteenth century, Burnell's Inn came into the hands of another outstanding churchman, Richard Clifford (d. 1421).[1] Like the Burnells, he was of a knightly family ; like the elder Burnell, he was an administrator-bishop, like the younger Burnell, he was a scholar (probably an Oxford graduate) and a patron of scholars. He had an even more impressive list of benefices : a deanery, two archdeaconries, prebends in six cathedral chapters, the headship of five royal chapels and of two hospitals, and six rectories, including one of the richest in England, Houghton-le-Spring, in county Durham (valued at £86, perhaps about £8,000 in modern money). He did not hold all these at once ; the archdeaconries and rectories he held in rapid succession, and the prebends were sinecures, so that at any given time he was holding only two or three benefices with cure of souls. Furthermore, he held these benefices because he was doing a job of work as an important royal official, not because he was somebody's son (like Bogo of Clare) or somebody's nephew (like William Burnell). To this extent pluralism had become controlled and rationalized. But it still meant that in 1399 he was dean of York, archdeacon of Canterbury, canon of York, Lincoln, Salisbury and Wells, and master of St. James's Hospital, Westminster, and no doubt performing any duties by deputy.

The reason for all this preferment was that Clifford was one of Richard II's most valued servants : clerk of the king's chapel, arrested by the Lords Appellant in 1388 but soon released, keeper of the great wardrobe, keeper of the privy seal, and finally one of the executors of the king's will. And he was the kind of indispensable administrator who survives revolutions. After 1399 he was kept in office, declared loyal by Parliament, sent by Henry IV on diplomatic missions, and made bishop first of Worcester (1401–7) and then of London (1407–21). He was one of the English representatives at the

[1] *B.R.U.O.*, I, 440 ff.

Council of Constance, where he was thought of as a possible candidate for the papacy, and, what is more, himself took the lead in expediting the election of pope Martin V and so helped to end the papal schism. It was at this point, at the peak of his career, that Clifford, like so many men of his type, planned an academic foundation at Oxford, which, if it had been followed up, might have put him among the Oxford college founders, comparable to Stapledon or Foxe, if not in the class of Wykeham or Wolsey. In January 1416 he rented Burnell's Inn from Balliol for ten years, with the option of purchasing it within that period;[1] and in August 1416, at Dover, when about to cross the Channel to go to Constance, he made his will, in which he left a sum of £666 : 13 : 4, to be spent at the rate of £40 a year, to maintain a body of scholars at Oxford, living in Burnell's Inn; this would provide for a dozen or more scholars for about sixteen years.[2] We cannot be certain whether Clifford intended this simply as a temporary measure — a hundred years later Cardinal Morton founded some similar scholarships to last for twenty years — or whether he envisaged the foundation of a permanent college, established in Burnell's Inn. The option of purchasing the Inn seems to suggest the latter, but it would have needed a much larger endowment for a permanent foundation, and in the event this was apparently not forthcoming, and the bishop of London's 'college' in time ceased to exist. But his good intentions struck the popular imagination, so that from now until its end Burnell's Inn continued to be known alternatively as 'London College'.

About the year 1410, just before Clifford's lease, Burnell's Inn seems to have been rented by some Benedictine monk-scholars;[3] and some time after Clifford's lease had come to an end, some Benedictines (whether the same or others) seem to

[1] *Oxford Balliol Deeds*, pp. 123 ff.

[2] *The Register of Henry Chichele*, ed. E. F. Jacob (Canterbury and York Society, XLII, 1937), II, 224-6.

[3] *General and Provincial Chapters of the English Black Monks*, ed. W. A. Pantin (Camden Third Series, LIV, 1937), III, 162.

have occupied it again. For in 1452 the matter came to the chancellor's court; the monks had apparently bilked Balliol by quitting the Inn without paying the rent. Accordingly the furniture they left behind was sequestrated to pay the rent, and an interesting inventory was drawn up describing the furniture of the chapel, the hall, the kitchen, and the buttery.[1] No description is given of the contents of the chambers of the monks — they probably had taken away their personal belongings with them; and we cannot tell whether they occupied the whole hall or only certain chambers. Benedictine monk-scholars were supposed to live in one of the three officially recognized monastic colleges, Gloucester College (now Worcester), Durham College (now Trinity), or Canterbury College (on the site of Canterbury Quad). Possibly these unsatisfactory tenants had migrated here because they had quarrelled with one or other of the monastic colleges, like the monk-scholars of Peterborough who migrated from Canterbury College to Gloucester College because of their 'ongoodly demenyng'.[2]

The end of Burnell's Inn (or London College) was as curious and instructive as its earlier history: it is the story of a Tudor take-over.[3] When Cardinal Wolsey founded his college in 1525, took over the buildings of the suppressed priory of St. Frideswide, and began to build his great quadrangle, he probably had no difficulty in acquiring the south-western tenements, between St. Frideswide's and the street, together with the suppressed parish church of St. Michael, Southgate, which may explain why he began by building the southern half of his quadrangle, with the hall and the kitchen beyond. The northern range of the quadrangle was left to the last, and in fact was not built until the seventeenth

[1] *Registrum Cancellarii*, ed. H. E. Salter (Oxford Hist. Soc., XCIII, 1932), I, 267-9.

[2] *Canterbury College, Oxford*, ed. W. A. Pantin (Oxford Hist. Soc., New Series, VIII, 1950), III, 121.

[3] *Oxford Balliol Deeds*, pp. 95 ff., 172 ff.

century. But it must have been quite clear from the beginning, from the layout of the quadrangle, that its completion would involve acquiring the large property on the north, namely the old synagogue (Dolphin Inn) and Burnell's Inn (London College), that belonged to Balliol College, as well as some property of Godstow and Studley priory further to the north-east. The cardinal, who was at this time in supreme control of both ecclesiastical and secular affairs, had the bright idea that instead of paying Balliol in hard cash, he would make it up to them by procuring for them the appropriation of ecclesiastical benefices or the like, which he was in a position to arrange ; thus he would get his land at no cost to himself. About December 1525 Wolsey wrote to his agents in Oxford, telling them to use 'such dexterity and policy as first they may, by good handling of the Master and company of Baly College and also the prioresses of Godstow and Studley monasteries, induce them, by good words and promises with hope that the said most reverend father shall by impropriation of benefices unto them or such other ways recompense the same, to be content to demand no other recompense for their houses, being now of so little profit and advantage unto them ;' only if that failed were they to agree to pay cash.[1] The college seem to have accepted the offer, but unfortunately for them, by the time Wolsey fell from power at the end of 1529, he had neither given them appropriated benefices nor paid them cash, and in 1530 Balliol threatened to resume possession of their property. Some years later Balliol even claimed that the conveyance of their land to the cardinal's college had only been sealed because the senior fellow of Balliol had secretly got hold of the college seal when the master and fellows were away in the country on account of the plague. But it was of no avail. The fact was that the king had taken over the cardinal's assets while disclaiming his liabilities. When the Benedictine tenants had defaulted a century earlier, Balliol could distrain on their

[1] *Oxford Balliol Deeds*, pp. 96-7.

furniture; when the cardinal and the king defaulted on a grander scale, there was no remedy.

So far we have been considering the great people who owned Burnell's Inn. How much can be known about the academic inhabitants who actually lived in Burnell's Inn and the other academic halls in this area? The Oseney rentals and the fifteenth-century chancellor's register [1] give us some information. In the early fourteenth century St. Edward Hall (just west of the present site of the Bear Inn) was rented by two well-connected scholars in succession: John de Orleton (in 1317), brother of Adam de Orleton, one of the leading political bishops in Edward II's reign; and John Trillek (in 1324), a nephew of Adam Orleton, and himself afterwards bishop of Hereford.[2] Trillek can only have been about 14 years old in 1324, so clearly he was just one of those wealthy scholars renting a hall as a private house, not managing it as a principal.

Since Burnell's Inn belonged to Balliol and Vine Hall belonged to New College, it is not surprising to find that a good many of the principals of those halls were Fellows of Balliol or New College respectively; probably the principalship of a hall was a useful college perquisite. Perhaps also such halls were already being regarded as a kind of college annexe, where undergraduates could be kept under the eye of a fellow, without going so far as to admit them into the college itself; certainly this was how Oriel used St. Mary Hall, by placing its exhibitioners there in the early sixteenth century. Some of the principals had notable or colourful careers. Nicholas Carent (or Caraunte), principal of Vine Hall in 1436–8, became secretary to Queen Margaret of Anjou. Dr. John Morton, principal of Peckwater Inn and lecturing

[1] *Oseney Cartulary*, ed. H. E. Salter (Oxford Hist. Soc., XCI, 1931), III, 102 ff.; *Registrum Cancellarii*, vols. I-II, *passim*.

[2] *B.R.U.O.*, II, 1404; III, 1906. Trillek afterwards acquired another house, in New Inn Hall Street, which subsequently became an academic hall called Trillock's Inn or New Inn Hall, and survived until the nineteenth century.

in the Civil Law School near by in the 1450s, went on into the king's service and ended up as archbishop Morton of 'Morton's fork'. Thomas Hope, a German by birth, and afterwards naturalized, was deprived of the principalship of Greek Hall in 1445 for not revealing disturbers of the peace to the chancellor; he seems to have aided and abetted his Welsh cook, Griffith, in beating up another man — perhaps an inter-hall feud. This did not permanently damage his career; he went on later to serve for many years in the Roman curia, and had a variety of benefices ranging from Constance and Speyer to Canterbury and Cloyne.[1] One of the last principals of Greek Hall (in 1521) seems to have been Edward Carne; a civilian, he was employed as a diplomat by Henry VIII and Mary, and after Elizabeth's accession lived on in Rome in the English Hospice until 1561.[2]

I have already mentioned the predominance of the lawyers' halls and the lawyers' schools in this area, and naturally the inhabitants of these halls, from the principals downwards, were students or graduates of canon or civil law. We can get some idea of how the principals employed themselves. Some of them taught in the neighbouring law schools; some of them practised in the chancellor's court, the university's jurisdiction, which was kept busy with numerous actions for debt, minor breaches of the peace, proving of wills and so forth. More interesting still, quite a number of these principals also acted as officials or commissaries to do the work of various bishops or archdeacons, being rewarded with prebends and benefices. Henry Corbridge, who rented Eagle Hall *c.* 1387–9, was commissary to the bishop of Salisbury; William Addsore (or Hadesors), principal of St. Edward Hall *c.* 1422, was commissary to the archdeacon of Meath; Walter Sandwych, principal of Peckwater Inn *c.* 1436–8, was commissary of the bishop of Lincoln and advocate in the court of

[1] The principals mentioned above will be found, under their names, in *B.R.U.O.*

[2] *Dictionary of National Biography*, *s.v.* Carne.

arches ; Owen Lloyd, principal of Vine Hall *c.* 1451–9, was official of the bishop of Lichfield and vicar general of the bishop of Exeter ; William Morgan, principal of St. Edward Hall 1479–80, and of Vine Hall 1485, was official of the bishop of Llandaff ; William Horsey, principal of Peckwater Inn *c.* 1499–1502, was official to bishop FitzJames in the sees of Rochester, Chichester, and London successively ; Edward Higgons, principal of Greek Hall and London College *c.* 1500–2, was registrar of the bishop of Hereford as well as a master in chancery.[1] The importance of these details is the light they throw on the curious medieval system by which one lot of men held the benefices while another lot of men did the work.[2] Bishops and archdeacons got their work done for them by men like these Oxford lawyers ; these were rewarded by prebends and lesser benefices, whose duties were performed, in turn, by a host of minor deputies, vicars, or stipendiary chaplains. It was a hierarchy of deputies and substitutes. This was not necessarily a bad thing ; the university of Oxford is no worse off because the work which was once done by the chancellor in person is now done by a vice-chancellor. It all depends on the quality of the deputies. Here we can gauge something of the quality of the middle men, the bishops' deputies, by identifying them with these Oxford lawyers and principals.

Occasionally we can get a fuller picture of these men. Archaeologists and historians have sometimes regretted that when people became Christians in the early middle ages, they stopped burying their dead with grave-goods. But the probate inventories, wills, and legacies that we find in the later middle ages are as good, and in some respects better, for they tell us something of a man's intellectual interests and tastes. One of the lawyers mentioned above, the Welshman Owen Lloyd, was principal of Vine Hall, practised in the chancellor's

[1] *B.R.U.O.* gives the details of the careers of these men.

[2] W. A. Pantin, *The English Church in the Fourteenth Century* (Cambridge, 1955), pp. 35 ff.

court at Oxford, and worked for the bishops of Lichfield and Exeter; his main preferments were in Exeter (two archdeaconries and a canonry), but he also held a canonry in Hereford, and when he died (*c.* 1478), he left his books to Hereford Cathedral library — perhaps it was nearer to his home country — and there the books still remain. They are an interesting collection of 22 manuscripts and 2 very early printed books.[1] Ten of the books represent the tools of his trade, the standard texts and commentaries in canon law and civil law. Another book is half canonical, half theological, the *Pupilla oculi*, a manual for parish priests. There is a little theology: two volumes of Peter Lombard's *Sentences*, some homilies on the Lord's Prayer, the great English mystic Richard Rolle's commentary on the psalter (one of the best-sellers of the period), and the Golden Legend. Then come an interesting number of books of more miscellaneous or general interest: Giles of Rome, *De regimine principum* (the standard medieval work on political science); two encyclopaedias, one by Isidore of Seville, the other by Bartholomeus Anglicus; a summary of Cicero's *Rhetoric* bound up with Boethius' *Consolation of Philosophy*; a moralized commentary on Ovid's *Metamorphoses*; and a treatise on agriculture by a Bolognese judge, Pietro de' Crescenzi (1231–1321), called the *Liber ruralium commodorum*, based partly on classical writers like Varro and Columella and partly on his own experience, a fairly popular work with several early printed editions, which was valued as much as a piece of elegant literature as for its technical use. Finally there are the two early printed treatises bound up together: an exposition of the Mass; and the *Isagogicon* or introduction to ethics of the Italian humanist Leonardo Bruni of Arezzo, together with his translation of Aristotle's *Eudemian Ethics*, one of the new style of translations; both were printed in 1475, the first at Strasbourg, the second at Louvain; clearly Lloyd, who died not later than 1478, lost no time in getting the latest books. Some of these

[1] Listed in *B.R.U.O.*, II, 1153–4, where his career is given.

books were standard works, common enough, some were more out of the way, most of them thoroughly medieval, one or two suggesting a slight contact with early Italian humanism ; the whole collection shows us a working lawyer with quite a wide range of interests.

We get a rather clearer picture of another Oxford lawyer from a probate Inventory entered in the chancellor's register just thirty years later. Master Robert Bryan, Doctor of Canon Law, of London College (or Burnell's Inn) died in 1508.[1] He practised in the chancellor's court and held a couple of rectories in succession ; there is no evidence as to whether he served as official to any bishop. At the time of his death he was at London College, not apparently as principal, but probably as one of the senior graduates who would sometimes rent a chamber in a hall. The inventory of his effects is a modest one ; the total value is £5 : 12 : 6 (perhaps about £500 in modern money), of which £3 : 3 : 6 represents his books. The garments and bed-clothes were few : two tawny gowns, one violet gown, a 'partlet' (a kind of collar), two coverlets, and a pair of sheets. There is no mention of any furniture ; perhaps he hired it from the hall. The most interesting part is the list of nineteen books. We are not told which of these were printed books, but no doubt some were ; a few years later John Dorne, the Dutch or German bookseller in the High Street, was doing a good trade in printed books.[2] As in the case of Owen Lloyd, about half of Master Bryan's books represent the equipment for his professional work. There are about eight books of canon law, the *Corpus iuris canonici*, some of the standard commentaries and apparatus, two copies of the *Speculum iudiciale* of William Durand, and the like, and a single book of civil law (Baldus Cinus on the Code). To these should be added a book described as '*Reparacionis legati*', a corrupt reading which seems to defy identification ; a

[1] *B.R.U.O.*, I, 291 ; his inventory is printed in Appendix (2) below, p. 57.

[2] *Collectanea*, I (Oxford Hist. Soc., V, 1885), 71 ff. ; *Collectanea*, II (*ibid.* XVI, 1890), 463 ff.

formulary of instruments, perhaps the *formularius instrumentorum ad usum curie Romane* (printed several times) which John Dorne was selling; and a treatise on witchcraft by Angelus de Gambilionibus of Arezzo (d. *c.* 1461)—I doubt if this was of much use in the chancellor's court, but it reminds us that the classic age of witch-mania had just begun on the continent and would be spreading to England before long. There is a solitary theological work, the letters of Ambrose, and two classical texts, Cicero's *Tusculan questions* and Valerius Maximus (a great favourite with medieval readers). Finally there is the most interesting group of all: five books which reveal a preoccupation with the art and practice of elegant Latin writing, and particularly letter-writing, as taught and exemplified by the Italian humanists of the fifteenth century. Three of these are treatises: the popular *Elegantiae linguae Latinae* of Lorenzo Valla (1407–57); one of the treatises on grammar and letter-writing by Augustinus Datus of Siena (1420–78); and an *Ars scribendi in epistolis*, which is probably the *Ars epistolandi* or *Ars scribendi epistolas* of Francesco Negri, a Venetian professor at Padua (d. 1513), a popular work giving twenty different kinds of letters, with rules and examples. The other two books are collections of letters: the letters of Gasperini Barzizza of Bergamo (*c.* 1370–1431); and the *Epistole Peii*, which must mean the letters of Pius II (Aeneas Silvius Piccolomini, 1405–64). All these 5 books of Bryan's may well have been printed; all of them were in print before 1500, some of them many times over. It is pleasant to think of Master Bryan sitting in his study in London College and reading the letters of Aeneas Silvius, which ranged over a variety of topics, such as the education of children (addressed to the King of Hungary), the commendation of the Friars Observant, the love-story of Eurialus and Lucretia (a product of Aeneas' unregenerate youth), as well as Poggio's famous letter on the death of Jerome of Prague (which found its way into the collection). A few years later a book-list of this kind would almost certainly have included Erasmus' treatise on letter-writing and the early instalments of his *Adagia*, and these latter had in fact already been published by 1508 ; but clearly to Master Bryan the latest authorities on polite and humane letters are still the fifteenth-century Italians, and he really belongs to a pre-Erasmian generation. It would be interesting to know whether Bryan had any semi-professional motive in this interest in letter-writing, that is to say, whether such a man might be called on to write elegant letters for clients or friends, as the secretaries of great men might do, or whether this was simply a disinterested amateur's taste for humane letters. If it should seem at all surprising to find a lawyer with these tastes, it should be remembered that Italian lawyers in the late thirteenth and early fourteenth centuries had been among the pioneers of humanism,[1] and that the greatest of the English humanists in the early sixteenth century was a lawyer.

As to the rank and file of those who lived in the halls, we get some information from the chancellor's registers in the fifteenth and early sixteenth century. The colleges had governing bodies and visitors who could deal with disputes ; they could keep their affairs to themselves. The halls were not corporate bodies ; their internal disputes and difficulties, however trivial, had to be brought into the chancellor's court. Consequently we hear a lot about such things as failure to pay the landlord's rent, failure to pay the manciple for battels, failure to pay chamber rent or lecture fees, transfers of scholars from one hall to another. And in the background there was an endemic turbulence, breaking out every now and then. In the thirteenth century this had taken the form of faction fights between the northerners and southerners, which had led to a peace treaty in 1274, formally abolishing the northern and southern 'nations'. But by the later middle ages the old turbulence had taken on a new form, feuds between neighbouring halls. In 1452 the Junior Proctor, Thomas Reynold, died of wounds received when intervening in a conflict

[1] B. Smalley, *English Friars and Antiquity* (Oxford, 1960), pp. 280 ff.

between the scholars of Peckwater Inn and St. Edward Hall.[1] In November 1512 we have a well-documented account of an affray between the manciple of Peckwater Inn and a servant of the principal of London College, both halls bordering on St. Frideswide's Lane. On a certain day, just after vespers, as the manciple was coming out of St. Frideswide's church, he was, it was alleged, attacked by the principal's servant; this seems to have happened in the lane, just outside the gate leading into the churchyard. Eight witnesses give their evidence:[2]

John Tregonwell, scholar of civil law, a witness sworn and examined . . . deposes that he saw the said servant of the principal of London College standing near St Frideswide' churchyard in the highway, and when he saw the manciple of Peckwater's Inn with other scholars of the same place coming from St Frideswide's church, he drew his sword and struck the said John Andrew (the manciple), and then the same John on his part drew his knife.

There follow the testimonies, in the same sense, of John Longe, John Vonsfelde (perhaps a German?), Richard Tyack, and Henry Trenacke, all scholars of civil law and all of Peckwater Inn, and Olyver, scholar of civil law, of Broadgates Hall. After this comes evidence from the other side:

Richard Edwards, layman, of the county of Somerset, witness produced in behalf of Master Stevyns [principal] of London College, . . . sworn and examined deposed that two scholars came out of Peckwater Inn and came against the servant of the principal of London College who was standing in the street, with sword and shield. Asked if he knew the persons, he said he did not rightly know the persons. Asked about their clothes, he says the principal's servant was wearing a blue tunic and the other two were wearing fustian tunics. Asked who struck first, he is doubtful. Asked about the place of the quarrel, he says near Frideswide's gate. Asked who were present, he says he knows that there were twenty present. Asked about the day and hour, he says Wednesday last [17 Nov.] about the hour of vespers. Asked whether he saw any arms placed at the gate of Peckwater Inn, he says he saw many men standing within the gate with arms, before the quarrel began,

[1] *B.R.U.O.* III, 1572. [2] Printed in Appendix (3), below, p. 58.

and the same was also seen, so he says, by two bakers of the prior of Frideswide's, that is to say, Hugh and Thomas. Asked whether he is bribed by entreaty or money, he says no. Asked whether he favours either side, he says no.

If we can believe the last witness, it is a grim picture of something rather like gang warfare, with armed men lurking in the gateway of Peckwater Inn — more like *West Side Story* than *Mr. Verdant Green*. It is characteristic of this area that most of the witnesses were law students. The first witness, John Tregonwell, was to be a man of some note in after life; he became principal of Peckwater Inn and Doctor of Civil Law, went on to practise in the court of Admiralty, was much employed by Henry VIII, and took a leading part in the visitation of the monasteries. It was he who in 1540 bought one of the most beautifully sited of the English monasteries, Milton Abbas in Dorset, and made his home out of it; his tomb is in the abbey church.[1]

I have left to the last Canterbury College, after St. Frideswide's the most important institution in the Christ Church area.[2] Unlike the halls, this was a genuine college, a corporate body with a common seal and endowments of its own, though it was a monastic college dependent on the cathedral priory of Christ Church, Canterbury. It occupied a site about 270 feet long (from north to south) by about 150 feet deep (from east to west) in the north-east corner of the area, on the site of the present Canterbury Quad and the eastern part of the Deanery garden. The site was built up by acquiring about a dozen tenements, some facing on to Oriel Street, some on to St. Frideswide's churchyard; some of these houses were

[1] *Dict. Nat. Biog.*, *s.v.* Tregonwell; A. L. Rowse, *Tudor Cornwall* (London, 1941), pp. 187 ff.; David Knowles, *The Religious Orders in England* (Cambridge, 1959), III, 273.

[2] *Canterbury College, Oxford* (Oxford Hist. Soc., New Series, VI, VII, VIII, 1947–50), vols. I-III, containing inventories, college accounts and miscellaneous documents; a summary of the history of the college is given in the Fifteenth Annual Report of the Friends of Canterbury Cathedral (March. 1942), pp. 33 ff.

said to have been demolished by the force of the wind (no doubt the great gale of 1366); here, as well as elsewhere in Oxford (as at Merton and New College), college expansion was made easy by the decay of houses in the fourteenth century. Canterbury College was founded by Archbishop Islip in 1363 as a mixed body of monk fellows from Canterbury and secular fellows; two years later he changed his mind and made it a wholly secular body, with John Wyclif as warden; and by 1370, after a lawsuit, the monks regained control, and thereafter until 1540 the college consisted of a monk warden and monk fellows (varying in number from two to eight), and five secular undergraduate scholars. There is a tradition that Sir Thomas More was for a time at the college; if so, he may have been one of these secular scholars, nominated by his patron, archbishop Morton. Such a small number of fellows and scholars would not fill the college, and here as in other colleges some of the chambers (about ten) were regularly let out to lodgers, mostly monk scholars of other monasteries, but with a few senior secular graduates. The college was able to resist absorption by Wolsey, but came to an end with the Dissolution of the monasteries in 1540. After that the buildings were taken over for use as part of Christ Church, and remained almost intact until the eighteenth century; they are shown in the top left-hand corner of Loggan's view of Christ Church (1683). The hall was on the west side of the quadrangle, the chapel on the south side, the gate on the east (where the present Canterbury Gate is); the rest of the quadrangle was occupied by staircases and chambers, and the library seems to have lain to the west of the quadrangle. Whereas Burnell's Inn was entirely obliterated by the north range of Tom Quad, and even Peckwater Quad does not quite occupy the site of the medieval Peckwater Inn, Canterbury Quad and Canterbury Gate, though entirely rebuilt by James Wyatt between 1773 and 1778, still reproduce the place and shape, as well as the name, of the medieval quadrangle of Canterbury College.

APPENDIX I

Letter to William de Yakesle, abbot of Thorney, from William Burnell, provost of Wells, c. 1289–92. British Museum, MS. Cotton Charter xiv. 13.

Religioso ac amabili Deo viro, domino Dei gracia abbati de T[horney], suus W[illelmus] B[urnell], Wellensis prepositus, salutem et se paratum ad sue beneplacita voluntatis. Quia dominus noster Batthoniensis et Wellensis episcopus, quem novimus pro constanti vos in sincere dileccionis visceribus confovere, literatorie vos exhortat, ut incepcioni nostre in artibus vobis placeat interesse, nos ipsius rogaminibus addimus preces nostras, consideracione consimili qua mari coniungitur rivulus ut conscrescat, vobis humiliter supplicando, quatinus die Lune proxima post octabas beati Iohannis Baptiste apud Oxoniam nostrum curetis principium vestra venerabili presencia decorare intuitu nostri domini memorati nostrique contemplacione rogatus. Nos etenim hac de causa habebitis arcius obligatos ad singula que nobis duxeritis iniungenda. Altissimus vos conservet.

APPENDIX 2

Inventory of Master Robert Bryan, of London College, c. Aug. 1503. Oxford University Archives, Reg. Canc. F (rev.), fo. 64v.

Inventorium honorum M. Bryan de collegio London.

1 In primis corpus iuris canonici magna[1] precium xviij s.
2 Willelmus in speculo in iure precium ix s.
3 Abbas in magna precium xviij s.
4 Cinis [2] super codicem precium xij d.
5 Iohannes de Ymola precium xx d.
6 Willelmus in speculo antiqua [3] precium iij s. vj d.

[1] *Sic MS., probably for* magna forma. [2] *Sic MS., for* Cinus.
[3] *Sic MS., probably for* antiqua forma.

7 Bartholus super extravagantes iij s.
8 Epistole Peii[1] xiiij d.
9 Angelus de maleficiis x d.
10 Laurencius de Valla xij d.
11 Epistole Grasperini[2] x d.
12 Tusculane Tullii xvj d.
13 Valerius Maximus x d.
14 Dinus de regulis iuris vj d.
15 Formularium instrumentorum viij d.
16 Epistole Ambrosii xij d.
17 Reparacionis legati vj d.
18 Augustinus Datus iiij d.
19 Ars scribendi in epistolis iiij d.
Item ij taune goundys xxvj s. viij d.
Item a violet gound vj s.
Item ij coverlettys viij s.
Item a partlet x s.
Item a peyyr of shetys iij s. iiij d.

APPENDIX 3

Evidence given in the Chancellor's Court about an affray between the manciple of Peckwater Inn and the principal's servant of London College on 17 November 1512. Oxford University Archives, Reg. Canc. F (rev.), fo. 178

Testes in causa mancipii Pecwaters Yn et servientis principalis collegii London. Eodem die [18 Nov. 1512] Iohannes Tregunwell, scolaris iuris civilis, testis iuratus et examinatus in causa precedente inter Iohannem Andrew mancipium Pecwaters yn et quendam servientem principalis collegii London', deposuit quod vidit dictum servientem principalis London' stantem prope semiterium beate Frydyswyde in regia via, et cum vidit mancipium Pecwaters yn cum aliis scolaribus eiusdem loci venientem ab ecclesia dive Frydiswyde, extraxit gladium et percussit dictum Iohannem Andrew, et tunc idem Iohannes ex parte sua extraxit cultum suum.

[1] *Sic MS., probably for* Pii. [2] *Sic MS., for* Gasperini.

Tercius testis. Iohannes Vonsfelde scolaris iuris civilis Pecwaters yn . . . deposuit ut primus testis. Et ulterius deposuit et dicit quod cum dictus serviens principalis percussit antedictum Iohannem, ipse extraxit cultellum suum et defendit seipsum et percussit eundem servientem principalis dicti collegii.

. . . .

Septimus testis. Olyverus scolaris iuris civilis Latarum Portarum . . . Interrogatus de tempore, dicit in die Mercurii proximo elapso statim post vesperas.

. . . .

fo. 178v

Testis in causa pacis inter Andrew et servientem principalis collegii London. Ricardus Edwardus, laicus comitatus Somersyde, testis productus ex parte magistri Stevyns collegii London', de et super quodam litigio pacis de quo supra inter Iohannem Andrew mancipium Pecwaters Yn et servientem principalis collegii London' iuratus et examinatus, deposuit quod duo scolares exierunt ab hospicio Pecwaters et veniebant adversus servientem principalis collegii London' stantem in platea cum gladio et scuto. Interrogatus de noticia personarum, dicit quod non recte novit personas. Interrogatus de vestimentis, dicit serviens principalis utebatur blodia tunica et alii duo utebantur tunicis de fusteyn. Interrogatus quis primo percussit, dubitat. Interrogatus de <loco> [1] litigii, dicit prope ostia Frydiswyde. Interrogatus quibus presentibus, dicit quod scit quod erant xx presentes. Interrogatus de die et hora, dicit in die Mercurii proximo elapso [2] et circa horam vesperarum. Interrogatus an vidit aliqua arma posita ad hostium Pecwaters Yn, dicit quod vidit multos stantes infra hostium cum armis antequam litigium erat inceptum, et illud etiam viderunt, ut dicit, duo pistores prioris de Frydswyth videlicet Hugo et Thomas. Interrogatus an sit correctus [3] prece vel precio dicit quod non. Interrogatus an favet alicui parti dicit quod non.

[1] *interlin.* [2] 17 Nov. [3] *Sic MS., for* corruptus.

3

E. F. Jacob

THOMAS BROUNS, BISHOP OF NORWICH 1436–45

My friend and former colleague at Christ Church, Sir Keith Feiling, in his earlier days one of Chichele's flock, may not think it an irrelevance to read here a few pages about one of the archbishop's ablest disciples and officers, Dr. Thomas Brouns, bishop of Rochester (1435), then Norwich (1436–45). It was a special mark of Chichele's rule at Canterbury that he was able to gather round him a staff of high distinction. William Lyndwood, the canonist, is known to all: Thomas Bekynton's letters have survived to prove his sure touch on public affairs; John Kemp, dean of the Arches, Chancellor of Normandy, archbishop of York, became a Cardinal; Richard Andrew, Auditor of Causes, King's Secretary 1433, was made the first Warden of All Souls (1438), then dean of York (1452), a constant negotiator in the royal service.

Two of the most active for church and king alike (for it was the fifteenth century) were John Stafford and Thomas Brouns. With Stafford I have dealt, although too summarily, in another place:[1] a royal servant of high connection taken from the Court of Canterbury to be bishop of Bath and Wells, Chancellor of England, and later archbishop; but Brouns is another story, if of a not dissimilar legal and diplomatic pattern: one that ended with a great East Anglian see as the crown of a long public career. Brouns must have been

[1] 'Archbishop John Stafford', *Trans. R. Hist. Soc.*, 5th Ser., XII (1962), 1–23.

one of the richer medieval bishops of Norwich — his will [1] is enormous, never of trifling bequests : but he was one of the more upright and humane of contemporary prelates, not a character like Polton or even Kemp.[2] Order, good sense, and flexibility were keynotes of his administration ; and he had a large circle of friends. Something of the peaceful moderation as well as of the methodical thoroughness of Chichele had pervaded his life.

Brouns was a native of Sutton Courtenay, near Abingdon. He was in all probability the son of William Brouns who held one-eighth of a knight's fee of the Courtenay earls of Devon, lords of the manor. Thomas in his will left £10 'for a memorial in the chancel of the Blessed Virgin Mary in the parish church of Sutton Courtenay where my parents and past members of my family (*maiores mei*) were wont to be buried' : and he left 108 marks in nine instalments for a chaplain to pray for him and his ancestors. To his nephew Richard Brouns, evidently his brother Richard's son, he bequeathed 100 marks for the repair of his houses in Sutton Courtenay and Dudcote (Didcot), and to stock them 'so that he may be sufficiently supported in his domestic economy (*in yconomia*)' ; as well as a good deal of valuable furniture.[3] The family was armigerous — but here is a difficulty. The late Mr. Dorling in giving the shield of Brouns in the *Victoria County History of Berkshire*, describes the bearings thus : Argent three hawks lures sable.[4] But these are the arms which occur in the cathedral of Norwich on a shield attributed by Blomefield to Brouns' predecessor John Wakeryng. Unquestionably Blomefield is correct.

[1] Lambeth Palace Library, Reg. Stafford, fos. 131v-4.

[2] See the letters written by Kemp, when he was trying to secure the archbishopric of York, to William Swan, proctor at the Curia : Brit. Mus., MS. Cotton, Cleopatra C.IV, fos. 160, 160v, 171-2v.

[3] Reg. Stafford, fo. 132 ; For the Brouns family, see *Victoria County History, Berkshire*, IV, 373. It is probable that the name was pronounced Bronns or Brunce, not Browns. Brown, as given in certain works of reference, it never was.

[4] *V.C.H. Berks.*, IV, 374.

At any rate Brouns' family were of middle estate, reasonably well off: of the kind that, in the fifteenth century, produced clerics who made their way to high office. It is a period of a rising middle class not merely in the towns, but in the countryside, and throughout the century the social structure of England was undergoing profound changes.

The date of Brouns' birth is not known, but he was sent to Oxford and was a master of arts by 1404.[1] If he went at the age of 16 in 1396, this makes him born about 1380. He was a jurist. He took his licentiate in the canon and civil law in 1411 and in due course the doctorate. His legal training is of outstanding importance. To positions in church and state, the study of the canon and the civil law opened the way; legal experience and the practice in the church courts was the most fruitful avenue, for the civil law was not practised in the courts, though it was required in foreign embassies and negotiations; but the canon law, which was the working law of the church, was the *sine qua non* for the ecclesiastical lawyer. A study of the secular prelates of the fifteenth century would show how large a proportion of them went up the ladder of promotion by their pleading and practice in the consistories. Chichele himself, as rector of St. Stephen's Walbrook, pleading in the London consistory, quickly came to the notice of Richard Medford of Salisbury and was made the bishop's chancellor; after that prebends came in, and all was secure.

Ten years were to elapse after taking his Master's degree at Oxford before Brouns received his first appointments to benefices. They were the livings of Appleton, Berks (probably 1403); Cranford St. John, Northants (1410); Ailby, Lincs (October 1410); St. Aldates, Oxford (1412);[2] the latter three rectories all in the diocese of Lincoln. In 1414

[1] A. B. Emden, *A Biographical Register of the University of Oxford, to* A.D. 1500, I (1959), 281. Hereafter cited as Emden.

[2] Emden, *loc. cit.*

bishop Repingdon of Lincoln brought him to the cathedral as sub-dean.[1] This was a dignity held in succession to Richard Hethe, archdeacon of Huntingdon. A strong successor was needed because of the tension prevailing between the bishop, the cathedral chapter, and the dean.[2] Between the chapter and the dean relations were extremely bad. In 1408 or 1409 Repingdon had held a visitation, which had not passed without criticism and opposition : the *comperta* showed that the conduct of the cathedral clergy and the order of the services lacked discipline and that ignorance of the cathedral statutes was general. It was necessary to have a canon who knew what statutes meant.[3] For this laxity the residentiaries said that the dean was responsible. In 1414 suspicion of heresy was added to the charges against the cathedral clergy. This was the year in which Repingdon had cause to be most active against the Lollardy pervading his diocese.[4] Significantly, it was the year when Brouns took his stall and later, in Convocation, he will be found prominent as commissary of the archbishop in the trial of Lollards. There was indeed good reason for having a competent lawyer. In 1412 the forty years of dean Mackworth's extraordinary régime had begun, and in November the president of the chapter and the eight residentiaries agreed to petition the bishop to convene the chapter in order to deliberate on the usages of the church and to settle disputes with the dean. Mackworth had already, on his own, varied the decanal oath by adding the words '*salvo iure meo decanali vel similia*'. Repingdon had to take notice of this and make a full enquiry. Brouns was one of his com-

[1] *Fasti Ecclesiae Anglicanae, Lincoln*, ed. H. P. F. King (1962), p. 4. He became archdeacon of Stow in March 1419 (*ibid.* p. 18), and prebendary of St. Botolph the same year (*ibid.* p. 39). In 1420 he was appointed by the Crown to the prebend of Langford Manor, but did not get it until 1423 (*ibid.* p. 76).

[2] M. Archer, 'Bishop Repingdon and his Chapter', *Univ. of Birmingham Historical Journal*, IV (1956), 91.

[3] In 1410 Repingdon (*Register of Philip Repingdon, Bishop of Lincoln 1405–1419*, ed. M. Archer, Memoranda, I (1963), 183), issued his injunctions on this ignorance.

[4] *Reg. Repingdon*, Memoranda, I, 362–3, 367–8, 379.

missaries for the purpose. The inquest led to a long-drawn-out series of meetings, resolutions, and compromises, Mackworth being usually absent, while an episcopal visitation of the chapter continued until 1418.[1] This was only the beginning of the affair. The later meetings Brouns did not attend; but he was still in the diocese. He held the prebend of Welton Westhall in 1416 which in 1419 he vacated for the archdeaconry of Stow and the prebend of St. Botolph's.[2] He must have given up the sub-deanery that year and he kept out of the mêlée in the chapter.

After 1419 he was being attracted south. The archbishop had begun to claim him. In August 1423 he was made warden of the altar of Goldes in the collegiate church of All Saints, Maidstone, and in 1427 he was given the Treasurer's prebend in South Malling.[3] As I have shown elsewhere, both these colleges in the diocese of Canterbury were largely reserved for the legal members of the archbishop's staff.[4] Brouns was in Chichele's *entourage* by 1423, when with Lyndwood, he was on the metropolitical visitation of the diocese of Chichester, visiting the clergy and people of Chichester, as well as the rural deanery of Boxgrove, in the cathedral itself.[5] In 1425 he became the archbishop's chancellor and auditor of causes; that means that he presided over the archbishop's court of audience, the court held by Chichele in virtue of his position as legate of the Holy See. With Lyndwood too in 1425 he carried out the metropolitical visitation of Merton College; the injunctions to the college were issued by him and Lyndwood in June that year and their careful economy shows the

[1] The complaints, long accumulated, against the dean's mismanagement are in A. Bradshaw and Christopher Wordsworth, *Lincoln Cathedral Statutes*, III (Cambridge, 1897), 372 f. Bishop Alnwick's award of 1439 is *ibid.* III, 186-207. Cf. K. Edwards, *The English Secular Cathedrals in the Middle Ages* (Manchester, 1949), pp. 68, 146.

[2] Emden, *op. cit.* I, 281; *Fasti Ecclesiae Anglicanae*, Lincoln, ed. King, p. 39.

[3] Emden, *op. cit.* I, 282.

[4] *The Register of Henry Chichele*, ed. E. F. Jacob, I (Oxford, 1943), lxxv-lxxvi.

[5] *Ibid.* III, 505.

character of the archbishop's chancellor. The number of the Fellows (44) must not be allowed to drop; the incautious felling of the woodlands of the College must be controlled; its books must not be sold; its manors must not be alienated in any way; and the details of its administration must be audited by a specially deputed Fellow who is to hear the *compotus* of the bursar and draw up in duplicate a full statement of the position annually. The chancellor was further commissioned to follow up the visitation by enquiring how the injunctions were in fact being observed and to correct defects revealed in the earlier part of the visitation.[1]

The years 1425–30 saw some of the great Lollard trials in which, as chancellor, Brouns played a conspicuous part. In that of William Russell he was both a judge and a commissary:[2] in 1425 he was on the committee of Canterbury Convocation deputed to consider 'the best and most expeditious way' of proceeding against the Lollards; in the long Convocation of 1431 he examined the proctors' certificates and pronounced the successive adjournments, and in 1432 was again examining the proxies and helping to determine the question whether Eugenius IV's dissolution of the Council of Basel was valid.[3]

Financially, during the period at Canterbury, he was doing quite well. He held for some time the rectory of St. Dunstan in the East (1425–31), and as a high legal dignitary of the archbishop he must have been residing in or near London, while drawing the revenues of his Lincoln prebend and of a further prebend, the Lancashire Flixton, belonging to the church of Lichfield. He therefore had three prebends and a rectory — as yet nothing like the position of the classical pluralists. In 1427 he added a further prebend, that of Ratfyn, along with the archdeaconry of Berkshire in the church of Salisbury, and in 1429 he was made a canon of Chichester.

[1] *Reg. Chichele*, IV, 265-8.
[2] *Ibid.* III, 119-20, 186-7, 191.
[3] *Ibid.* III, 220, 226, 232 (the Basel debate).

In 1431 he was appointed by the Crown to the deanery of Salisbury.[1]

Thus, materially fortified, he was entering the rat-race for the episcopate. His early experiences were unfortunate. Bishops may indeed have been elected by a chapter, but in fact the issue lay with the king (and under Henry VI, with his Council) or the Pope, the one party initiating, the other consenting. Usually it was the king in his Council who determined on their man and sent the name to the Pope, who then provided him to the see.[2] Occasionally it was the Pope who got his way, and sometimes there was a compromise on a third name. In 1429, Brouns, now with five canonries and the chancellorship to his credit, was elected by the chapter to Chichester with royal support ; but the Pope preferred another member of the Salisbury chapter, the dean, Simon Sydenham, whose place, two years later, as just mentioned, Brouns was chosen to fill. In 1433 on the death of Thomas Polton, Brouns was provided by the Pope to Worcester, but this time the king's Council intervened to cancel the appointment because its acceptance without leave offended the Statute of Provisors, and Brouns had to withdraw.

That was the ostensible reason : the real was more characteristic and less creditable. Young Thomas Bourchier, son of William Bourchier, earl of Essex and his wife the Lady Anne, daughter of Duke Thomas of Woodstock and part inheritor of the Bohun fortunes, was born in 1412 ; rapidly advanced, by the age of 15 was offered the deanery of St. Martin le Grand. He was made Chancellor of Oxford at the age of 22 (1434–5). Thomas was now put forward by the Court party and when Brouns was provided by the Pope, the *congé d'élire* nominating

[1] Elected 4 July 1431, confirmed 17 July : *Fasti Ecclesiae Anglicanae, Salisbury*, ed. Joyce M. Horn (1962), p. 4. Emden, who gives his prebends, omits the deanery.

[2] 'Under Henry VI. bishops were recommended not so much by the king as by the lords who dominated his council' : R. J. Knecht, 'The Episcopate and the Wars of the Roses', *Univ. of Birmingham Historical Journal*, VI, 2 (1958), 110.

Bourchier was issued to the dean and chapter of Worcester, which, on 9 December 1433 complied.[1] This created tension between the Pope and the Crown which was not finally resolved until the see of Rochester fell vacant on the death of John Langdon and Brouns was appointed by papal provision. The Worcester election was a bad business and Brouns, who had merited the position, must have felt it keenly.

He had already deserved well of the government. In 1420 he was one of the envoys arranging for an interview between Henry V, the King of France, and the Duke of Burgundy (April 1420);[2] in July that year he was sent on a mission to treat with the bishop of Nantes and others about the release of Arthur of Brittany.[3] It was in the 'thirties that he became involved in conciliar politics, his absorption in which is reflected in the later part of his Register, mainly after 1440. In 1432 he was among the first royal ambassadors to be named in the English delegation to Basel.[4] He was with the delegation which arrived late in February 1433 and in the late spring of that year was one of the English ambassadors protesting in the king's name against the Council's procedure by deputations instead of through 'nations'.[5] Most of the delegation seems to have returned to England in the summer of 1433, but Brouns was not with them.[6] In 1434 he was named as an ambassador for the second English delegation to the Council,[7] the members of which, when it arrived, were incorporated. Brouns was not with it long. In November 1434 he left Basel along with Edmund Beaufort, earl of Mor-

[1] These transactions are analysed by A. Hamilton Thompson, *Interim Report of the Appointment of Bishops Committee* (Church Assembly 282), 1929, App. IV, pp. 42-3.

[2] Rymer, *Foedera* (3rd ed., 1740) IV, iii, 169; where he is termed Thomas Brous (probably a misreading for Brons).

[3] *Ibid.* IV, iii. 182.

[4] *Proceedings of The Privy Council*, IV, 123, 125; Rymer, *Foedera* IV, iv, 183, 184.

[5] A. Zellfelder, *England und das Basler Konzil* (Berlin, 1913), pp. 248-50.

[6] P.R.O. *Lists and Indexes*, nos. XI, p. 81, and XXXV, p. 202.

[7] Rymer, *Foedera*, V, i, 12; *Calendar of Patent Rolls, Henry VI*, II, 342.

tain.[1] He appears to have taken no further part in the work of the second English delegation which stayed in Basel until the summer of 1435. What was he doing in the winter of 1433–4, when the rest of the English had gone back and why did he leave prematurely before his colleagues returned? He seems to have remained abroad but the nature of his employment is unknown. As I mentioned above he had already been provided, in vain as it turned out, to the see of Worcester by Eugenius IV and, as Dr. Schofield suggests to me, he may have wished to be out of the tensions and complications at home which his acceptance of the provision involved.

Perhaps his most important assignment was his membership of the English party sent in May 1439 (after he had become bishop of Norwich) to negotiate peace with France: our last resort after the rebuff the English suffered at the Council of Arras in 1435. The hope faded: but Brouns did useful work in negotiating a commercial treaty with Flanders the same year.[2] He was out of his diocese from 9 June to 5 October 1439, leaving its care to his devoted vicar general John Wygenhale. But we are anticipating and must go back a little. While bishop of Rochester, he was translated to Norwich by a papal bull of 19 September 1436. He received the bull while at the Council of Basel, but had to apologize to the king for doing so before the royal assent had been obtained. The difficulty was surmounted and Brouns had the temporalities restored to him on 16 February 1437. He held the see until his death on 6 December 1445.

I do not propose to consider his short Rochester episcopate, but to make only one general observation. Rochester was a monastic cathedral and had had a monk of Christ Church, Canterbury, as its last bishop. Here Brouns would acquire valuable experience for dealing with a monastic chapter of

[1] *Monumenta Conciliorum Generalium* (Vienna, 1873), II, 771; *Concilium Basiliense, Studien und Quellen zur Geschichte des Konzils von Basel*, ed. J. Haller (Basel, 1895 cf.), V, 411.

[2] *Foedera*, V, i, 61, 62, 63.

monks, such as he was to need at Norwich Priory. The Prior of Norwich, as will be seen, was to give him a lot of anxiety.

For Norwich recourse must be had to his register.[1] This is the official record of his acts. Its entries follow the pattern of his predecessors, John Wakering and William Alnwick, but without any section of testaments; this means, very roughly: commissions to his officers; institutions and exchanges, ordinations, 'memoranda' of all kinds, both relating to his diocese and the church at large. Early in Wakering's register appears the unmistakeable hand of that bishop's new scribe and register, John of Exeter, notary public, whose autograph and notarial mark are found in various places. Exeter continued to direct and, with assistance, to write the register throughout Alnwick's pontificate and worked for Brouns the whole of his time. The note of Brouns' death on St. Nicholas Day 1445 at the end of a page of institutions is in his hand.[1]

It is a fine, bold register hand, notable for the magnificent marginals with the large capitals and for the scrolls in which he places the month in which the institution took place. These marginals are fully four times the size of the rest of the writing, but he left himself space in the margins too for financial notes to be made on each institution: 14 marks; 20l, and with these almost invariably come the letters P, sometimes PA, M, sometimes MI. These figures and notes probably refer to the first-fruits of the benefice, to collect which from the new incumbent one of Brouns' staff was duly commissioned. The figures correspond with the assessment of the living that formed the basis of taxation payments and is sometimes above, rarely below, the figure given in the *taxatio* of Nicholas IV. Where the benefice was unassessed the marginal *non taxatur* is written. What then do *M* and *P* mean? The latter is certainly *pagavit* (he paid). M may stand for *man-*

[1] I am much indebted to the bishop of Norwich for permission to consult this (1962) under the best of conditions, and to Mr. T. F. Barton, F.S.A., his honorary archivist, for valuable help. The Registers have now been deposited by the bishop in the Archive Department of the Norwich Public Library, where they are classified as 'Institution Books'.

datum (mandate to be sent for the payment). Possibly, but less likely, for *mutuum* (*i.e.* the clerk borrowed the dues), but *MP* or *MI PA* which occurs occasionally may mean *minus pagavit* (he paid less than he should). Sometimes *M* is repeated four times, noting the collector's irritation. I think that these are notes by a collector, not by Exeter himself.

In his administration of the diocese Brouns relied on his vicar general, John Soresden, alias John Wygenhale, doctor of canon law, who was also commissioned as the president of his consistory, *i.e.* official principal.[1] Wygenhale who was rector of Barton Bendish (a fine church north of Stoke Ferry) was given two prebends in the bishop's collation. In 1441 he was master of the Chantry of the Exaltation of Holy Cross, Attleborough (founded by Sir Robert Mortimer, *c.* 1390), a secular college of a master and three Fellows,[2] and later (1444) of the deanery of the collegiate church of the Blessed Mary of the Fields (*i.e.* Chapel Fields), the bishop's own college which he had endowed.[3] The register is almost as much his book as Brouns'. Commissary general, corrector of offences, and sequestrator was Master Nicholas Dorman who had to supervise the residence of the incumbents, correct abuses in the clergy and laity, and had the proof of all testaments of lesser people in the diocese; the larger being reserved to Wygenhale and in the case of magnates and clergy to the bishop or his commissary.[4] Dorman was also the bishop's official in his temporal property.[5] Master Richard Doket was made receiver of first-fruits.[6] Besides the four archdeacons of Norwich, Norfolk, Suffolk, and Sudbury, there was a special official in the archbishop's liberty of Lynn, Master William Cote, bachelor of canon law.[7] It was a much bigger diocese than the present, for it included both east and west Suffolk, an area rich in religious houses, a number of them exempt from the archbishop's jurisdiction, including, of course,

[1] Institution Book 10, Reg. Brouns, fos. 2v (a shorter form is on fo. 5), 3.
[2] *Ibid.* fo. 41v. [3] *Ibid.* fo. 55. [4] *Ibid.* fo. 3. [5] *Ibid.* fo. 3v.
[6] *Ibid.* fo. 4. [7] *Ibid.* fo. 6.

the huge liberty of St. Edmund. To perform all episcopal acts, *e.g.* ordination, confirmation, making of chrism, etc., bishop Robert of Grado, now beneficed in the diocese, was again commissioned as suffragan.[1] The bishop was Robert Ringman, a Franciscan employed in the diocese from 1425–52. Robert never collated nor instituted ; these duties were reserved for the bishop and his official. The medieval suffragan of Norwich, it should be said, was quite different from the modern version. He was not attached to any area or town, but was purely an assistant to the bishop. He did not institute : he ordained, and that was one of his principal uses. Out of the 38 ordinations in Brouns' time 22 were taken by the suffragan, 16 by the bishop.

The main burden of the institutions — the entire burden when Brouns was away — fell on Wygenhale, who in addition examined and conducted all exchanges, confirmed elected religious where non-exempt, and instituted new Superiors. He was normally resident in Norwich but also went on circuit. The bishop was only periodically at the palace, though he used the palace chapel for ordinations and the house itself for various episcopal *acta*. His manors of Hoxne, Thorpe by Norwich, and South Elmham were his normal resort. Frequently in London on royal business and in convocation, he lived in his manor or inn at Charing Cross where there was a garden and ponds looked after by a keeper, one John Strange, paid 14 pence a week with his lodging in the gardener's house from the revenues of the bishop's Essex manor of Lambourne.[2] Brouns did not personally reside in the diocese until 2 September 1438 when according to the register 'the said reverend father first came to his manor of Hoxne'.

Brouns' institutions followed the pattern of Alnwick's. On an average there were 10 to 12 a month.[3] For the first year there were 121, for the second 111, for the third 128. These include the *prefecciones priorum*, appointments of the heads of

[1] Institution Book 10, Reg. Brouns, fo. 3v ; commissio suffraganei.
[2] *Ibid.* fos. 98, 98v.
[3] There were 16 in March 1440.

religious houses which are recorded in some detail. The bishop pronounces the election valid, confirms it judicially, issues a certificate enabling the newly appointed abbot or prior to administer the spiritualities, receives from him the oath of canonical obedience and orders the new prelate to be installed by the archdeacon or his official. Certain entries here suggest that 'election' did not necessarily have the sense which we give it today. On 20 September 1438 Thomas Pope, canon of Flitcham, was appointed prior of that small Augustinian house, a dependency of Walsingham. The convent had submitted to the bishop's nomination in high and low (they compromised on Brouns), and the words Brouns used of Pope's appointment are *nominamus et eligimus*. I find only one instance of a private patron exercising his right to present a religious house in his own patronage : the Trinitarian house or Ingham where in February 1440 Milo Stapleton Esquire, in certifying that it was '*nostre fundacionis et patronatus*', asked the bishop to exercise his authority for him and appoint John Blakeney as a priest brother.[1]

Concerning the institutions, two facts impress the mind : the substantial number of livings in the gift of religious houses (outnumbering those of private patrons) and the proportions of exchanges both within and without the diocese, which in the early years of the episcopate is comparatively high, *e.g.* monthly, four to five out of ten to twelve, but falling off during the 'forties. It is still difficult to know how all the exchanges were originally arranged without opining that there must have been some sort of clerical agency to give the information to clerks who wanted to move. This was Professor Hamilton Thompson's guess and it may be right. But there is a sort of regional boundary. Those coming into the diocese of Norwich by exchange did not have to travel far : there are few from distant dioceses. Some came from Ely where Louis of Luxembourg, archbishop of Rouen, the President of the English Council at Rouen, was administering the

[1] Reg. Brouns, fo. 31v.

see which he held *in commendam* ; some (particularly Essex incumbents) from London diocese ; some from Lincoln. Salisbury seems the most distant. It was on the whole an East Anglian clientèle. Coming to the benefices themselves, I have noted that the statistics in Wakering's register reveal how large a proportion of the parish churches belonging to the monasteries had no vicarage ordained within them, and it was the bishop's constant care to watch that the incomes of the incumbents were adequate, especially in view of the fact that remissions from the tenth were hard to come by. Decline in income of smaller churches, particularly of moieties, might lead as they do today to a union of benefices and a number of such unions were carried out by Brouns, obviously on the advice of the archdeaconry — no pastoral committee existed as today.

Either personally or through Robert of Grado, Brouns held ordinations at the *quatuor tempora* (four times a year). During his episcopate 1343 orders were conferred. That does not imply 1343 separate clerks, for there were three stages in Holy Orders — sub-deacon, deacon, priest. There are 360 ordinations as priest, 498 as deacon, and 476 as sub-deacon. There is no note of the examinations held by the archdeacons. The registrar gave only the names of those entering Holy Orders and no first tonsure or acolyte is mentioned. Eighty per cent of those instituted to livings were already in priest's orders ; I have only counted one acolyte instituted. There were very few cases of clerks under age becoming rectors or vicars. Brouns was apparently able to resist family or noble pressure there. It is hard to estimate the proportion of men with degrees ordained. The number of those described as *magister* is small and Brouns granted very few licences for study ; but he was anxious that the diocese should send growing youth to the university and in his will left a sum of money to provide funds. As a disciple of Chichele, Brouns would want to promote the graduate, but for those with

[1] *E.g.* Reg. Brouns, fo. 94 (Langley).

higher degrees the prebends in his collation were scanty, all the more so since his cathedral was monastic and those prebendal posts, *e.g.* stalls in Stoke by Clare, had to be reserved for people who acted as his helpers or commissioners in the diocese. Probably the rectors and vicars in the Norwich diocese were not a particularly academic lot, less so than in Lincoln, Chichester, or Canterbury dioceses. They belonged, as far as one can trace them, to the yeoman or husbandman class and to families of traders and merchants in the towns and ports of East Anglia. I have found only two villeins or *nativi* being manumitted but there is no mention of ordination in their cases.[1]

The examiner of clerks to be ordained, besides enquiring into the birth, morals, and learning of a candidate, had to ask what title he had, *i.e.* what were his means of support. The clerk could say that he had means of his own or that his title was his patrimony, his family's goods, or that he could live on the proceeds of his benefice. Mr. H. S. Bennett has pointed out that, at any rate, by 1427 there wer every few patrimony titles. This is certainly true for Brouns' register. The predominating title is given by religious houses : only few are returned as having the title of their benefice. In view of the overwhelming bulk of the candidates ordained having monastic titles, Mr. Bennett asks :

> 'is it possible that they [the monasteries] may have given nominal title to candidates on condition that they paid the monastery a proportion of their benefices when they were obtained, rather like a modern scholastic agency ?'[2]

Brouns' institutions show that the monasteries were under no obligation to appoint these ordained clerks to their own churches. On occasion they did so, for in any larger church there was more than one position going. If one studies the

[1] Thomas Burdene of Lingwood 'nativum nostrum ad manerium de Beytham cum tota sequela', fo. 98v ; and Adam Ponyant, villein of the priory of Norwich, fo. 99.

[2] *Studies presented to Sir Hilary Jenkinson*, ed. J. Conway Davies (1937), p. 29.

large numbers of titles provided by St. Giles Hospital, Norwich, one inclines to agree with Mr. Bennett that there may well have been some financial arrangement. This Augustinian hospital was not rich; it had an income of £58 in 1535, but the number of benefices in its control was nothing like the number of clerks whom it provided with titles. The suggestion that to get a title you made a subscription to a religious house, *e.g.* St. Benet Hulme, Ixworth, or Carrow (for the nunneries were prominent) is not to be rejected. It would have been a good way for an impoverished house to add to its revenues for the year.

The memoranda of Brouns' register are more interesting even than those of Wakering's or Alnwick's for the variety of interests covered both within and without the diocese. There is nothing so scandalous as the episode, in Alnwick, of the prioress of Redlingfield who had to be ejected from her priory for immorality and bad government. John of Exeter recorded the whole case with care, even to the extent of recording the remark of the prioress about the bailiff with whom she had misconducted herself, 'that he was a free man and of free condition and of the best family (*de optima stirpe*) of the village'.[1] But the case of Sir Thomas Tudenham, who had left his wife Alice (Woodhouse), which ends Brouns' register, does not fall appreciably below this standard.[2] Much of the memoranda was the result of cases heard by Brouns in his own *audientia*, many begun upon petition and some requiring the testimony of local jurors who would be neighbouring incumbents summoned by the archdeacon. All property business where the immovables of the see were concerned was taken by the bishop and the prior sitting *capitulariter*, for the prior was equally the guardian of the property of the see

[1] Institution Book 10, Reg. Alnwick, fo. 104. Noted by J. C. Cox, *Victoria County History*, *Suffolk*, II, 83-4. They made love 'subtus le heggerows'.

[2] Reg. Brouns, fo. 113 ff. This tremendous case, ending in divorce and involving well-known Norfolk people, was begun at the end of Alnwick's régime and was heard by John Wygenhale at the bishop's promotion. Alice was the daughter of Sir John Woodhouse of Kimberley.

and full chapter decision was necessary for acquisitions, alienations, and financial acts of importance.

Relations with the prior were a difficult subject upon which there are a number of entries. Before 1433 bishop Alnwick had had great trouble with his prior, for the latter was responsible for ordering the services of the monastic cathedral; next to the exempt abbot of St. Edmunds he was the leading conventual in the diocese; socially and tenurially he was the biggest man in Norwich, always there while the bishop was not; and the bishop was not his abbatial superior though he could be visited by the bishop and though the bishop handled the amoval of the monastic obedientiaries.

The friction came mainly over the service. Brouns was determined to assert the dignity of his office and much space in the memoranda is given to the omission by the prior of the *reverencialia* or marks of respect which the bishop demanded as his due.[1] The registrar inserted the direction of Eugenius IV to all non-exempt religious houses that, when the bishop visited them, the bells should be rung and marks of reverence paid.[2] In 1440 Brouns petitioned Eugenius that no one below him in dignity should, while he was present, use full pontificals or give solemn Benediction, and the Pope himself granted the petition. Brouns further drew up a list of the liturgical *reverencialia* on which he insisted: the exact position of the prior when walking with the bishop in procession — the prior on the right but a little behind the bishop (*non tamen pari fronte cum episcopo sed paulo retractus*), and holding the hem of the bishop's cope; that when the bishop made his ordinary visitation of the priory there should be a solemn reception at the western entrance and a bell should be rung. These and other demands of the bishop were agreed at a meeting of both sides in the bishop's palace — the bishop, his lawyers and the notary Exeter, and the prior and senior obedientiaries of the monastery — when a further point was added: whenever the bishop moved through the cathedral wearing

[1] Reg. Brouns, fos. 109-10v. [2] *Ibid.* fo. 101.

pontificals by night or by day, the prior if he was there, or person next in dignity, should cense the bishop.[1] But the liturgical point which raised the worst storm was the kissing of the text of the gospels, *sive aliud deosculatorium*, and it was owing to the prior's denial of this to the bishop that Brouns made a tuitorial appeal to Rome and for the protection of the court of Canterbury.[2] This mark of respect had apparently been agreed upon but had not been carried out. Brouns, in his appeal (12 October 1443), complained that when he had gone in procession to the high altar, the prior, after the prayers had been said, refused to minister to him the crucifix *vel osculatorium, i.e.* the pax. The prior's position evidently was that this was a special mark of honour not payable except when the bishop had been away from his cathedral for a substantial time, and in the end it was agreed that he should do this whenever the bishop came to his cathedral after an absence of two continuous months or more.[3]

Brouns' interest in liturgical matters and his desire for uniformity can be seen in a letter to the priory of Redlingfield. He has been told, he says, that its service books are in a worn and frail condition and that the priory has been acquiring works of various uses, the variety of which does not induce proper devotion in the convent. He is aware that these religious can acquire books of the use of Salisbury at less cost than would be involved if they bought others of divers uses. Accordingly he ordains that from 1 May 1440 Salisbury shall be the one and only use permitted in the convent and he enjoins the prioress to take steps accordingly.[4] He was nothing if not practical, and in his will Brouns left the priory a copy of the use.[5] In this he was following the example of archbishop Chichele who in his metropolitical visitation of the cathedral of Chichester enjoined the Salisbury pattern upon the dean and chapter.[6] It was, as he states, the most easily available: the stationers and book-sellers were evidently trading in it.

[1] Reg. Brouns, fo. 110v. [2] *Ibid.* [3] *Ibid.* [4] *Ibid.* fo. 101v. [5] Reg. Stafford, fo. 132v. [6] *Reg. Chichele*, III, 505.

Brouns was far from being a local bishop ; his training and diplomatic experience pointed the other way. His interest in the struggle between the Council of Basel and pope Eugenius IV is expressed in a number of entries under 1440 and relates to the campaign of Eugenius to dissuade England from taking the side of the conciliar majority. In 1439 Eugenius had concluded at the Council of Florence the union of the Greek and Latin churches. This is a subject of a special oration made at the court of Rome by Vincent Clement, the Spanish Dominican, who conducted from time to time much of Henry VI's diplomatic business in the Curia and as a sympathetic go-between had the confidence of the English episcopate. Brouns had entered this as the 'speech made in the presence of the pope before he presented the letters of our lord King'.[1] The letters were Henry VI's congratulations to the Pope upon securing the union of the churches. The envoy praises Henry VI as one of those who offer themselves for the truth and for the faith, one 'whom neither the revolutionary arguments of the men at Basel nor the bland letters of that portentous body, nor the clever reasoning of many have been able, I do not say to prevent, but to cause for a moment to hesitate in declaring his obedience to the Roman Father'.[2] The long and flowery discourse testifies to the king's abhorrence of the Basel majority and of the dangers of following it.

This is followed by a letter of Eugenius IV to Henry VI referring to the royal letter which Clement presented. Henry had told the Pope that he had sent to Basel an envoy *ad reprimendam vesanam eorum temeritatem* and had written to other princes in the same strain like a good truly catholic prince.[3] The registrar then copied in a letter of Charles VII signed by the French monarch in his Council at Bourges on 2 September 1440 urging obedience to the Roman See.[4] None of the documents, to my knowledge, have seen the light. They bear out the English dislike of the Council of Basel in which

[1] Reg. Brouns, fo. 104.
[2] *Ibid.* fos. 104v–5.
[3] *Ibid.* fo. 105.
[4] *Ibid.*

the first of our two delegations to that assembly declined to be incorporated. This was shrewd diplomacy, for the English church had much leeway to make up with Eugenius who was constantly suspicious of the opposition to papal provisions and reservations that existed in the king's Council,[1] a body indeed which was to show its dislike of paying taxation for papal crusades whether against the Hussites or against the Turks.

Brouns' later years at Norwich were darkened by the famous struggle between the citizens and the ecclesiastical owners of property of the city. The dispute, familiar to all students of Norwich history, had been going on for many years. The underlying cause was the various interpretations placed on the unwarily drawn charter of Henry IV (1404) creating the city of Norwich a county and exempting the citizens from the jurisdiction of the sheriff of Norfolk. In Norwich and its periphery what was city and what was county? Where were the boundaries to be drawn? Were the great franchise-holders — the bishop, the prior, the abbot of St. Benet Hulme and others — to be included in the city, or could they plead that their franchise exempted them from its jurisdiction? The claim of the radical progressives was that the *whole* city came under their jurisdiction. This the conservative element of the place, quite apart from the ecclesiastical franchise-holders, utterly denied.[2] The struggle between the leading conservative, Thomas Wetherby, and the radicals, as Mr. Blake recently reminded us,[3] must be seen in the light of an internecine feud. By 1440, when the citizens had received various rebuffs from royal commissioners who

[1] Cf. Raymonde Foreville, *Le Jubilée de saint Thomas Becket* (Paris, 1958), pp. 63-4; E. F. Jacob, *Henry Chichele and the Ecclesiastical Politics of his Age* (1952), pp. 15 f.

[2] An account is given in Blomefield, *Essay towards a topographical Study of the City of Norwich*, III (1806), 150 f.; W. Hudson and J. C. Tingey, edd., *Records of the City of Norwich* (1906–10), I, nos. LXXXIX–XCII, and 340-1.

[3] W. J. Blake, 'Thomas Wetherby', *Norfolk Archaeology*, 32 (1958–60), 60-72. Mr. Blake's defence of Wetherby is interesting and a useful correction to Hudson's partisanship but needs fuller documentation.

tried to settle the territorial question,[1] the situation was acute and the townsfolk were resorting to violent attacks upon the bishop's palace, the priory, and other religious houses.

There are two documents in the register relating to these disturbances. In the first, dated 18 March 1443, Brouns directs his vicar general and the archdeacons to publish in sermons and on other occasions of general concourse the excommunication sent by archbishop Chichele and directed against those who were in rebellion against the peace of our sovereign majesty the king and against the church of Norwich. The document is in English and relates primarily to the attacks on the bishop himself and on the priory which had been going on in that particular year. Chichele's intervention is important: it was a general excommunication not only of all ring-leaders, but also of all citizens participating in the assaults, and must reflect the anxiety of the king's Council. Brouns had to interpret this, and did so in a mandate to his official principal and his archdeacons:[2] having transmitted the sentences, he at once reserved to himself the absolution of all who had fallen under the ban. All lesser penitenciars were excluded. He could indeed lay an interdict on the city, but this, he said, he was not prepared to do, provided that persons who knew themselves to be guilty would come to him and seek absolution. This was a sagacious provision, for he must have known many of the offenders. The second document, undated, is in fact part of the first: it is the verdict of twelve jurors on the encroachments made by the citizens upon lands and property of the bishop. The issue in dispute was whether these properties lay within the city of Norwich or the county of Norfolk. Enquiries into alleged encroachments began, as Blomefield, and later Hudson and Tingey show, in 1417.[3] It was this issue that various judicial commissions appointed by the Crown were asked to determine. The most important of these was the enquiry held at Thetford in July 1441 before

[1] Blomefield, *op. cit.* III, 151–2. [2] Reg. Brouns, fos. 92, 92v.

[3] Hudson and Tingey, *Records of the City of Norwich*, I, 288.

John Fray, William Paston, and Sir Thomas Tudenham, knight, which found the burgesses were wrongfully claiming rights over the bishop's land and various hospitals and the hamlets adjoining ; in short, claiming and acting as if the central religious buildings and much of the suburbs lay within their own jurisdiction. Brouns is stated by Blomefield to have offered to mediate between the conservatives and the radicals of the city.

He had been a good friend to the citizens. Between 1437 and 1444, the year when a royal patent gave the definite topographical ruling upon the claims of the citizens and of the bishop and religious houses, he had intervened with the king on behalf of the city. In 1437 when the franchises and liberties of the city were taken into the king's hands and a new mayor and sheriffs were appointed, Brouns besought the king to restore the franchises of the citizens, with success : the new officers were discharged.[1] Again in 1439 he joined his predecessor William Alnwick in requesting the Council to restore the liberties and franchises which once more had been seized by the Crown on the grounds that the citizens were using unauthorized weights and measures.[2] In 1443–4, in conjunction with the Earl of Norfolk he was again asked by the citizens to use his good offices with the king for the restoration of the liberties of the city.[3] And in his will he left 40l. to help them to pay the tenth — the normal borough taxation. These acts of clemency had not been repaid, as the documents we have just cited show. The citizens had adopted a violent course, and the royal patent of 8 February 1444 shows what some of the encroachments were : *e.g.* appropriation, by the citizens, of St. Gregory, Norwich ; the acquisition of Connisford Meadows, without royal licence. In the end the king had to issue a declaration that follows clearly the terms of the Award of Thetford, the second of the documents quoted here,

[1] *Calendar of Patent Rolls*, 1436–41, p. 123.
[2] P.R.O., E. 28/63 ; *Cal. Patent Rolls*, 1436–41, p. 357.
[3] Hudson and Tingey, *op. cit.* I, No. XLIII, 114.

and further granted full regalian rights to the bishops of Norwich, not only to be keepers of the peace and justices in Norwich, but in their own lands to appoint commissioners and justices of the peace :[1] 'to hear and determine all cases arising within the Priory, the palace, Lynn and all their lordships'. Brouns had evidently done his best to get a peaceful solution of the dispute, but it had been unavailing.[2]

We can think of Brouns as an alert, liberal-minded, and thorough diocesan and as one loyal to his friends and servants. In his will he remembered not only the prior and the monks, not only the canons of his collegiate churches, but the vergers and the bell-ringers. He made liberal bequests to his squires, to his yeomen and his grooms, and all members of his household who had been with him two years. He left 5 marks to Henry Bonor, his cook ; a hundred pounds (a large sum) was to be paid to the tenants of his demesnes 'when the 15th of the lord king happens', *i.e.* towards the taxation. He left 100 marks to subsidize six boys from his demesne lands, who were to be exhibited to grammar and logic (*sophistriam*), in the University of Oxford, each receiving 40s. or more a year, as his executors should decide.[3] In the codicil to his will he deputed the choice of these to Wygenhale and John Mildwell, his confessor, and put in Cambridge as an alternative.[4]

[1] *Cal. Patent Rolls, 1441–1446*, pp. 232–3.

[2] The submission of the citizens to the bishop and the Earl of Suffolk is printed Hudson and Tingey, *op. cit.* No. XLIV, 116.

[3] Reg. Stafford, fo. 132v.

[4] 'In altero studiorum Oxon' vel Cantabrigie' ; fo. 134.

4

H. R. Trevor-Roper

THE FAST SERMONS OF THE LONG PARLIAMENT

IT was an observation of that time', wrote Clarendon of the Puritan Revolution, 'that the first publishing of extraordinary news was from the pulpit; and by the preacher's text, and his manner of discourse upon it, the auditors might judge, and commonly foresaw, what was like to be next done in the Parliament or Council of State.'[1] Clarendon himself took a great interest in the techniques both of parliamentary management and of political preaching. He had himself, in the first eighteen months of the Long Parliament, ample opportunities of watching the 'tuning of the pulpits' by Pym; and indeed, I shall suggest, his first tactical defeat by Pym may have been in one such matter. Though some of his particular illustrations are incorrect, his general statement is, I believe, true. In this essay I wish to show how the leaders of the Long Parliament, while there was effective leadership, used the pulpit both for strategic and for tactical purposes: both to declare long-term aims and to inaugurate temporary shifts of policy; and I shall do so particularly with reference to those sermons over which the parliamentary leaders had direct control, the regular 'fast sermons' which were preached before Parliament on the last Wednesday of every month from 1642 to 1649.

General fasts, with appropriate sermons, were, of course,

[1] Edward, Earl of Clarendon, *The History of the Rebellion*, ed. W. D. Macray (Oxford 1888), IV, 194.

nothing new in 1640. Great occasions had always called them forth. There had been a general fast on the approach of the Armada in 1588, a weekly fast in 1603 until the plague was over, and another general fast for the great plague of 1625. More recently, fasts had also been held at the beginning of Parliament. There was always something a little distasteful to the Crown about such proposals: they emphasized the gravity of affairs and implied that Parliament, with God's support, provided the means of solution. Consequently Queen Elizabeth never allowed them. In 1580, when the House of Commons suggested a public fast for the preservation of the queen's life and the better direction of the actions of the House, she was furious. The proposal was very modest, and the House proposed to leave the choice of preacher entirely to the Privy Councillors in the House 'to the end they might be such as would keep convenient proportion of time and meddle with no matter of innovation or unquietness'. Even so, the queen expressed her great misliking and astonishment at such rashness and made the House eat the humblest of humble pie. That done, she graciously allowed that their rash, unadvised, and inconsiderate error had proceeded from zeal, not malicious intent, and forgave them provided that they never misbehaved in that sort again.[1]

They did not; and it was not till the last Parliament of James I that a more formidable House of Commons revived the proposal. On 23 February 1624 Sir Edward Cecil moved that there be a general fast, with a collection for the poor, as in Holland. The House was to choose the preachers. But of course the king must give the authority: Parliament could only prescribe for itself. So the Commons conferred with the Lords and together they moved the king. James I agreed, saying that he would consult the bishops as to the best time. After that the practice became regular. There were general

[1] Some early fast-days are mentioned in a later fast sermon by William Gouge, *The Right Way . . .* (1648). See also *Commons' Journals* (hereafter referred to as *C.J.*), I, 118 foll.

fasts, proclaimed by the king on the motion of both Houses, at the beginning of each of the first four parliaments of Charles I.[1]

Apart from fasts, or 'days of public humiliation' in times of crisis, there were also special sermons on certain anniversaries and on days of thanksgiving for great victories or deliveries. The accession-day of the reigning monarch was one such anniversary; another was 5 November, the day of the Gunpowder Plot; a third, which rose in popularity as the Stuarts fell, was 17 November, the accession-day of Queen Elizabeth. This was an unofficial day of thanksgiving, on which the Stuart kings, not unnaturally, tended to frown.[2]

Thus when the Long Parliament met, in November 1640, it was perfectly natural that one of its first acts should be to propose a general fast, and it was, by now, perfectly natural that the king should agree to it. It was also perfectly predictable that particular crises or particular triumphs might elicit special days of 'public humiliation' or 'thanksgiving'. What few would have predicted was that such occasions would have been converted into a regular system in order to sustain the unity of Parliament and the fulfilment of an ever more radical programme over several years; that Pym would learn to 'tune the pulpits' as effectively as ever his heroine Queen Elizabeth had done; and that well-timed sermons would not only declare the general party line but also, on particular occasions, prepare the way for dramatic episodes. They would foretell the death first of Strafford, then of Laud; declare the Civil War; initiate the iconoclastic programme; and, finally, they would announce the most dramatic, most revolutionary gesture of all: the execution of the king himself.

The first episode in this history comes at the very beginning of the Parliament. When Parliament met, its very first act

[1] *C.J.* I, 671, 715, 869, 873-4, 922-6.

[2] For the celebration of 'Queen Elizabeth's day' under the Stuarts see J. E. Neale, *Essays in Elizabethan History* (1958), pp. 9-20.

was to propose a general fast. The procedure followed the form which was now usual. Both Houses, in agreement, requested the king to authorize the solemnity. Each House chose its own preachers. All business was to be suspended. There were to be sermons morning and afternoon. The Lord Mayor was to make arrangements in the City. At the same time the House of Commons, following earlier precedents, also appointed a day on which all its members should take the sacrament and listen to further sermons. This was an internal matter requiring no royal authority. When these plans were agreed, the dates were chosen. Symbolically, the date chosen for the joint fast was 17 November, Queen Elizabeth's day; the date for the taking of the sacrament was to be 29 November. The preachers chosen by the Commons were, for the first ceremony, Stephen Marshall and Cornelius Burges; for the second, John Gauden and George Morley.

These arrangements were not casual. Nothing, in those early days of the Long Parliament, was casual. After all, this great meeting of Parliament had been planned long ago. For three years 'the great contrivers', as Clarendon called them, had been planning their tactics, preparing their programme. They had a political programme and a social programme, and they intended to realize them both by certain clearly defined steps. First, they had to force the king to summon Parliament; then they had to secure the return of their friends to Parliament; then they had to dismantle the existing royal government; finally, they had to persuade the king to accept the reformers into his counsels. For this purpose the great peers — the Earls of Warwick, Pembroke, Bedford — had used their clerical and borough patronage. For this purpose the great strategists — Bedford and his supporters, Pym and St. John — had devised their strategy. Naturally, now that the moment for parliamentary action had come, they were not unprepared. The function of the first sermons was to lay down the policy of Parliament, and the preachers chosen already knew their parts.

By far the most important of the preachers was Stephen Marshall, minister of Finchingfield, Essex, the most famous political parson of the Revolution. Like so many of the political clergy, Marshall was a client of the Earl of Warwick, and he had served his master well, preaching for his parliamentary candidates throughout Essex. He had already preached the fast sermon at the beginning of the Short Parliament, that first false start of the reforming programme.[1] In the Long Parliament he would emerge as the inseparable political and spiritual ally of Pym, the interpreter of Pym's policy after Pym's death. At every stage of the Revolution we can see him. Now he is thumping his pulpit on great occasions; now he is meeting with Pym, Hampden, and Harley to prepare parliamentary tactics; now he is bustling through Westminster Hall to push voters into the Parliament before the division; now he is retiring, exhausted, to recuperate in the well-appointed house of his good friend 'my noble Lord of Warwick'. Later he would be the Parliament's envoy to Scotland, its chaplain with the captive king; he would pass unscathed from Presbyterianism to Independency; and if he always appeared as the spokesman for the winning side, his changes can be explained by one consistent aim, which was also the aim of Pym: to preserve the unity of opposition against royal and clerical reaction.[2]

From beginning to end, Marshall was the clerical tribune of the Parliament. Others accompanied him for stretches of the road only. At the beginning, his constant companions were Cornelius Burges, who now preached with him on the fast-day, and Edmund Calamy. They too were both clients of the Earl of Warwick. As a political parson Burges at least

[1] *Calendar S.P. (Domestic) 1639–40*, p. 609.

[2] There is no adequate biography of Marshall, whose importance, at least as the spokesman of policy, seems to me greater than has been allowed. The particular details which I have mentioned come from two passages in the diary of Sir Simonds D'Ewes, both quoted in F. A. Shaw, *A History of the English Church . . . 1640–1660* (1900), I, 81–2, and from *A Copy of a Letter written by Mr. Stephen Marshall* (1643), p. 1.

was hardly less active than Marshall. His greatest achievement would be the ingenious financial device of 'doubling' on bishops' lands to pay off the Scottish armies. That busy Scotch minister, the Rev. Robert Baillie, who so piqued himself on his political ability, recognized 'good Mr. Marshall' and 'my dear friend Dr. Burges' as kindred spirits — at least until he found that they were even sharper than he. From the opposite side Clarendon would also single them out. 'Without doubt', he would write, 'the archbishop of Canterbury had never so great an influence upon the counsels at court as Dr. Burges and Mr. Marshall had then upon the Houses.' [1]

Thus from the start the stage was set. By the time that Burges and Marshall mounted their pulpits, their message was predictable. Strafford was in prison, his plans to break the Parliament frustrated, at least for a time. But for how long? All depended on the cohesion of Parliament, its refusal to be divided by royal manœuvre or internal strains. This had always been Pym's message: from his earliest days in Parliament he had advocated a 'covenant' among the enemies of popery and tyranny. Now both Burges and Marshall sang to the same tune. In the universal peril, said Marshall, all hope lay in a covenant such as had been made to defend religion in the days of Queen Elizabeth. It was not enough, added Burges, 'to pull down and cut off some of the Nimrods' who had invaded English laws and liberties: 'there must be a thorough joining of themselves to God by covenant'. And each in turn looked back to the same day eighty-two years ago, 'the auspicious entrance of our late royal Deborah (worthy of eternal remembrance and honour) into her blessed and glorious reign'.[2]

Marshall and Burges laid down the political conditions of parliamentary survival. The next sermons, the sermons of 29 November, showed something of the social programme

[1] Clarendon, *op. cit.* I, 401.

[2] C. Burges, *The First Sermon Preached to the House of Commons . . .* (1640); S. Marshall, *A Sermon Preached before the House of Commons* (1640).

envisaged. They also gave a further glimpse of the mechanics whereby the pulpits were tuned. John Gauden was another clerical *protégé* of the Earl of Warwick. George Morley was, as far as we can see, unconnected with the 'great contrivers'. He was an intimate friend of Hyde and Falkland, an Anglican of 'Socinian' views like Falkland himself, and a regular member of Falkland's circle at Great Tew. His future was to be as a royalist ally of Hyde. But in 1640 Hyde and Falkland were reformers and Morley had incurred the dislike of Laud: they could therefore propose him in a loyal but anti-Laudian Parliament, and he could be chosen along with the candidate of the 'great contrivers', Gauden. But even at this early stage the distinction between the real party leaders and their 'moderate royalist' allies was made apparent. When the sermons were over, the House voted its thanks to Gauden, and invited him to print his sermon. The thanks, and the request, were conveyed by Sir Thomas Barrington, the brother-in-law of the Earl of Warwick. But Morley fared differently. His sermon, we are told, 'was so little to their gust and liking' that no such message was sent to him. His sermon was not printed and we do not know what he said.[1]

On the other hand, Gauden's sermon, the sermon which the leaders of Parliament blessed, is a very revealing document. It was a plea for a peaceful, social, and religious reformation in England, and it ended with a positive suggestion. If Parliament wished, said Gauden, to carry out this reformation, it could not do better than to consult 'two great and public

[1] The fate of Morley's sermon is described by Anthony Wood, *Athenae Oxonienses* (ed. P. Bliss, 1813–1821), iv, 150. Wood does not date it precisely: after mentioning 'the wars', which, he says, commenced in *anno* 1641 [*sic*], he says 'at the beginning of which he [Morley] preached one of the first solemn sermons before the Commons. . . .' Since 'the wars' began in 1642, the *D.N.B.* (*s.v.* Morley) says that his sermon was in 1642. But in fact Morley was never invited again after November 1640, and the *Commons Journals* for Nov. 1640 confirm that he was not invited to print his sermon then. It therefore seems clear that this is the episode to which Wood refers. In writing 'at the beginning of which' Wood was no doubt thinking rather of 'the troubles' generally than 'the wars' particularly.

spirits who have laboured much for truth and peace', John Dury, the apostle of Protestant unity, and John Amos Comenius, the Bohemian reformer of education, 'both famous for their learning, piety and integrity and not unknown, I am sure, by the fame of their works, to many of this honourable, learned and pious assembly'. In the published version of his sermon Gauden added a note. It might not seem easy, he wrote, to fetch these men to England since Comenius was in Poland and Dury in Sweden. However, 'there is a fair, easy and safe way of addresses to them both': they could be reached via Samuel Hartlib of Duke's Place, London.

Certainly Hartlib, Dury, and Comenius were 'not unknown' to the leaders of Parliament: they were far better known to them than to the preacher who now uttered their names. Hartlib was a close friend of Pym, and for the last few years most of the 'great contrivers' had been in touch with them, directly or indirectly, circulating their works, supporting their projects, supplying them with money. Those three men were the philosophers of the 'Country Party', and in naming them Gauden was stating in advance the social programme of the parliamentary reformers. And once the programme had been thus indicated, the rest followed. Hartlib was requested to fetch Dury and Comenius to England in the name of 'the Parliament of England'. Next year they came; and although the deterioration of politics made it impossible to realize their reforms, and Comenius would retire, disillusioned, to Sweden and Holland, their names would never be far from the lips of the parliamentary leaders. Whenever political peace seemed (however falsely) to have returned, Hartlib and Dury would be summoned to draft the new social millennium; and when Oliver Cromwell had at last, among the debris of Crown and Parliament, established some kind of order, it was from their circle that he would accept advice on religious reform, social and educational policy, even foreign affairs.[1]

[1] I have dealt more fully with this episode and its significance in my essay 'Three Foreigners' in *Encounter*, vol. XIV (1960), no. 2.

So much for the first fast sermons, the sermons of 1640 At that time there was no thought of repetition. The ceremonies were inaugural ceremonies ; the sermons charted the course ahead ; the rest should be plain sailing. Unfortunately it was not in fact plain sailing. What Bedford called the great rock of Strafford's case thrust itself up and threatened to wreck the Parliament. For the trial of Strafford did not go according to plan. The legal charges were hard to prove and yet it seemed suicide to acquit him. Bedford himself wished to spare Strafford for the sake of ultimate compromise with the king ; but would the king ever compromise if he had Strafford to advise him ? Was it not safer to knock that fatal adviser on the head as a beast of prey, even if it alienated the king for ever ? That was the view of Bedford's more radical allies. Between these two policies the parliamentary leaders wavered. Then, at the beginning of April, events occurred to decide them. On 1 April Bedford and Pym learned of the Army Plot, the plot to rescue Strafford from the Tower by force. At first Bedford, in his desire to keep tempers down, persuaded Pym to say nothing to the Commons. But Pym, it is clear, was now converted. On 3 April he caused the remaining Irish charges against Strafford to be hastily depatched so as to push forward the more damaging English charges ; and next day, being Sunday, he once again used the pulpit to declare policy.

The preacher of this ordinary Sunday sermon was Samuel Fairclough, a country clergyman from Suffolk. The patron of his living there was Sir Nathaniel Barnardiston, a close ally of Pym ; and the preacher himself acknowledged that only the favour and command of his patron could have brought him from his rural obscurity to address so exalted a congregation. When the sermon was over he would return to that obscurity and only come to our notice again twelve years later, when he would preach at his patron's funeral. Nevertheless, this demure and humble parson was not afraid, on this occasion, to pronounce a very remarkable sermon. It was about the 'troubler of Israel', Achan, whose sins lay heavily on the whole people of God, until they were relieved of it by his prompt execution on the orders of Joshua. For 'troublers of the state', said the preacher, though they must have the benefit of 'due trial and examination', must always be despatched 'without any unnecessary delays or procrastination'. Thereupon, with revolting relish, he repudiated in turn every argument of justice or humanity. Death, only death, would satisfy the remorseless preacher, death without time for repentance on one side or for reflection on the other. And then, lest he should seem to be speaking of too abstract a case, he dropped the case of Achan, whose punishment was more apposite than his crime, and turned to other 'troublers of Israel' who had deserved the same fate. In particular he turned to Achitophel, the treacherous councillor of King David, who, having wormed his way into his master's confidence, and then stirred up armed revolt, finally offered himself to suppress the rebellion he had raised, in order 'that, as he had been President of the Council in peace, so now he might feed his ambitious humour in making himself general of the forces in war'. In this capacity Achitophel, said the preacher (who seemed remarkably well informed about Strafford's speech to the Privy Council on 5 May 1640), had urged 'all haste and expedition, no further counsel but his own: he would not have the battle delayed one day'. Therefore let there be no delay in his despatch, which will give such joy to the church as Israel felt when the Egyptians were drowned in the Red Sea, when Sisera was beheaded, when Haman was hanged.[1]

At this time, it should be noted, Strafford, though on a capital charge, was still legally presumed innocent. The knowledge of the Army Plot was still confined (it seems) to Bedford and Pym. The details of Strafford's advice in Council would not be revealed to Parliament till the next day. It is hardly

[1] S. Fairclough, *The Troublers Troubled, or Achan Condemned and Executed* (1641).

conceivable that this country clergyman, so submissive to his patron, so dazzled by his momentary publicity, should have dared, on his own initiative, to dictate to Parliament, while the great trial was still *sub judice*, a new and more sanguinary course. And yet from that date this was the course which would be followed. The conclusion is forced upon us that Fairclough's sermon was the means of declaring a new party line.

Perhaps it was the usefulness of that sermon which suggested to Parliament a more frequent use of solemn fast-days; for only a fortnight afterwards a proposal for another joint fast was referred to a committee, and the committee, on 28 April, reported that there indeed were grounds enough for such a solemnity. Notwithstanding the former day of public humiliation, progress had been slow, dangers and fears remained, plague threatened. . . . However, the proposal seems not to have been pursued. No doubt it was lost in the press of business. And when Strafford's head was at last off, and the king, it seemed, had surrendered on all issues, the occasion for sackcloth and ashes was over. In the summer of 1641 Pym even felt able to disband the Scottish armies on which Parliament had hitherto relied and which had now become a liability. The next special religious demonstration was therefore not a fast but a day of thanksgiving for the peace with Scotland. To celebrate that event, the sign of victory, the basis of a purely English reformation, on 7 September 1641 the church bells were rung all over England; and Parliament listened to ecstatic sermons from Stephen Marshall and Jeremiah Burroughes. To both of them 1641 was '*annus mirabilis*', 'this wonderful year', greater than 1588, the year of the Armada, the 'return of the prayers of forty and forty years' since the accession of Queen Elizabeth: the year which had silenced all critics, would enable swords to be beaten into ploughshares and spears into pruning-hooks, and would begin 'a very jubilee and resurrection of Church and State'.[1]

[1] Jeremiah Burroughes, *Sion's Joy* (1641); S. Marshall, *A Peace Offering to God* (1641).

The euphoria of that autumn was general. It was then that Milton's great pamphlets were written, then that Dury and Comenius met in England to plan the new social reformation for which the political basis, it now seemed, was secure. The disillusion caused by the Irish rebellion and its consequences was therefore profound. By the middle of December the affairs of Parliament looked blacker than ever. The king was now back in London. He had won over the City, the House of Lords, the 'neuters' in the country. He was preparing to strangle the parliament. So we need not be surprised to find the leaders of Parliament, on 17 December, proposing once again (as well as certain more practical measures) a 'day of humiliation'. This time it was to be not only a parliamentary but a general fast, to renew and re-emphasize the solidarity of Parliament and people. The fast was to be celebrated by the two Houses and the City on 22 December, by the country on 20 January. The preachers to the Commons were to be, as so often, Stephen Marshall and Edmund Calamy. The Lords and the City would choose their own preachers. The arrangements in the country were to be made by the local authorities on the instructions of their members of Parliament.

By the day of the parliamentary fast, London was already in turmoil. Pym had won one great victory: the city elections had given him control, through his radical ally alderman Penington, of the Common Council. The king had counter-attacked by putting a notorious cavalier in command of the Tower. At any moment, it now seemed, the crunch would come. If Parliament was to survive, it must keep left, disdain no weapons, draw on the radical spirit of the City mobs, exalt their radicalism by ideological gestures. In the previous winter, Pym had contained the City mobs, diverted their attacks on episcopacy, on images, on 'popish' ceremonies. Now he must appeal to these forces. The sermons of 22 December reflected this mood. While Calamy deplored the delay in reformation caused by the sins of the City, which made it, like Sodom, ripe for destruction, Marshall beat the drum ecclesiastic and urged his hearers to hunt out the sinners. They should remember good king Josiah, who not only broke down 'all the images and reliques of idolatry' but also 'executed the justice and vengeance of God upon the instruments of the kingdom's ruin, the idolatrous priests, digging the bones of some of them out of their graves'. No nice scruples of prudence or legality had hindered that good work. Josiah 'consulted not with flesh and blood': it was God's work and he did it without question, 'with zeal and fervency'. Parliament should now go and do likewise.[1] For these seasonable sermons the preachers were duly thanked and voted a gratuity of £20 apiece in plate.

So the fierce struggle for London was launched. Massive processions demanded justice against 'bishops and popish lords', the obstacles to reform; 'images' were denounced and attacked, Westminster Abbey and the House of Lords invaded; the impeachment of the queen was threatened. The king retaliated with his attempt on the Five Members and, failing, left London, resolved only to enter it again as a conqueror.

To the leaders of Parliament the king's flight was a declaration of war. At the time, neither side might be prepared for war, and it would take eight months before the necessity of it could be admitted and the armies raised. The great problem was created by the 'neuters', that solid body of men throughout the country who insisted, and would long insist, that there was no cause for civil war and demanded that king and Parliament make concessions to each other to restore the old 'mixed monarchy'. All through these first eight months of 1642 the 'neuters' bombarded both sides with their appeals. But on both sides the leaders had already decided. On the king's side, we see it if we look behind his formal statements to his private correspondence with the queen. On Pym's side

[1] Edmund Calamy, *England's Looking-Glass* (1641); S. Marshall, *Reformation and Desolation* (1641).

we see it, once again, in his tuning of the pulpits, and, in particular, in the utterances of his spiritual oracle, the true amplifier of his master's voice, Stephen Marshall.

For on 24 December, at the height of the struggle for London, when Marshall's last sermon was still echoing in their ears, the Commons once again turned their attention to public 'fasts'. Recognizing that they were now faced by a permanent crisis, and that their survival depended on continuous contact with the country, continuous propaganda, they invited the Lords to join them in proposing to the king that as long as the troubles in Ireland remained unsettled, there should be a regular monthly fast. The ground was well chosen. The Lords agreed ; the king could not demur ; and a royal proclamation was duly published. By its terms, the last Wednesday of every month was to be kept as a fast-day 'as well by abstinence from food as by public prayers, preaching and hearing the word of God . . . in all cathedrals, collegiate and parish churches and chapels' throughout England and Wales. The fast already arranged for the country on 20 January was confirmed. Thereafter Parliament, City, and country would celebrate the fast on the same day, beginning on 23 February 1642.[1]

The parliamentary sermons of 23 February thus marked the beginning of a new regular system, a standing covenant between Parliament and people. Ostensibly linked to the rebellion in Ireland, which king and Parliament pretended equally to deplore, it was in fact tied to the English crisis which was sustained by that rebellion. By agreeing to the system, Charles I had put into the hands of his enemies a means of co-ordination and propaganda to which he himself had no parallel. What kind of an engine it was would be shown from the very start, in the opening sermons of those two star performers of the Parliament, Stephen Marshall and Edmund Calamy.[1]

As before, Edmund Calamy, the unpolitical clergyman,

[1] For the proclamation see Rushworth, *Historical Collections*, III, i, 494.

looked to the past. Hitherto, he pointed out, the new English reformation had been carried out in a peaceable, parliamentary way. While the other nations 'travailed through blood to a reformation', the building of the new England had gone forward, like Solomon's Temple, without the noise of hammer or axe.[1] It was all very satisfactory — so far. But what of the future? At this point Stephen Marshall, the politician, took over. As before, he looked forward; and he looked forward, quite clearly, to war. The bloodthirsty sermon in which, six months before the outbreak of hostilities, he denounced the 'neuters' and called for total war would become the most famous of all his works. It was also the sermon which he himself most admired. According to his own account, he afterwards preached it, up and down the country, sixty times, and it was several times printed. It caused him to be known as 'the great incendiary of this unhappy war'. When he published it, he entitled it *Meroz Cursed*.

For there are times, explained the minister of Christ, when 'God's blessed servants must come down from mount Gerizim, the mount of blessing, and go up on mount Ebal, the mount of cursing, and there curse, and curse bitterly', as the angel of the Lord once cursed the men of Meroz for failing to join in the battle 'against King Jabin and his general Sisera, who for twenty years had mightily oppressed the children of Israel'. 'For all people are cursed or blessed according as they do or do not help the Church of God in its need.' Does not the holy writ expressly say, 'cursed is he that doeth the work of the Lord negligently?' And what is this imperative work of the Lord? 'The next words', replied the preacher, 'will tell you: cursed is everyone that withholds his hand from shedding of blood'. For the Lord, he explained, 'acknowledges no neuters'; 'he that is not with me is against me', and 'public neuters' shall receive from the hand of Christ the same bloody doom and execution which Gideon very properly imposed upon the men of Succoth and Penuel when

[1] Edmund Calamy, *God's Free Mercy to England* (1642).

they refused to co-operate in catching and killing his enemies. Then, moving on from the barbarities of the Old Testament to the barbarities of the middle ages, Marshall invited his hearers to admire 'that brave Bohemian captain', John Zizka, 'who not only was willing to fight while he lived but bequeathed his skin, when he died, to be made a drum-head for the service of the war'.

Meroz Cursed was the first of a long series of incendiary sermons which, from now on, scandalized royalists and moderate men alike. 'No good Christian', wrote Clarendon, 'can without horror think of those ministers of the Church who, by their function being messengers of peace, were the only trumpets of war and incendiaries towards rebellion.' The Scriptural phrases used by Marshall, the texts concerning the men of Meroz, the curses upon those who did the work of the Lord negligently or held back from the shedding of blood, would become the commonplaces of many a later preacher.[1] So would some other choice Scriptural examples : the virtue of Phinehas, the grandson of Aaron, who did not wait for authority but slew the transgressors with his own hand and thus stayed the plague that had visited Israel ; the vices of Saul, who ignored the orders of Samuel to hew Agag, king of the Amalekites, in pieces, and of Ahab who similarly defied the orders of a prophet and spared Ben-Hadad, king of Syria. They were part of the horrible propaganda with which Pym found it necessary, at times, to rally his forces in order to

[1] 'There was more than Mr. Marshall who, from the 23rd verse of the 5th chapter of Judges, *Curse ye Meroz* . . . presumed to inveigh against, and in plain terms to pronounce God's curse against all those who came not with their utmost power and strength to destroy and root out all the malignants who in any degree opposed the Parliament.' (Clarendon, *op. cit.* II, 320-1.) Clarendon's editor, W. D. Macray, remarks on this passage that 'prolonged search has failed to trace the other sermons to which Clarendon refers'. In fact the curse upon Meroz for neutrality is explicitly repeated in numerous fast sermons, *e.g.* Thomas Wilson, *Jericho's Downfall* (28 Sept. 1642) ; Thomas Case, *God's Rising, His Enemies Scattering* (26 Oct. 1642) ; Charles Herle, *A Pair of Compasses for Church and State* (30 Nov. 1642) ; John Ley, *The Fury of War and Folly of Sin* (26 April 1643), etc.

resist, and bring into 'a good correspondency' with Parliament, a king whose circumstances happily dispensed him from such disagreeable language.

Thus the regular series of 'monthly fasts' began. They would continue for seven years. The routine was soon established. When one ceremony was over, the next would be prepared. The two Houses would separately choose and invite their preachers. The invitation of the Lords was impersonal, that of the Commons conveyed by named members — neighbours, friends, kinsmen : presumably their original sponsors. Sometimes, of course, there were refusals and substitutes had to be found. When the fast-day came, official parliamentary business was omitted or cut down to a minimum. The Lords normally gathered in King Henry VII's chapel of Westminster Abbey, the Commons in St. Margaret's, Westminster. The two preachers delivered the sermons, one in the morning, one in the afternoon. The ceremonies were open to all : unless expressly excluded by a parliamentary order, the public was free to attend and (according to the fashion of the time) to take notes of the sermons. Next day, or within a few days, votes of thanks would be passed and conveyed to the preachers, generally with a request to print their sermons, by named members, generally their original sponsors. Then the process was repeated. Similar ceremonies took place all over the country. Nor was it only on the last Wednesday of the month that Parliament subjected itself and the people to this heavy dose of religion. Special crises called forth special fasts also : fasts to celebrate the opening of the Westminster Assembly, to desire blessings on the parliamentary armies when in difficulty, to persuade God to remove 'a great judgment of rain and waters' or 'abundance of rain and unseasonable weather', and to abate such calamities as the miseries of Scotland during the triumphs of Montrose, the incidence of the plague, divers crying sins and enormities of the church, the spread of heresies and blasphemies, etc. There were also, when occasion called for them, special days of thanksgiving. All these entailed special sermons, whose preachers were chosen, thanked, and invited to print in the same way.

Of course the procedure looks smoother in the parliamentary journals than it was in fact. In fact the fasts were always regarded as party propaganda and, in consequence, were often resented in the country. From the beginning there were complaints. Even members of Parliament were accused of foregoing abstinence and sermons in order to drink and dine in taverns, and royalist pamphleteers and poets made merry at the sleek, black-robed, well-paid Marshall who lifted his nose like a whale to spout, and beat and banged his pulpit as he thundered damnation to the absentees. In the country the inattention was even worse, and a constant stream of orders and ordinances, imposing new burdens of enforcement and new penalties for omission, showed that the parliamentary example was ill followed. Still, at the centre a good appearance was kept up. There was also, in London, a good supply of preachers. From the start, as 'scandalous' ministers were ejected, country preachers, encouraged by their local members of Parliament, poured in to compete for their places, and from 1643 the Westminster Assembly provided a constant reservoir of clerical talent, eager to display itself to the new, many-headed patron of the church. For the first few years, therefore — as long as the Parliament was united — the system reflected parliamentary policy. It also reflected the shifts in that policy. Out of many possible instances, a few must suffice.

The first great test of Pym's leadership, after the outbreak of war, came in the early months of 1643. At first, both sides had expected a quick victory: neither was prepared for a long war. Consequently, when both had failed in their first objectives, the pressure towards compromise was irresistible and Pym was obliged to negotiate with the king. But as he had little faith in the king's peaceful intentions, it was essential that the 'treaty of Oxford' should not be interpreted as a sign of weakness on the parliamentary side. If the conservatives on Pym's right were willing to accept a treacherous peace, he must rely on the radicals on his left and show that, with their support, he would fight on for a more stable settlement. This resolution was clearly shown, on the very eve of the negotiations, by one of the fast sermons of 25 January 1643. It was a sermon which might seem, to anyone unaware of the real situation at Oxford, singularly inappropriate to the opening of a peace treaty.

The preacher was John Arrowsmith, who had been proposed by Pym's step-brother, Francis Rous. His text was Leviticus xxvi, 25, 'I shall bring a sword upon you, that shall avenge the quarrel of my covenant', and his message was that bloody civil wars were peculiar signs of God's blessing on a country, and that England, having now been singled out for this favour, must fight it out, exacting 'like for like and, particularly, blood for blood (Rev. xvi, 5-6)'.[1] After listing the sins which called most loudly for blood, and which included especially the neglect of God's covenant and disrespect for its messengers, the clergy, he gave his specific instructions. He reminded his hearers that the English victory over the Scots at Musselburgh, a century before, had been won at the hour when Parliament, in London, ordered the burning of 'idolatrous images'. Thus if Pym held out his right hand to treat with the king, with his left he pointed the way to a more radical war and a new campaign of iconoclasm. Five days later he emphasized his threat by pushing through Parliament an ordinance abolishing episcopacy and including the ratification of the ordinance in the terms of the treaty. No doubt this paper ordinance was as yet merely a threat, to be withdrawn if necessary : Pym would always have settled for 'moderate episcopacy' ; but such withdrawal presupposed a real settlement. At present he suspected the king's motives and was determined to negotiate only from the appearance of strength and radical resolve.

The event justified him. In fact the king had no intention

[1] John Arrowsmith, *The Covenant's Avenging Sword Brandished* (1643).

of making peace. He was playing for time till the queen should arrive from Holland with the means of victory. And in fact, all through the first three weeks of the treaty, as he spun it out, he was waiting for news of her arrival at Newcastle upon Tyne. Finally, after a series of dramatic adventures at sea, her little fleet arrived at Bridlington. By that time Parliament had been able to draw the moral, and on 22 February, as she drew towards land, the fast-preachers made it clear. They were John Ellis, invited once again by Rous, and William Bridge, whom bishop Wren had driven abroad but who had now returned, like the queen, from Holland, to be 'one of the demagogues of the Parliament'.

Ellis was chiefly concerned to expose the dangers of 'a false peace' — that is, one which did not guarantee the future by 'putting Christ into the treaty'. He urged his hearers to remember the message of his predecessor Mr. Arrowsmith and make no peace till the false brethren and enemies of Christ had been trodden down like straw in the dunghill. Bridge was more explicit. Kings, he explained, were sometimes, like King David, too indulgent to their families, and he thought it necessary to warn King Charles against this fault. 'Sir,' he exclaimed, 'your Absalom and your Adonijah, you may love them well, but not better than your own peace, your own people. If the Queen of your bosom stand in competition with your kingdom, you must not love her better than us, than it.' He then quoted an edifying story from Turkish history. A Turkish emperor, he said, was charged by his subjects with neglect of his kingdom, 'moved thereto (as they alleged) by the too much love of a lady, his concubine ; whom in a great assembly the emperor showed to all his people on a time, and they concluded that, in regard of her excellent beauty, they could not blame him for being misled. But, saith he, that you may know how little I regard her in comparison with you, he drew his scimitar and killed her before them all.' [1]

[1] John Ellis, *The Sole Path to a Sound Peace* (1643) ; Wm. Bridge, *Joab's Counsel and King David's Seasonable Hearing It* (1643).

Such was the example which Mr. Bridge held up to Charles I, preparing to welcome, after a year's absence, his beautiful queen.

So the attack was launched on the queen, as the fomenter of civil war, the irreconcilable enemy of 'settlement'. In March, while still formally treating with the king, Parliament invaded the queen's chapel, broke up its furniture, expelled its priests. Then, on 16 April, the treaty was broken off, and radical passions had to be enlisted in earnest for the renewal of a more desperate war. On 24 April Sir Robert Harley asked for a committee to destroy superstitious monuments in London churches and himself at once set about the work. Two days later, it was among headless statues and shivered stained-glass windows that the Commons gathered in St. Margaret's to hear the monthly fast sermons. The first, appropriately enough, was by a *protégé* of Harley himself, a country clergyman from Cheshire who served up the now familiar texts 'Curse ye Meroz' and 'Cursed be he that keepeth his sword back from blood'. The second was by William Greenhill, another of bishop Wren's victims, famous for his commentary on Ezekiel. His sermon once again was a pointer to immediate policy. He chose the ominous text, 'The axe is laid to the root of the tree'.

Like Samuel Fairclough two years before, Greenhill demanded 'justice on delinquents'. Indeed he referred back explicitly to the execution of Strafford. 'When your justice fell upon that great cedar-tree above a year and a half ago', he cried, 'did not all England tremble?' And now too much time had passed without a second stroke. Though great 'delinquents' still lived, the executioner's axe had culpably been allowed to rust. That was most improper. However, he added, regretfully, 'if justice be at a stand and cannot take hold of living delinquents to keep the axe from rust, let justice be executed upon lifeless delinquents. Are there no altars, no high places, no crucifixes, no crosses in the open street that are bowed unto and idolised? Lay your axe to the roots and hew them down!'[1]

The message was clear, and was instantly obeyed. Two days after the sermon, the terms of Harley's committee were extended to include the destruction of idolatrous monuments in streets and open places. On 2 May, Cheapside Cross, that bugbear of the Puritans, the pride and glory of the City, was at last ceremonially hewn down. Thereafter, Parliament turned to 'living delinquents'. There can be no doubt who was in the mind of Greenhill when he spoke of living delinquents whom justice could not yet reach. It was the queen. And sure enough, on 23 May, Henry Darley proposed her impeachment. Darley was Pym's oldest ally and agent, and Pym himself intervened often in the debate and finally himself carried the resolution up to the Lords. Another member who intervened was Sir Peter Wentworth who stated that it was high time to lay the axe to the root. The reference to Greenhill's sermon is obvious; and indeed it was Sir Peter Wentworth who had proposed Greenhill as preacher to Parliament. A week later, another more accessible 'living delinquent' felt the consequences of the same sermon. In the small hours of the morning, a party of musketeers commanded by the implacable William Prynne, breaking into his room in the Tower, seized the documents, the diary, even the devotions of the Parliament's forgotten prisoner, archbishop Laud. His impeachment too, long laid aside, was now to be resumed.

The spring and summer of 1643 was Pym's most radical period. He had to be radical. The position of Parliament seemed desperate, and at times his own position in Parliament seemed desperate too. Unless he kept left, he would lose control of it to the real radicals, Henry Marten, Alderman Penington, and their friends. But Pym by himself was not a real radical. Always he saw past the immediate radical gestures to the ultimate conservative settlement. Therefore he

[1] William Greenhill, Ἀξίνη πρὸς τὴν Ῥίζαν (1643).

never yielded anything substantial to the radicals on his left. Radical gestures could be forgotten, radical ordinances reversed, broken windows repaired. In the autumn of 1643, thanks to the Scottish alliance and the failure of Waller's Plot, Pym recovered his central position; his chief rival, Henry Marten, was expelled from Parliament; and a new policy could be adopted. When Pym died, in December 1643, nothing irrevocable had been done. The queen was still unimpeached, archbishop Laud was still alive, the episcopal church was destroyed on paper only. A stroke of the pen could restore it: its lands were unsold. So when Stephen Marshall preached his master's funeral sermon, its message was neither radical nor sanguinary. It did not need to be. It was merely a plea for perseverance in the long, just, necessary civil war.[1]

If 1643 had begun as the year of the radicals, 1644 began as the year of the Scots. In December 1643 the Scotch commissioners and Scotch ministers returned to London and at once showed their resolution by boycotting Pym's funeral sermon. In 1641 they had been sent empty away, but this time they meant business. 'Nothing for nothing' was their rule. If they were to come as deliverers, they must receive the price; and the price had long ago been stated: in order to guarantee the revolution in Scotland, England too must adopt a full Presbyterian system, on 'the Scots model'. That meant, incidentally, that the English Parliament, like the Scotch, accept the orders of a General Assembly of the Church. The Westminster Assembly, from a mere advisory body, a reservoir of preachers chosen by the lay parliament, must assume command. As practised hands in clerical and political intrigue, the Scotch ministers were confident that they could bring this about. They obtained seats in the Assembly; they organized a party, gave orders, reported home. And they secured invitations to preach not merely, as in 1640–1, to the gaping

[1] S. Marshall, Θρηνῳδία, *The Church's Lamentation* (1643).

populace of London, but to the Parliament itself. This was an opportunity not to be missed.

The Scotch ministers preached to the Commons on the four successive fast-days after their arrival. The series was opened by Alexander Henderson, the framer of the national covenant of Scotland. He delivered, according to his colleague Robert Baillie, 'a most gracious, wise and learned sermon' urging the English legislature to repair its past errors and now, though late, build the house of the Lord in England. The other three ministers, Samuel Rutherford, Baillie himself, and George Gillespie, pressed the same message. England, said Gillespie, had been culpably slow in following the good examples of Scotland. The whole nation was guilty of scandalous laxity in the past, still unredeemed. Why had not the idolatrous high places been taken away? The trouble was, England was intolerably Erastian: it put its trust in the laity, not the clergy: 'it did even make an idol of this Parliament and trusted to its own strength and armies'. No wonder God had been greatly provoked and had visited the guilty country with defeat, until it had drawn the correct deductions and appealed to Scotland. From now on, given due obedience, all would be well: 'Christ hath put Antichrist from his outer works in Scotland and he is now come to put him from his inner works in England'. Baillie, in printing his sermon, rubbed it in even deeper. He was astonished, he told Francis Rous, the chairman of Parliament's committees on religion in England, that 'the wheels of the Lord's chariot should move with so slow a pace'. This 'wearisome procrastination to erect the discipline of God' was inexplicable 'to mine and every common understanding'. It caused millions to live in every kind of carnal sin 'without the control of any spiritual correction'. All this was the result of a deplorable freedom of speech in the Assembly. Such things could not happen in Scotland. . . . By a happy irony, Baillie sent an inscribed presentation copy of the sermon to 'the most lernit, his noble friend Mr. Selden, in testimony of his high respect', adding the words *τὸ μέλλον ἀόρατον*, 'the future is invisible'. It was indeed. Long and loud Baillie would afterwards lament the ruin of all his plans by 'the insolent absurdity' of that 'head of the Erastians', John Selden.[1]

So the Scots, from the parliamentary pulpit, laid down the new party line, their party line. Unfortunately, as they soon found, the line was not followed. They had been invited merely out of civility, and once civility was satisfied, they were ignored. Except for an invitation to Alexander Henderson to preach on the day of thanksgiving for Marston Moor, a Scotch victory, they were never invited to preach to the Commons again; and their English successors were lamentably tame and 'Erastian'. On one occasion, indeed, Baillie could report 'two of the most Scottish and free sermons that ever I heard anywhere'. This was in the autumn of 1644, on the special fast-day for the armies of the Lord General, 'Essex, then in straits in the west: the two preachers then laid well about them and charged public and parliamentary sins strictly on the backs of the guilty'. And frequently the London clergy, responding to Scottish pressure in the Assembly, and excited by the prospect of clerical power, let fly at the error of toleration, at antinomian doctrines or at preaching tradesmen. But in general the Scots found that their labours were in vain. They colonized the Westminster Assembly only to find the Assembly itself ignored by the Parliament. The Parliament insisted on choosing its preachers; naturally it chose those whom it could trust; and the preachers thus chosen, as Baillie lamented, spoke 'before the Parliament with so profound a reverence as truly took all edge from their exhortations and made all applications to them toothless and adulatorious'.[2]

However, one occasion should be recorded which may be regarded as a Scottish victory. In the autumn of 1644, while

[1] Alex. Henderson, *A Sermon Preached to the House of Commons* (1643); S. Rutherford [same title] (1644); R. Baillie, *Satan The Leader in Chief*... (1644); G. Gillespie, *A Sermon before the House of Commons* (1644). Baillie's inscribed presentation copy to Selden is now in the Bodleian Library, Oxford.

[2] Baillie, *Letters and Journals* (Edinburgh, 1841), II, 220-1.

the Scots could boast of Marston Moor, the English armies were everywhere in difficulties. At Westminster tempers were frayed, Cromwell was attacking his commanding general, the Earl of Manchester, and the Scots were throwing themselves eagerly into the quarrel. Some radical gesture was needed to emphasize ultimate solidarity, some scapegoat, on whom all could agree, must be sacrificed. It happened that, at this time, the long, desultory trial of archbishop Laud had at last reached the point of decision. All the evidence had been heard, and it seemed that, legally, he must be acquitted. But in fact the old archbishop was too good a scapegoat to miss. Presbyterians and Independents alike hated him. The Scots, in particular, pressed for his death. So the leaders of Parliament decided that he must die. And once again, as with Strafford, their decision was made clear through official fast sermons.

22 October was the day of a special fast for the union of the parliamentary armies. On that day Laud's room in the Tower was once again vainly raided for evidence on which to destroy him. At the same time Edmund Calamy, preaching before the Commons, reminded them of 'all the guilty blood that God requires you in justice to shed, and you do spare'.[1] A few days later 'many thousand citizens' petitioned for 'justice' on delinquents, and members of Parliament who sought to reject the petition were voted down. Then, on 30 October, came the monthly fast. 'When your gins and snares catch any of the bloody birds', cried the Rev. Henry Scudder, 'dally not with them : blood will have blood ; contract not their bloodguiltiness upon your own souls by an unwarranted clemency and mildness.' Would God, exclaimed the Rev. Francis Woodcock, the robe of justice were often 'dyed in a deeper colour with the blood of delinquents. It is that which God and man calls for. God repeats it, *Justice, Justice* ; we, echoing God, cry *Justice, Justice*.' [2]

[1] Edmond Calamy, *England's Antidote against the Plague of Civil War* (1644).

[2] Henry Scudder, *God's Warning to England* (1644) ; Francis Woodcock, *Christ's Warning Piece* (1644).

These were the sermons to the Commons. But sentence must be passed by the Lords, and the Lords were still sticklers for legality. What preacher, in these circumstances, would the Lords choose ? In fact, they found a way of evading the problem. For the fast day of 30 October they did not choose their own preachers but, only five days before the ceremony, invited the Westminster Assembly to appoint them.[1] The Assembly, of course, was glad to do so ; the Scots, naturally, were delighted by this unusual subservience of a lay body ; and the Lords heard a predictable sermon. The Rev. Edmund Staunton admitted that he had had 'short warning' ; but he did not have to look far for his matter. The City petition for the blood of delinquents he said, had suggested his subject. So he sang the praises of Phinehas, who did not wait for legal authority before spearing Zimri and the Midianite woman, and of the eunuchs who threw down Jezebel so that 'her blood was sprinkled on the wall' ; he lamented the wickedness of Saul who omitted to hew Agag in pieces ; 'and now', he ended, 'could I lift up my voice as a trumpet, had I the shrill cry of an angel which might be heard from east to west, from north to south, in all the corners of the kingdom, my note should be *Execution of Justice*, *Execution of Justice*, *Execution of Justice* ! That is God's way to pacify wrath : *Then stood up Phinehas and executed judgment, and so the plague was stayed*.' [2]

Next day, with mechanical precision, the House of Commons dropped the impeachment of Laud and proceeded by way of attainder, to destroy him, guilty or not, and cast his head before the king as a preliminary to the treaty of Uxbridge, just in case he should doubt their radical resolve.

But if the destruction of Laud represented a victory for the Scots, it was a very slight victory compared with the defeat inflicted on them in the same months by the internal revolution in the English Parliament. For those were the months in which Vane and Cromwell, the 'Independents',

[1] *Lord's Journals*, VII, 44.
[2] Edmund Staunton, *Phinehas' Zeal in Execution of Judgment* (1644).

established their authority and, in the New Model Army, forged a weapon which would soon eliminate the Scots from England and defeat them in Scotland. How deeply the Scots committed themselves to the losing side in that internal English struggle is vividly shown in Baillie's letters, and much of the hatred of Cromwell for the Scots, and their consequent misfortunes, dated from those days when they had sought to have him impeached, like Laud, as an 'incendiary' between the two kingdoms. The climax of the struggle came in December 1644 with the proposal of the 'Self-Denying Ordinance'; and in the methods by which Vane sought to carry this crucial ordinance he showed himself, in tactics if not in spirit, the true disciple of Pym.

The immediate chain of events began on 9 December 1644. On that date a report was due from the committee to which the bitter quarrel between Cromwell and the Earl of Manchester had been referred. The chairman of the committee was Zouche Tate. Instead of reporting on the particular issue, Tate submitted a general conclusion 'that the chief causes of our division are pride and covetousness'. Thereupon Cromwell delivered his famous speech about the moral decline of Parliament and the necessity for self-denial; Tate proposed a resolution that no member of Parliament should, during the war, hold military or civil office; Vane seconded the proposal; and in the mood of the moment it was accepted by the House. A committee was instructed to bring the resolution forward as an ordinance.

This was a good beginning, but as yet it was only a beginning. The ordinance still had to be framed and read three times by the Commons. Meanwhile the mood of the moment might pass. And even if the ordinance passed the Commons, the Lords would certainly see it as an attack upon their authority. It was therefore essential to Vane and his friends to prolong the confessional mood and to spread it, if possible, to the Lords. For such a purpose they resolved, in Clarendon's words, 'to pursue the method in which they had been hitherto so successful, and to prepare and ripen things in the Church that they might afterwards, in due time, grow to maturity in the Parliament'. On 11 December, the day on which the ordinance was first read, the Commons agreed to hold a solemn fast in which they would humble themselves for their 'particular and parliamentary sins' and so secure divine support for their future measures. This fast was fixed only a week ahead — a sure sign of immediate political necessity. Moreover, it had certain special features. First, the Lords were invited to celebrate it together with the Commons: instead of choosing their own preachers, they would thus have to listen to the preachers already chosen by the Commons. This also entailed a change of place. Neither Henry VII's chapel nor St. Margaret's would hold both Houses together, and Lincoln's Inn Chapel was finally chosen. Secondly, the whole service was invested with a peculiar secrecy. Cries for the blood of 'delinquents' might serve to rally the people, but the sins of the Parliament could only be opened in private. Strict measures were therefore devised to exclude the public from Lincoln's Inn chapel on 18 December while Lords and Commons listened 'for eight or ten hours' to Thomas Hill, Obadiah Sedgwick, and the inevitable Stephen Marshall. And these preachers, though thanked by both Houses, were not invited to print, and did not print their sermons.

For this reason we do not know exactly what they said, but there is no reason to distrust the general account which has been preserved by Clarendon.[1] After appropriate preliminary orisons, the preachers, he tells us, delivered their

[1] Clarendon, *op. cit.* III, 456–60. S. R. Gardiner (*Great Civil War*, 1901, II, 91) refers to Clarendon's 'blundering account' which, he says, is 'plainly inaccurate' because Clarendon presupposes a fast of which there is no record in the Parliamentary Journals and which could only have taken place on a Sunday [*i.e.* 8 Dec.], a day 'on which no fast was ever appointed'. But this criticism, which suggests that Clarendon, on the basis of mere 'Oxford gossip', invented a non-existent fast, is in fact based on a misunderstanding: a misunderstanding which is at once cleared up when it is realized that Clarendon has confused the initial debate of Monday 9 Dec. with the second debate, and passage of the Ordinance in the Commons, on Thursday 19 Dec. As so often, Clarendon has interpreted the situation correctly, in spite of confusion of detail.

sermons, in which, 'let their texts be what they would', they told the Houses plainly and at great length that all their troubles sprang from private greed and ambition which was alienating the people and postponing all hope of reformation. Finally, 'when they had exaggerated these reproaches as pathetically as they could . . . they fell again to their prayers, that God would take his own work into His hand, and if the instruments He had already employed were not worthy to bring so glorious a design to a conclusion, that He would inspire others more fit, who might perfect what was begun and bring the troubles of the nation to a godly period'. Next day, in the Commons, Vane dwelt on the lesson of the preachers. If ever God had appeared to the Parliament, he said, it was in the exercises of yesterday. And having enlarged on the holy theme he sped the Self-Denying Ordinance through its third reading and passed it up to the Lords.

It was a brilliant manœuvre ; but in politics there are no short cuts and the Lords, in spite of their heavy religious battering, were not stunned into submission. It would take another three months, and other methods, before they would finally accept a much modified Self-Denying Ordinance. Nevertheless, the struggle over the Self-Denying Ordinance marked a crucial stage in the eclipse of the Scots. From then onwards they were gradually pushed out of English politics and forced to witness the success of that 'high and mighty plot of the Independents', which Baillie had foreseen, 'to have gotten an army for themselves under Cromwell' and so to push on with a purely English revolution.[1]

The Scots did indeed find one opportunity of fighting back, at least from the pulpit. This came in the summer of 1645. By that time their own position had become very delicate. On the one hand they had, as they felt, triumphed in the Westminster Assembly and, through it, were demanding the instant, overdue establishment in England of a Calvinist theocracy, complete with all-powerful General Assembly, ruling

[1] Baillie, *op. cit.* II, 246.

elders, and full powers of excommunication. On the other hand, even as they pressed their claims abroad, their position at home was in jeopardy. While Cromwell was winning victory after victory in England, in Scotland Montrose was master of almost the whole country. It was therefore significant that at this moment the Commons appointed as fast-preacher a man who, in the Westminster Assembly, was already known as an 'Erastian' friend of Selden, an enemy of Scotch claims. This was Thomas Coleman, formerly a rector in Lincolnshire, now — as once before — sponsored by the two members for his county, Sir John Wray and Sir Edward Ayscough. In his sermon Coleman urged that the lay legislature of England 'establish as few things *jure divino* as can well be', allow no rules to have divine sanction without clear Scriptural warrant, and 'lay no more burden of government upon the shoulders of ministers than Christ hath plainly laid upon them'. The clergy, he said, should be content to be secured in learning and supplied with maintenance : church-government they should leave entirely to Parliament, for 'a Christian magistrate, as a Christian magistrate, is a governor in the Church'. In this manner the English Parliament, triumphant at Naseby, gave its answer to the Scotch General Assembly, reeling under the victories of Montrose.[1]

Coleman was not an Independent. He explicitly opposed Independency. He was a Presbyterian — but an English Presbyterian, and the Scotch Presbyterians were aghast at his doctrines. They had already been very busy in the Assembly : a 'blasphemous book' had taken up much of their time 'before we got it burnt by the hand of the hangman'. Now they found themselves faced by Coleman. To be silent under such an attack was impossible ; but where could they counter-attack ? The House of Commons was no good : the majority there were 'either half or whole Erastians'. But by good luck another opportunity presented itself. The House of Lords, commiserating with the military disasters of the Scots,

[1] Thomas Coleman, *Hope Deferred and Dashed* (1645).

had invited the four dominies to preach at four successive fasts and the last of these occasions was still to come. It was to be on 27 August, and the preacher was to be the youngest, most learned, most argumentative of the four, George Gillespie.

Gillespie seized his opportunity. Instead of lamenting the miseries and perhaps acknowledging the sin of his country, as the occasion required, he turned on Coleman. Coleman, he said, had been neither active nor passive on the side of reformation 'but will needs appear on the stage against it'. His views struck at the root of all church-government, were contrary to the Word of God, the Solemn League and Covenant, the opinions of other Reformed Churches, and the votes of Parliament and Assembly. They had given no small scandal and offence. . . . But Gillespie soon found that he himself had caused no less scandal, especially by misusing such an occasion. The controversy thus roused rumbled on, with increasing acrimony, for six months. Sides were taken ; pamphlets proliferated. But whatever the power-hungry clergy of London thought, inside the Parliament the views of Coleman prevailed. Never again, even in the period of 'Presbyterian' domination, was a Scotsman invited to preach to the English Parliament.[1]

Indeed, 1645 saw the end of Scotch influence in England. As the English 'Presbyterians' asserted themselves, it became clear that they were not really Presbyterians at all — the Scots had merely imposed the label on them. Even Stephen Marshall, Baillie now discovered, was really little better than an Independent : he 'miskens us altogether', Baillie lamented : 'he is for a middle way of his own'. And meanwhile, even Marshall was finding his position as the oracle of Parliament challenged by more radical preachers imposed upon Parliament by the triumphant Cromwell. In 1645–6, the year of final victory, new names begin to appear as fast-preachers. The old regulars, Calamy and Burges, Sedgwick and Case, and

[1] G. Gillespie, *A Sermon Preached before the House of Lords* (1645). See also Baillie, *op. cit.* II, 306 ; *Cal. S.P. Dom*, 1645–7, p. 127.

many others who will soon abandon the revolution, are joined by their future supplanters, William Strong, Peter Sterry, Thomas Goodwin, John Owen, Nicholas Lockyer, Walter Cradocke, William Dell, Hugh Peter.

Above all, Hugh Peter. What Marshall was to Pym, Hugh Peter is to Cromwell. If Marshall preached electioneering sermons before the Parliament of 1640, Peter would ride round the country 'making burgesses for Parliament' before the 'recruiting' elections of 1646. If Marshall declared the reforming, political programme of Pym in 1640, Peter would declare the radical, social policy of Cromwell in 1647. If Marshall preached the thanksgiving sermon for the peaceful victories of 1641, Peter would preach the thanksgiving sermon for the military victories of 1646. If Marshall holloa'ed the parliamentary pack onwards into war in 1642, Peter, in 1647, would holloa the Army onwards into revolution. If Marshall pressed his unwanted spiritual services upon archbishop Laud as he was led to the block in 1645, Peter would utter his hideous, vindictive texts in the ears of a yet greater victim, as he was sent to the block in 1649. Both were great emergency preachers. In delicate crises, when other men hung back, they would come forward. But the occasions were different. Marshall, like Pym, sought always to preserve the Parliament, to carry it forward, armed and united, on the old path to reform ; Peter, like Cromwell, would seek, with new allies, to hack a shorter, bloodier way to what he valued above any political form : a new society.[1]

Only one of Peter's fast sermons was ever printed. It was the thanksgiving sermon for victory preached on 2 April 1646. Like Marshall in 1641, when the Parliament seemed to have won its bloodless victory, he announced the present year as *annus mirabilis*, the most glorious year since the year of the Armada. 'Oh the blessed change we see, that can travel from Edinburgh to the Land's End in Cornwall, who not long since

[1] For Peter, see especially R. F. Stearns, *Hugh Peter, The Strenuous Puritan* (Urbana, 1954).

were blocked up at our doors ! To see the highways occupied again ; to hear the carter whistling to his toiling team ; to see the hills rejoicing, the valleys laughing!' Even Germany, by now, seemed to be 'lifting up her lumpish shoulder' ; even 'the thin-cheeked Palatinate' looked hopeful ; the 'over-awed French peasant' was studying his liberty, and the Dutch remembered how they had 'bought their freedom with many, many thousands of good old Elizabeth shillings'. 'All Protestant Europe seems to get new colour in her cheeks' ; why then should not England too flourish again ?[1] And just as Marshall's thanksgiving sermon had been followed by blue-prints for the new society which men believed to be within their reach, so Peter's thanksgiving sermon also announced a new spate of social pamphlets. Hartlib and Dury, the original prophets of the Country Party, rushed into print again ; Dury had been invited to preach before Parliament ; and Hugh Peter himself, in pamphlet after pamphlet, projected the new social reforms which could be achieved, if not by the Parliament, then directly, outside Parliament, by the Army.

As yet, these new preachers of 1645–6 had to be discreet. To the Parliament, political settlement came before social change, and the pace must not be forced. Peter kept his social pamphlets distinct from his parliamentary sermon. John Owen attached his scheme of church-government to his fast sermon only when printed. William Dell went too far and paid the price. He kept his fast sermon within bounds but then published it with an outrageous preface. He was summoned before the House of Commons and disciplined. Nor was he ever allowed to preach before Parliament again. Even the Rump Parliament, which made him Master of Peterhouse, refused to have him : when his name was suggested, the House, for the only time on such a matter, divided ; and he was voted down.[2]

[1] Hugh Peter, *God's Doing and Man's Duty* (1646).

[2] Dell's sermon (25 Nov. 1646) was printed as *Right Reformation* ; the *Commons' Journals* report the sequel (V, 10 etc.). The abortive attempt to invite Dell to preach to the Rump was made on 28 Jan. 1653 (*C.J.* VII, 252).

Political settlement or social reform, an imperfect political compromise as the basis for future reformation or a social reformation now, without tarrying for any — that was indeed the issue of 1646–7, the issue on which Parliament and Army ultimately divided and through whose division revolution came in. And in that revolution, which wrecked the Parliament, the old methods of parliamentary business were wrecked too. Pym and his friends, even Vane, St. John, and Holles, might 'tune the pulpits' in order to keep Parliament and people together along a prepared line ; but how could this be done when Parliament was at the mercy of its own warring parties, and of military force ? By now the London clergy, the natural source of fast-preachers, were more 'Presbyterian' than the 'Presbyterians' in Parliament, and the Army was more radical, more 'Independent' than the 'Independents' in Parliament. In such circumstances clergymen hardly knew what to say. There were too many tuners and no agreement about the musical notes. This became painfully clear in June 1647 when the mutinous Army, having seized the king, was hovering ominously around London, uncertain as yet whether to strike.

One of the preachers for the June fast was Nathaniel Ward, recently returned from New England. He was, as he afterwards wrote, 'Truly unwilling to come upon any public stage, knowing how perilous and jealous the times are' ; and in fact he contrived to give universal offence. He urged Parliament to restore the king to his authority and establish the church on a sure basis : 'till these two wheels be set right, all the lesser are like to go wrong' ; and so he proposed that the Parliament pay off the Army, reassert military discipline, correct the extremer forms of heresy in the ranks, and remedy some obvious grievances. It was eminently sensible advice, but unfortunately timed : only two days earlier the Army had forced the eleven 'Presbyterian' leaders to withdraw from the House and presented a series of much more radical demands. Ward's commiseration of the king did not please the

Presbyterians; his proposals for dealing with the Army infuriated the Army. His sermon 'gave offence' to a terrorized House; in the Army it was described as 'worse than Edwards his *Gangraena*'; and he was neither thanked nor asked to print.[1]

Next month the fast-day was even worse timed. It was due to fall on 28 July. But on 26 July the City mob invaded the Parliament and forced the House of Commons to reverse its recent votes and recall the eleven members; after which both Houses adjourned themselves till 30 July. The preachers thus delivered their sermons in a moment of 'Presbyterian' counter-revolution. How the London preachers took advantage of that counter-revolution is recorded in the diary of Lord Lisle, a member of Parliament: 'on that day Mr. Edwards and divers other ministers in London stirred up the people in their sermons to raise arms to suppress the army, abusing the day which was set apart for the calamities of bleeding Ireland and exciting the people to put this kingdom again into blood, and so to make it bleeding England also'.[2] But two days later, the illusion of Presbyterian victory faded. The Speakers of both Houses fled to the protection of the Army, the Army marched on London, and by 4 August Parliament and City alike were in its power. Fortunately the parliamentary preachers seem to have been very prudent, for they were thanked not only by the 'Presbyterian' Parliament of 2 August but also (since the proceedings of those days were afterwards annulled) by the 'Independent' Parliament of 25 August. They showed their prudence still further in omitting, though invited, to print any of their sermons.[3]

The man who did publish was Stephen Marshall who once

[1] *C.J.* V, 205, 228; Rushworth, *Historical Collections*, VI, i, 596; *Clarke Papers I* (Camden Soc., 1891), 150. The sermon was afterwards printed 'without the knowledge, or consent of the author', but containing a 'Letter to some Friends' signed by him.

[2] *Sidney Papers* (ed. R. W. Blencowe, 1825), p. 26.

[3] The preachers on 28 July were, to the Lords, Christopher Love and Henry Langley and, to the Commons, Benjamin Whichcote and Thomas Jaggard.

again, in a moment of crisis, emerged as the politician of the hour. Like other men who were neither Cromwellians nor radicals,[1] Marshall believed that, at that moment, the unity of Parliament and Army was all-important and that the alternative would be confusion leading to unconditional royal reaction. So, in these last days of July, he flung himself into action. He made a party in the Westminster Assembly, worked on the aldermen of the City, darted to and fro between Lords, Commons, and Army headquarters, and finally, with seventeen supporters in the Assembly, presented a petition to the Houses offering to mediate between the City and the Army. His efforts were successful. The City militia offered no resistance, and the Army entered London without a struggle. When all was over, the defeated party recognized Marshall as the chief architect of their ruin. 'In that nick of time', wrote Baillie, when 'one stout look more' would have established Presbyterianism for ever, it was Mr. Marshall, 'the main instrument' of the Solemn League and Covenant, who, with 'his seventeen servants of the Synod . . . put presently in the Army's power both Parliament, City and nation'; and Denzil Holles, the twice-purged leader of the 'Presbyterians' in Parliament, never failed to denounce the former zealot for Presbyterianism who, on that occasion, became 'a principal instrument' of Cromwell '. . . going and coming between Westminster and the headquarters, or the Parliament doors soliciting the members of both Houses, persuading them by all manner of arguments, sometimes assurances, sometimes terrifyings, to agree to those things which the Army desired'. To Skippon, the commander of the City militia, and 'to his chaplain Marshall', wrote Holles, 'we must attribute all the evil that has befallen king and kingdom.' Naturally, when the purged Parliament obediently

[1] *E.g.* like the Earl of Manchester, who had strong personal grounds for opposing Cromwell and who is generally regarded as a Presbyterian, but who nevertheless joined the Army on this occasion and, being Speaker of the House of Lords, gave it the authority which it needed to overpower the Parliament.

voted a day of thanksgiving 'for the restoration of the honour and freedom of the Parliament' — *i.e.* for its rescue by the Army from the 'most horrible and abominable rape and violence' of the City mob — it was Stephen Marshall who was invited to preach the main sermon ; and he preached it, as we should expect, to some tune. 'That apostate', commented Holles, who now found himself accused of dividing king from Parliament, Parliament from City, and City from Army, 'went beyond Ela, making the deliverance a greater one than the Gunpowder Treason, as I have been credibly informed by those that heard him.' [1]

To Marshall it seemed that the old unity of Parliament had been restored. Once again, thanks to the Army, the old policy of his master, Pym, could be pursued. In fact it was not so. In fact the intervention of the Army proved the end of Parliament as an effective body in politics. This breach is indicated, incidentally, in the fast sermons. For five years the system had worked smoothly. Every month preachers had been chosen, had preached, had been thanked, had been invited to print their sermons, and had printed them. But from that date onwards all changes. Preachers are harder to find ; refusals are more frequent ; the Parliament becomes more dependent on a few reliable servants. Until 1647 no preacher had preached to either house of Parliament more than once a year, except Marshall and his understudy, the learned Greek and Hebrew scholar Joseph Caryl,[2] who had sometimes preached twice or thrice. But in 1648 Marshall would be called upon seven times, Caryl four times and one other clergyman four times.[3] Finally, even those clergymen

[1] For Marshall's part in the events of July-Aug. 1647 see *Lords' Journals*, IV, 368 ; Baillie, *op. cit.* III, 17, 302, 306 ; Denzil Holles, *Memoirs* (1699), pp. 88, 110, 123, 143, 160, 168. S. Marshall, *A Sermon Preached to the Two Houses of Parliament* . . . (1647).

[2] Caryl accompanied Marshall as chaplain to Charles I at Holdenby House. He was one of the very few ministers who, like Marshall, preached regularly to Parliament during the whole period from 1642 to 1653.

[3] The other clergyman was John Bond. Caryl and Bond remained, with John Owen and William Strong, the main preachers of the Rump.

who could be prevailed upon to preach fast sermons showed a remarkable reluctance to print them. From the beginning of the monthly system until June 1647 every preacher had been asked to print his sermon, and had printed it. Nathaniel Ward, on 30 June 1647, was the first not to receive such an invitation. Even so, he printed his sermon. But from then on, though invitation remained the rule, printing was the exception. Only five out of the last fourteen fast sermons of 1647 were published, and thereafter the proportion steadily declined.[1] From July 1648 even Marshall forbore to print. It is clear that, from the revolution of 1647, the fast sermons, like the Parliament itself, had lost their purpose.

Nevertheless, on one last occasion the system returned to life. First in April 1641, when Pym had decided to change from legal impeachment to political attainder in order to destroy the life of Strafford, then in October 1644 when Vane had decided, in the same way, to destroy the life of Laud, the preachers had been brought in to announce, and to justify, this fearful change ; and how could the grim masters of the Parliament now do less when the victim was both greater and, by now, in their eyes, guiltier than either Strafford or Laud ? This time, because of that difference, the pace was slower, the pressure greater ; but the method was the same. The same careful choice, the same exact timing, the same bloodthirsty message indicated the continuity of technique between the judicial murder of the servant and of the master.

It was on 16 November 1648 that the Council of Officers, gathered at St. Albans, received from Henry Ireton the *Remonstrance of the Army* which he had drawn up during Cromwell's absence in the north. It demanded that the king, as the sole and capital author of all the troubles of the kingdom, be speedily brought to trial. On the very next day the House of Commons had to appoint a preacher for the next fast, for the preacher nominated over a fortnight ago had suddenly

[1] Only 13 out of 48 such sermons were printed in 1648, and only 10 out of 56 for the years 1649–53.

withdrawn. This defaulting minister was that same Samuel Fairclough who, in 1641, had first called for the death of Strafford, and who had now, once again, been nominated by his patron. But in the face of these new developments his patron found himself more conservative, and perhaps Fairclough shrank from such a double triumph. In his place a radical member of Parliament proposed a young clergyman, George Cokayne, minister of St. Pancras, Soper Lane. This was a famous 'Independent' church whose minister was appointed by the parish and whose parishioners included the three pillars of radicalism in the City : Rowland Wilson, who would become sheriff, and Robert Tichborne and John Ireton, who would become Lord Mayors of the Republic. John Ireton was the brother of Henry Ireton, the moving spirit of the Revolution. Three days later, Henry Ireton presented the Remonstrance to a trembling Parliament, which sought to bury it by postponement. Then, on 29 November, came the fast-day, and the newly appointed Cokayne followed his senior colleague Obadiah Sedgwick into the pulpit.

His message was predictable. In every respect it echoed the Remonstrance. From the procrastinating Parliament, Cokayne demanded judgment and that quickly. 'Delay not to act for the people's good who have intrusted you.' He did not predetermine the method — 'we leave that entirely to your wisdom' — nor the sentence — justice should still be 'mingled with mercy' ; but then neither did his brief, the Remonstrance. But his language, like that of the Remonstrance, was ominously firm : he reminded the Commons, as they had by now been reminded *ad nauseam*, of Saul and Ahab, who had 'ventured God's displeasure' by sparing their captive kings. 'Honourable and worthy, if God do not lead you to do justice upon those who have been the great actors in shedding innocent blood, never think to gain their love by sparing of them.' [1] When the sermon was over, the thanks

[1] George Cokayne, *Flesh Expiring and the Spirit Inspiring* (1648). The full and laudatory biography of Cokayne by John B. Marsh, *The Story of Hare-*

of the intimidated House were boldly conveyed by Cokayne's parishioner, Rowland Wilson.

The order was given ; from now on the events followed. On 1 December 1648 the person of the king was seized. On 6 December the Parliament was purged of its resisting members. It was the greatest purge of all, Pride's Purge. On the very next day the machinery was put in motion. A special fast was declared, and it was declared at once. There was to be no question of waiting for the ordinary monthly fast, whose preachers had already been appointed before the Purge, no chance of counter-organization. The fast was to be on the morrow, on 8 December ; and the preachers were carefully chosen. They were Stephen Marshall and Joseph Caryl, the two preachers most acceptable to the Army, and 'the grand journey- or hackney-man of the Army', the 'stalking-horse and setting-dog of the grandees of the Army', Hugh Peter.

None of the three sermons was afterwards printed, but the gist of them is clear from contemporary newspaper reports. Marshall and Caryll, the old parliamentary preachers, urged the broken remains of the Parliament, now as in 1647, to preserve harmony with the Army. Hugh Peter, more bluntly, told them to obey their masters. In particular, he advised them 'to adjourn till Monday or Tuesday, that they may know how to steer their debates by the resolutions of the soldiery'. The Rump of Parliament recognized the voice of its ruler. It adjourned for four days, till Tuesday.[1]

All through the next month Hugh Peter worked hard in favour of the Army and its violent proceedings. This was the time when he earned his sinister reputation as a tribune of revolution, a buffoon-preacher who dragged religion through the gutter and used it to sanctify every incidental

court, being the History of an Independent Church (1871), curiously omits any reference to this part of his sermon, or to any detail which links him with the trial of the king.

[1] Stearns, *op. cit.* p. 328. *C.J.* VI, 95.

indecency of naked power. His next opportunity to preach to the Parliament came on 22 December. This was a special fast-day, hastily appointed 'for removing the heavy judgment of God now upon the kingdom'. It was celebrated by both Houses together, in St. Margaret's (they could all fit into it comfortably now). The whole churchyard was filled with musketeers and pikemen, to guard the Parliament, and soldiers surrounded the pulpit to guard the preacher. Our accounts of the sermon are imperfect and perhaps exaggerated: they come from contemporary pamphlets and later recollections; but in substance they are no doubt true.[1]

Once again Peter gave the Rump of Parliament its immediate orders. He bade it (as if it had any alternative) put its trust in the Army, which would lead England out of its Egyptian bondage. But how was that to be done? it might be asked. 'That', replied Peter, 'is not yet revealed to me.' Then, placing his head on the pulpit-cushion, he pretended to sleep until a voice from Heaven awoke him with a start, and with the answer. 'Now I have it', he exclaimed, 'by Revelation! Now I shall tell you. This army must root up monarchy, not only here but in France and other kingdoms round about. This is to bring you out of Egypt. This Army is the corner-stone cut out of the mountain, which must dash the powers of the earth to pieces.' As for the objection that such a revolution was 'without precedent', Peter soon disposed of that. The Virgin Birth was also without precedent, but it happened. 'This is an age to make examples and precedents in.' Then the preacher showed what precedent he would establish. He demanded the immediate trial of the king. The citizens of London, the London preachers, were all opposed to such a trial. Peter soon dealt with them. 'Those foolish citizens', he said, were like the people of

[1] Theodorus Verax [Clement Walker], *Anarchia Anglicana* (1648), *or the History of Independency, part II*, pp. 49–50; 'The Trial of Hugh Peter', in *An Exact and Most Impartial Accompt of the Indictment . . . of 29 Regicides . . .* (1660).

Jerusalem at the time of Christ's crucifixion: 'for a little trading and profit they will have Christ (pointing to the redcoats on the pulpit-stairs) crucified and this great Barabbas at Windsor released; but I do not much heed what the rabble says. . . . My Lords, and you noble gentlemen of the House of Commons, you are the Sanhedrin and the Great Council of the Nation, therefore you must be sure to do justice and it is from you we expect it. . . . Do not prefer the great Barabbas, murderer, tyrant and traitor, before these poor hearts . . . the army, who are our saviours.'[1]

Next day the gentlemen of the House of Commons at least obeyed their orders. They set up a committee to consider how to proceed by way of justice against the king. But only four days later, before that committee could report, and before Cromwell himself had made up his mind, another fast-day had come round. This time it was the regular monthly fast, whose preachers, unlike those of 22 December, had been chosen a month before — in fact, before Pride's Purge. This, as it turned out, was unfortunate: it showed that, in revolutionary times, special fast-days, at short notice, were safer than an independent regular routine.

One of the ministers chosen proved sound. He was Thomas Brookes, a radical minister whose sponsor, Sir John Bourchier, would survive the purge and become a regicide. Brookes preached a fire-eating sermon demanding justice, whatever the cost. Parliament, he declared, should ignore the clamour of kindred and friends, ignore the 'ignorant, sottish people

[1] Mr. Stearns (*op. cit.* pp. 330-2) makes two separate sermons out of this material, ascribing the passage about Barabbas to a later sermon preached at the time when the Rump was hesitating to pass the Act setting up the High Court of Justice — *i.e.* between 3 and 6 Jan. But the source — a Mr. Beaver, who heard the sermon and gave evidence at Peter's trial in 1660 — is quite clear. He says that the occasion was 'a fast at St. Margaret's' in Dec. 1648 'a few days before the House of Commons made that thing called an Act for his [the King's] Trial' (*i.e.* the ordinance which passed the Commons on 28 Dec.). It is also clear from the text that Peter was preaching to both Houses. All this evidence points conclusively to Peter's official fast-sermon of 22 Dec.

who think that the doing of justice will undo a land', and recognize that, on the contrary, neglect of justice will provoke God 'to throw all your religious services as dung in your faces'. He therefore recommended to them the classic examples of holy murder and impious clemency : Phinehas who did not wait for judgment ; Saul and Ahab who spared the kings whom God had commanded them to kill.[1]

So spoke the morning preacher. It was an echo of the sanguinary sermons of Fairclough, calling for the blood of Strafford, of Scudder and Woodcock and Staunton calling for the blood of Laud ; and the Rump Parliament duly approved his sermon. But in the afternoon a different, discordant voice was heard. Thomas Watson, pastor of St. Stephens, Walbrook, was a 'presbyterian' who had been proposed by the 'presbyterian' London merchant John Rolle. But the Revolution which had occurred since he had been nominated, and which had probably excluded his sponsor from the House, did not deter him. To a congregation of furious or frightened men, hurrying or hurried blindly forward, he preached one of the boldest sermons that was ever uttered to the Long Parliament. It was a sermon against hypocrisy, and the preacher sketched, in apposite detail, the character of the hypocrite. The hypocrite, he said, is 'zealous in lesser things and remiss in greater, . . . zealous against a ceremony, a relic or painted glass . . . but in the meantime lives in known sin, lying, defaming, extortion, etc.' He is zealous against popery, but makes no conscience of sacrilege, starving out the ministry, 'robbing God of his tithes'. Then he drew nearer and struck deeper. The hypocrite, he declared, 'makes religion a mask to cover his sin'. So 'Jezebel, that she may colour over her murder, proclaims a fast'. Already the congregation of parliamentary saints must have begun to tremble for what would come next. And well they might, for it came hot and strong, even personal. 'Many', said the preacher (and there could be no doubt of whom he was

[1] Thomas Brookes, *God's Delight in the Progress of the Upright* (1648).

thinking) 'make religion a cloak for their ambition. Come see my zeal, saith Jehu, for the Lord. No Jehu, thy zeal was for the kingdom. Jehu made religion hold the stirrup till he got into the saddle and possessed the Crown. This is a most exasperating sin.'

Predictably, the Rump did not thank Watson, nor invite him to print his sermon. Even the Levellers, who would soon echo his sentiments about Cromwell's 'hypocrisy', rejected such an ally. 'This Presbyterian proud flesh', they said, 'must down with monarchy, one being equal in tyranny with the other.' But Watson ignored the implied veto. He published his sermon himself. He had no difficulty in finding a printer. The sermon came out under the same *imprimatur* as the *Serious and Faithful Representation*, the protest of the London clergy against the trial of the king and the charge that they, by their opposition, had ever intended the destruction of the monarchy.[1]

Immediately after the fast-day, Cromwell made up his mind, and on 28 December the obedient Rump passed the ordinance for the King's Trial. Two days later it chose its preachers for the next fast, which was due to fall on 30 January 1649. This time there was to be no chance of error. The two preachers were proposed by two safely radical members, Gilbert Millington and Francis Allen, both of whom would sign the king's death warrant. They were John Cardell and John Owen.

So the most dramatic month of the whole Revolution began. At every stage the courage of the regicides was sustained by the shrill voice of the preacher, and the preacher, in that month, was always the same ; for if there were several ministers who would press the Parliament to try the king, there was only one who would openly demand his execution. Between 26 December and 30 January there was no official

[1] Watson's sermon was published as *God's Anatomy upon Man's Heart*. The Leveller comments are from *The Moderate* (nos. 25, p. 235, and 26, p. 248).

parliamentary fast, but there were plenty of unofficial opportunities, and Peter used them to the full. Every stage of the personal tragedy of Charles I was punctuated by his gleeful exclamations. When the king was fetched from Windsor to St. James' Palace, Peter rode before his coach 'like a bishop-almoner . . . triumphing'. Himself placed in charge of the palace, he pestered the king to confess his crimes, as he had pestered archbishop Laud at his trial and the Marquis of Winchester in the smouldering ruins of Basing House. At the solemn fast with which the High Court of Justice began its proceedings he exclaimed rapturously that, 'with old Simeon', he could now cry *Nunc Dimittis* ; for after twenty years of prayer and preaching his eyes had seen salvation. Then he preached his famous sermon on the 149th Psalm :

> Let the saints be joyful in glory : let them sing aloud upon their beds.
> Let the high praises of God be in their mouth, and a two-edged sword in their hand ;
> To execute vengeance upon the heathen, and punishments upon the people :
> To bind their kings with chains and their nobles with fetters of iron . . .

At critical moments in the trial, Peter preached to the soldiers, encouraging them to hope for a bloody verdict ; he gave them cues to drown all murmurs of dissent with rhythmical cries of 'Justice, Justice !' or 'Execution, Execution !' ; and when sentence had been given, he preached a final sermon at St. James's Palace itself, choosing as his text Isaiah's famous denunciation of the King of Babylon :

> All the kings of the nations, even all of them, lie in glory, every one in his own house.
> But thou art cast out of thy grave like an abominable branch, and as the raiment of those that are slain, thrust through with a sword, that go down to the stones of the pit : as a carcase trodden under feet.

Thou shalt not be joined with them in burial, because thou hast destroyed thy land, and slain thy people : the seed of evildoers shall never be renowned.

This savoury text Peter had hoped to utter to the face of the king himself; but, as he afterwards regretted, 'the poor wretch would not hear me'. Three days later the monthly fast was postponed for one day in order that London might witness a more spectacular ceremony : the execution of the king.

Next day the more prudent clergy emerged again. Messrs. Cardell and Owen duly congratulated the Rump on its great act of justice ; they paraded, in retrospective vindication, the old gory texts about the wicked kings of Israel ; and then they looked forward to the long delayed reformation, the social reformation of which men had dreamed in 1640, in 1641, in 1646–7, only to be blocked by recurrent obstacles : Strafford, the Irish rebellion, the revolutionary crisis, and the second Civil War. Now at last, it seemed, all the obstacles, even the greatest, had been destroyed : the way was clear. The Rump, said Owen, was God's instrument of justice which it was sin to resist ; and when he published his sermon he appended to it a treatise on the religious reforms which were required in order to vindicate this title. The kingdom, said Cardell, was 'an old ruinous house', ready, unless repaired or rebuilt, 'to drop down upon your heads' : there were 'worm-eaten beams', 'rotten posts and studs . . . that will never serve again, that must of necessity be removed'.[1] On the same day Stephen Marshall preached to the Lords. Unlike his colleagues, he was too prudent to print his sermon, but we can hardly doubt its gist. Marshall had travelled the whole way with the Revolution hitherto. The spiritual ally

[1] J. Owen, *A Sermon Preached to the House of Commons . . .* (1649) ; J. Cardell, *God's Wisdom Justified and Man's Folly Condemned* (1649). Owen's sermon, in the preface to which, as Wood says (*Athenae Oxonienses*, IV, 103), 'he doth insolently father the most hellish notion of the preceding day', was among the books formally condemned and burnt by the University of Oxford in 1685.

of Pym had become the spiritual ally of Cromwell. From a 'Presbyterian' he had become an 'Independent'. Like Cromwell, like all the 'Independents', he was indifferent to 'forms of government'.[1] By agreeing to preach on the very morrow of regicide, even though it was to the reluctant Lords, he to some extent condoned the act. As the Presbyterian Robert Baillie afterwards wrote, 'he was more satisfied with the change of government, both civil and ecclesiastical, than many of his brethren' ; and the moderate royalist Thomas Fuller, no unfriendly biographer, noted that 'he was of so supple a soul that he brake not a joint, nay sprained not a sinew, in the alteration of the times.'[2]

Marshall's sermon to the House of Lords was its epitaph. When Cardell had spoken to the Commons of the rotten posts and studs of the kingdom which must be removed, there could be little doubt of his meaning. In fact, within a week, the House of Lords was abolished ; but the House of Commons went on, and Marshall went on with it. But how different it must have seemed to him since the great days when, with Calamy and Burges, he had laid down its tactics and preserved the unity of its 400 members : when he had instructed them in St. Margaret's how to vote and then shepherded them busily into Westminster to register their votes ; when he had trumpeted them into war and carried them, dwindling but still united, through the years of misfortune ! By now all his old colleagues had fallen away. Calamy and Burges had joined the 'Presbyterian' opposition ; Gauden had passed through Presbyterianism to royalism and had compiled the most famous, most effective of royalist tracts. In order to find fast-preachers, Parliament now had to draw on radical Army chaplains and furious sectaries. And in any case, it might be asked, what was the point of regular

[1] As he put it in *A Letter to a Friend in the Country* (1643), 'among the divers kinds of lawful governments, monarchy, aristocracy and democracy, no one of them is so appointed of God as to exclude the other from being a lawful government'.

[2] Fuller, *The History of the Worthies of England* (1672), II, 52.

fast sermons now? Parliament had shrunk to a mere handful of commoners. Marshall himself had done his best to stay the shrinkage. He had protested against Pride's Purge — though, as always, he had clung to the winning side.[1] He would be used by Cromwell to woo back the 'Secluded Members', but in vain.[2] Those who now sat at Westminster were so firmly held together by common interest, even common crime, that the old device of parliamentary sermons seemed hardly necessary.

Indeed, at such a time, political sermons were an added risk. The Rump had had one taste of the danger in Watson's sermon of 26 December. It had another on 25 February when Thomas Cawton, a London minister, publicly prayed before the Lord Mayor and Aldermen for Charles II and all the royal family. For this 'treasonable prayer' the Council of State promptly sent him to the Gatehouse. Meanwhile *Eikon Basiliké* was circulating everywhere to encourage misguided religious devotion to the Stuarts. Nor was it only the royalist and Presbyterian enemies of the Republic whose views were expressed in religious form. Levellers and Anabaptists on the left of the precarious new government were already preaching a 'second revolution'. Faced by this double danger, the Rump Parliament began to think that political sermons had lost something of their charm. Like so many revolutionary parties, it decided that liberty of expression was a luxury only to be allowed in the days of opposition; and at the end of March it acted accordingly. On 28 March it decided to bring in an Act ordering preachers in London not to meddle with matters of government but 'only to apply themselves to their duty in preaching Jesus Christ and his Gospel for the edification of their congregations'. A convenient precedent for such a measure had been given by the states of Holland and West

[1] That Marshall remonstrated against Pride's Purge appears from a marginal note in *A Serious and Faithful Representation of . . . Ministers of the Gospel within The Province of London* (1648), p. 1.

[2] Wood, *Athenae Oxonienses*, III, 964.

Friesland which had acted a month ago to forbid the expression of any political opinion by the clergy.[1] Next day, a timely pamphlet reinforced this decision. It was by John Dury, one of the original prophets of the social reformation which was now, at last, to be realized; and it was entitled, *A Case of Conscience Resolved, concerning Ministers meddling with State Matters in their Sermons.*

Dury admitted that the 'court chaplains' of Charles I had preached political sermons, and that since 1640 'the popular preachers have paid them back in their own way'; but in the end what good, he asked, had come of all this political preaching, this confusion of the minister with the magistrate? On both sides it had 'wrought nothing else but animosities and confusion'. To those who insisted — and how often the puritan preachers had insisted! — that men must not be lukewarm neutralists but zealous in the cause of God and for the public good, Dury replied that we must also beware lest we mistake the cause of God. It was the voice of religion disgusted with politics: the voice which would ultimately lead so many disillusioned men, and Dury himself, into the new, quietist gospel of Quakerism.[2]

In all these circumstances we can hardly be surprised that doubts began to assail the Rump as to the desirability of continuing the regular monthly fast. After the king's execution, the old procedure was followed and the usual preparations were made for a fast on 28 February. Stephen Marshall was once again invited, but refused. So did another clergyman. Two preachers were ultimately found, and preached, but did not print their sermons. Then the House decided to change the date of the next fast to 22 March, and set up a committee,

[1] *C.J.*, VI, 175. The orders of the states of Holland and West Friesland had been procured by de Witt in consequence of clerical denunciations of the execution of Charles I. They were published in England on 26 February 1649 as *An Extract out of the Register of the Resolution of the States of Holland, etc.*

[2] Dury's tract inevitably landed him in controversy. He amplified it next year in *A Case of Conscience concerning Ministers Meddling with State Matters in or out of their Sermons, resolved more satisfactorily than before.*

including Scot, Ireton, and Cromwell to draw up reasons for the change. Ten days later the committee was strengthened and the date of the fast was postponed to 5 April. On 17 March an Act was brought in accordingly, but in discussion the date was once again postponed, this time to 19 April. With this change the Act was published; but at the same time the committee was ordered to bring in, with all convenient speed, another, more general Act. On 23 April this Act was duly brought into the House. It was an Act to repeal the Act for the observation of the monthly fast.

The reasons given were no doubt true enough. The Parliament of England, it was said, had found by sad experience that the observation of the monthly fast had, for divers years, in most parts of the Commonwealth, been wholly neglected and in other places had been very imperfectly celebrated. Therefore, from now on, the said fast was abolished and all men should, on the last Wednesday of the month, follow their lawful callings. In future, instead of the regular fast, there would only be such special fasts as might from time to time be ordered. In particular, there was to be a special fast on 3 May in the London area, and on 17 May in the country, to pray God to pardon the sins of the nation, its unthankfulness for recent mercies, its proneness and endeavour to relapse into its former tyranny and superstition, and 'the iniquities of the former monthly fast-days'.

Meanwhile the Parliament was concerning itself with political preaching in general. All through the early months of 1649 both royalists and radicals continued to use their opportunities. At first the great danger had been counter-revolution; but before long the threat of a second revolution seemed more imminent, as the Levellers roused their followers against the new 'juggling junto' of Cromwell and Ireton. To a timid spirit even some of the official fast sermons might seem dangerously radical. The preachers on 19 April, for instance, gloried in the prospect of further convulsions and looked forward to the triumph of radical heresy and the cause of the poor.[1] On the special fast-day of 3 May, the sermons were even more radical. The preachers, we are told, declared 'that after the oppressor was taken away, the oppression ought not to be continued' and that true patriots would prefer 'to be poor in a rich Commonwealth than rich in a distracted, poor and almost ruined nation'. At the time of the last Leveller mutiny these radical sentiments were not relished and the preachers, though thanked, were not invited to print their sermons. Next day Parliament ordered that the Act prohibiting the clergy from meddling in politics be reported. The Levellers believed that this Act was directed against them;[2] but in fact, when it was passed, on 9 July, the threat from that side was over; the last Leveller mutiny had been crushed, and the text was openly directed only against royalist propaganda and, more generally, against those who directly or indirectly preached or prayed against the power, authority, or proceedings of the Parliament.[3]

With these two measures of 1649, the abolition of the regular monthly fast and the order against political preaching, we may conclude this study of the political sermons of the Long Parliament. Of course it was not a final end. If the monthly fast had ceased, special fast-days or days of thanksgiving continued to be declared, and it would soon be clear that political sermons were by no means extinct. It was not even a tidy end. The monthly fast had originally been designed to continue as long as the troubles in Ireland. How much more satisfactory it would have been if it could have been kept going for those few remaining months! For, in fact, now that the troubles of England, however temporarily, were settled, the Irish troubles would soon be ended. On 1 November 1649 Parliament would learn of Cromwell's sack and massacre of Drogheda and Marshall and Sterry would

[1] John Owen, *Οὐρανῶν Οὐρανία, The Shaking and Translating of Heaven and Earth* (1649), John Warren, *The Potent Potter* (1649).

[2] *The Moderate*, No. 43, 1-8 May 1649, p. 492.

[3] *Resolves of the Commons concerning such ministers as shall preach or pray against the Present Government* (9 July 1649).

be appointed to preach at the day of thanksgiving. If only the monthly fasts could have been kept up till then, they could have been called off with a ceremonious, triumphant flourish. But perhaps their premature end was really more appropriate. The connection with Ireland was, after all, accidental. The real purpose of the monthly fast had been to provide a constant sounding-board of parliamentary policy, a regular means of contact with, and propaganda to, the people. By the spring of 1649 none of those purposes could be fulfilled. A Parliament which had shrunk into an oligarchy no longer needed such a sounding-board, and an oligarchy which had lost touch with the people could no longer exploit the means of propaganda. Though we have few texts of the special fast sermons or thanksgiving sermons preached from 1649 to 1653, the circumstances in which they were preached sufficiently show the changed spirit behind them. The careful preparation, the narrow definition, the penalties threatened for non-conformity, all indicate a defensive spirit very different from that which had animated a national Parliament fighting for liberty; and by ceasing even to authorize the printing of the sermons, Parliament renounced the hope of using them to influence the country. In the hands of Hesilrige and Scot, Pym's broadcast propaganda had become a private lecture.[1]

Meanwhile others were taking up the discarded weapon. Already, during the rule of the Rump, the new political preachers were emerging. Once again, as in 1645–7, it was in Cromwell's army — that moving, restive body of men, rendered nervous by constant tension, exalted by successive victory — that they discovered their power. They were the 'Anabaptist' chaplains, the 'Fifth Monarchy Men'. Stepping into the gap left by the ruin of the Levellers, these men quickly

[1] Formal thanks and invitations to print were the rule until March 1651, though preachers seldom took advantage of the invitations. From March 1651 thanks are rare and invitations to print rarer still, gradually ceasing altogether.

captured the old machinery of propaganda. Thanks to the patronage of Harrison, they even penetrated into St. Margaret's and uttered their disconcerting doctrines to the Parliament. Just as Cromwell, in 1645–6, had introduced Hugh Peter and Peter Sterry to alarm the followers of Holles and Stapleton, so Harrison now brought in the revolutionary Fifth Monarchy tribunes to alarm the followers of Hesilrige and Scot. It was he who sponsored Vavasour Powell in February 1650, John Simpson in March 1651, and Christopher Feake in October 1652. The Parliament shrank away from these radical preachers. It voted down a proposed vote of thanks to Simpson, avoided offering one to Feake ; and in January 1653, when Harrison proposed the radical William Dell, divided to defeat him. But the radicals, at the beginning of 1653, were not to be defeated by mere parliamentary votes. They had patrons more powerful than Hesilrige and Scot, congregations more numerous than the Rump ; and they were determined to use both. If Parliament would not use them, they would overturn Parliament itself.

On 3 March 1653 the Long Parliament held what was to be its last solemn fast : a fast to implore God's blessing on the counsels and armed forces of the Commonwealth. The preacher, once again, was Stephen Marshall. That faithful servant, 'the arch-flamen of the rebellious rout', 'the trumpet by whom they sounded their solemn fasts', had begun the long series ; now, accidentally, he was to end it : to pronounce the epitaph of the House of Commons as he had already done for the House of Lords. We do not know what he said. But while he uttered to his diminished congregation his unthanked, unrecorded sermon, a new force was mustering out of doors. In the churches and open places of London, Vavasour Powell, Feake, and Simpson would soon be addressing massive audiences demanding the end of Parliament and a new system of government in which the pulpits should not be tuned by any man, but all power should be exercised direct by the preachers, the Saints.

5

J. Steven Watson

ARTHUR ONSLOW AND PARTY POLITICS

'The Speakership of Arthur Onslow', Mr. Philip Laundy justly remarked in his recent book, 'was of immeasurable importance, not only in relation to the evolution of the office itself, but also to the broader course of parliamentary history.'[1] The special interest of this broader course of parliamentary history in the eighteenth century is the emergence, slowly and confusingly, of party politics. No feature of the constitution is so intimately involved with this as the Speakership. A study of the Speakership should therefore illuminate the growth of party. It is a measure of the failure to chart this growth that no writer on the office — not even Mr. Laundy — has been able to see the significance of Onslow's success or of the failure of his successors.

The older writers — Manning,[2] Lummis,[3] Dasent,[4] MacDonagh,[5] were unanimous in telling a story which had that clarity which is produced by ignoring the facts. And authorities of less specialization but greater eminence have found this clarity compulsive ever since. Dr. Redlich, the Porritts, Sir William Holdsworth, and Sir David Keir have all, in their turn, accepted an account of Onslow's work between 1728 and 1761 which obscures his real achievement and makes nonsense of the political developments of the century.

[1] P. Lundy, *The Office of Speaker* (1964), p. 261.
[2] J. A. Manning, *The Lives of the Speakers of the House of Commons* (1850).
[3] E. Lummis, *The Speaker's Chair* (1900).
[4] A. I. Dasent, *The Speakers of the House of Commons* (1911).
[5] M. MacDonagh, *The Speaker of the House* (1914).

The legend is that Walpole 'appreciated in advance the value of appointing an incorruptible man to the Chair, for though not above venality himself he was fundamentally dedicated to the interests of the country'.[1] Onslow was the one just man in a muck-raking world. In the Chair he more than came up to expectation. But after his retirement there came a bad period in which Speakers were party men. Fletcher Norton and Manners Sutton are singled out as the glaring examples of partisanship in the Chair, but we are left to suppose that Cust, Cornwall, W. W. Grenville, Addington, Mitford, Abbot, and Abercromby were weak if not wicked, though never so partial as to provoke the Commons to unseat them. Then, so goes the legend, with Shaw Lefevre in the office of Speaker (1829–57) 'its holders attained the standard set by Onslow'.[2]

But was this 'standard set by Onslow' comparable with that at which Shaw Lefevre eventually arrived? In Sir David Keir's phrase: 'During the long tenure of the Chair by Arthur Onslow the office came first to be set above party',[3] does 'above party' there carry the same significance as it did in 1839? We know very well what the impartiality established by Shaw Lefevre means; for it is still with us: it has become a leading feature in the constitutional ideas we offer for export. The Speaker, like an umpire at a tennis match, must sit aloft — ruling which shots are fair and which balls are out of court — while the champions of the political parties struggle for victory on the floor below. The only favouritism he is permitted to show is that he will call on minority spokesmen more frequently than can be justified by their numbers. His concern has to be with the rules and never with the players. For this reason he resigns from political clubs when he is chosen for the Chair. For this reason also he expects to be re-elected to Parliament without effort on his part. His

[1] P. Laundy, *op. cit.* p. 263.

[2] W. S. Holdsworth, *The History of English Law* (6th ed. 1938), X, 535.

[3] D. L. Keir, *Constitutional History of Modern Britain* (1938 ed.), 480.

impartiality in fact is politically negative, sterilized; it is a neutrality in the constant war of parties.

Little of this is true of Onslow's speakership. For a good part of his time in the Chair he held office under the Crown:[1] he spoke in Committee:[2] he attended partisan meetings. His was an active, not a cloistered virtue. Certainly he was fanatical in his zeal for the dignity and independence of the House of Commons. No one who reads his autobiographical fragment[3] or Hatsell's *Precedents of the House of Commons*[4] can fail to see that he was suspicious of the power of ministers and dedicated to the protection of ordinary members. He believed that pedantry was the best barrier against tyranny. He claimed for himself a patriotic impartiality in politics. But this impartiality, if it is to be understood, has to be seen in a context quite different from that of the last hundred years. Onslow never thought of his House as a tourney between opposing sides. On the contrary his emphasis was always upon its unity, a unity which he strove both to inspire and express by his own actions. No member might criticize past decisions of the House — 'Mr. O. in this case, whenever a member was proceeding to argue against a former decision of the House, always stopt him by saying, "This question is over, the majority of the House have determined upon it, and you, sir, are included in that majority: it is the declared sense of the House"'.[5] Even in ascertaining this sense of the

[1] He did not decline to hold office under the Crown, as Sir David Keir has it (*op. cit.*, p. 480) but was forced to resign his office in circumstances which appear below.

[2] According to E. and A. Porritt, *The Unreformed House of Commons* (1909), I, 447, speeches in Committee by the Speaker disappear between 1714 and 1770. This is an error. Many such speeches are recorded in the *Parliamentary History* and in memoirs.

[3] Hist. MSS. Comm. *14th Report*, Appendix, IX (Onslow MSS.), [hereafter cited as *Onslow MSS.*], 473-520.

[4] Hatsell, as Clerk, produced in 1781 a full account of Procedure as Onslow had fixed it by his rulings. The edition produced in 1818 is enriched by footnotes based on information obtained from Onslow and Abbot.

[5] John Hatsell, *Precedents of Proceedings in the House of Commons* (1818), II, 234 n.

House he did his best to avoid any sense of party conflict. He disliked the taking of decisions for it was 'a very unparliamentary proceeding' to insist upon divisions except in cases where the issue was really in doubt:[1] he preferred to decide questions by his own judgment of opinion after acclamation.

Onslow boasted that he had reached the Chair not through St. James but through his independence of character.[2] He was nevertheless acceptable to the king and to Walpole. Walpole sought in 1727–8 to conciliate his critics and was willing to have a man of independent views in the Chair. At the same time it was not in his interest to have someone of vaulting ambition there. He had, after all, only just survived the threat to replace him by the last Speaker, Spencer Compton. For more than a century to come, the Speaker was able to use his position as the adviser and guardian of back-benchers to build up a following for himself in any struggle for power.[3] Walpole conceded that the Speaker had a right to expect the honour and profits of office: he advised Onslow to sit for a borough rather than for the county of Surrey, for this would make his re-election (under the terms of Anne's Regency Act) simpler when he accepted further offices;[4] but he wanted an associate, not a rival in the Chair. This point Hervey made with the characteristic insinuation that Onslow was chosen only because Walpole expected compliance from one with so little claim to the office.[5]

Onslow came of a family which had already produced two Speakers and a Clerk of the Commons. His parliamentary

[1] Hatsell, *Precedents of Proceeding of the House of Commons* (1818) II, 199–201, and notes.

[2] *Onslow MSS.*, p. 516. The king of course could never dictate to the House who should be chosen Speaker. His disapproval, however, would probably be an effective veto as it seems to have been to Grenville's chances in 1761 (*Grenville Papers*, ed. W. J. Smith, 1852, I, 411) and to Rigby's in 1770.

[3] This 'Speaker's following' is the real source of Addington's rise.

[4] *Onslow MSS.*, p. 518.

[5] John, Lord Hervey, *Memoirs of the Reign of George II* (ed. R. Sedgwick, 1931), I, 74, 75.

seat was safely maintained by the standing of his family in Surrey.[1] He had been trained in the Law but had left the profession to act as secretary, in 1714, to his uncle who was then Chancellor of the Exchequer, and this had led to his obtaining a position as Treasurer of the Post Office.[2] For a while after this he had despaired of advancement and had retired to devote himself to the affairs of Surrey. He had entered Parliament in 1720. There was no doubt of the staunchness of his Whig views or of his support of Walpole. Indeed he maintained that corruption was worse before the rise of Walpole to leadership, for Sir Robert could command support for himself and his policies and had less need to buy it.[3] Yet even Sir Robert felt the corrupting influence of power. Onslow criticized Walpole's vindictiveness towards Catholics and the way he took advantage of the Atterbury plot.[4] In the same spirit he expressed admiration for the talents of Wyndham while deploring his adoption of set opposition.

Thus Onslow's political views (when he was pulled, protesting his unworthiness, into the Chair) were those of a true independent Whig. He accepted the necessity of having a sovereign and despotic authority in the constitution, and that this body must be Parliament, but at the same time he believed that this sovereign authority must be kept in reserve, usually inactive. For *stare super vias antiquas*, preserve the ways of the Common Law, should be a sufficient motto for the ordinary government of England. The function of the House

[1] The Onslows had been members for Surrey in all but five Parliaments since 1627 and had represented Guildford for all but two years since 1660. Arthur Onslow was unopposed in all general elections after he became Speaker not because there was any recognition of a Speaker's right to an undisputed return but because he took care of his family influence. In 1780 therefore, while attacking the right of C. W. Cornwall to become Speaker, T. Townshend argued that a Speaker should be a man with a seat made safe not by official arrangement (Cornwall sat for a Cinque port) but by local weight and connection. This is in contrast to the modern view.

[2] *Onslow MSS.*, pp. 500, 501.

[3] *Ibid.* pp. 473, 509–13.

[4] *Parliamentary History*, VIII, 52.

of Commons as a part of the sovereign body should be to scrutinize and to check all proposals for change, to apply itself judicially to problems as they arose, to maintain a balance against the hand of power ; to legislate only when an overwhelming case had been made out for a change. At the same time the Commons should not cause a breakdown in administration but should maintain the necessary (and usual) means by which the king carried on the executive government. This theory of the balance of the constitution could only be worked so long as there was basic agreement upon fundamentals. Such agreement would be jeopardized by political faction, by party. Onslow was prepared to protect minority views but he condemned both formal opposition and overbearing executive authority.

The procedural forms of the House emphasized its legalism : they made positive action impossible unless members of the House were prepared to operate the rules in a gentlemanly and unobstructive way. There is no need to explore them here,[1] though their study and expression was the life-work of Onslow. The point here is that Onslow, by making himself the embodiment of parliamentary forms and the spokesman for a united House, vastly increased his own weight in the constitution. He claimed, and was granted, the position of the regulator of the balance in it. But this was not to make him less influential politically. On the contrary the greater his authority as an uncorrupted pundit the more influential he could be in shaming an opposition into decency and so the more valuable his assistance once Ministers had secured his agreement to a course they proposed. It was for this reason that Onslow — at first to the surprise [2] and then amid

[1] For some of their significant features see my essay 'Parliamentary Procedure as a Mirror of the Constitution' in *The Burke Newsletter*, vol. III, No. 4, 108 (1962).

[2] In the 1730s Doddington, for instance, believed that Onslow was building up his own middle party to replace Walpole and baulk the opposition. Hist. MSS. Comm., *Diary of 1st Earl of Egmont* [hereafter cited as *Egmont Diary*], I, 31.

the admiration of his contemporaries — declared his ambition satisfied with the Chair so that he would never leave it for other office.

Onslow's political feelings were not limited to this worship of the idea of a balance in the legislative organs. He was an independent Whig also in his general views on policy. He regarded the Hanoverian kings as the foundation of our liberties, but he disliked (as will be seen) continental entanglements. In January 1730 the Speaker spoke in Committee to make an attack on Henry Pelham for having expressed favour of the idea of a standing army. While an army might be a necessity of the moment it could not, he said, be accepted as a permanent feature of the constitution.[1] He preferred the militia. He was interested in overseas expansion and in the colonization of Georgia. He had a patriotic fervour for the Navy and the deep-blue-sea sentiments often called Tory. Instinctively he supported that middle policy which had commended itself to Harley and was in his own time expressed by Walpole. Accordingly he distrusted Carteret and hated Bolingbroke. When he told Henry Pelham not to expect him to be compliant to ministerial demands, it was a warning of independence which gave no offence because his support of the Pelham system was well known[2] — and indeed gained importance from his sympathy with the quirks of country gentlemen.[3] Pelham's answer was that he would not want a Speaker 'in a *set* opposition' but 'I shall as little like a Speaker over-complaisant, either to me or to them'.[4]

Onslow's income reflected his double allegiance, to the House of Commons and to the Crown. He received £5 a day from the Exchequer for his normal duties in the Chair. But for every Private Bill — and Private Bills were still an important part of the parliamentary process — he received fees.

[1] *Egmont Diary*, I, 12. [2] *Ibid.*

[3] This is what Hervey means by saying that his 'true Whig and laudable principles were daubed by country, fulsome, bombast professions'.

[4] *Onslow MSS.*, p. 517.

He also had profits from the sale of the Votes and various other perquisites.[1] Payment from the Crown marked for Onslow the fact that he was the agent of the Crown. He was, so to speak, the only elected minister of George II. But his service of the king had this peculiarity also, that a greater part of his duty was to express the doubts or objections freely formulated in the Commons. Formally he did this when making an annual speech presenting money bills of the year to the king.[2] Informally he did it in confidential ministerial councils or in what Horace Walpole called 'his pompous pathetics', statements from the Chair.

Because Onslow's care for minorities and suspicion of the intentions of ministers was the part of his work on which he laid stress himself, his activity in government requires particular attention. In 1730 Walpole appointed a Committee to meet with the Dissenters who were pressing for amendment of the Test Act. Its purpose was to satisfy them of the government's sympathy while avoiding any action in Parliament. On it served the Lord Chancellor, the Lord President, the two secretaries of state, Walpole himself, and Mr. Speaker Onslow. In the discussion Onslow took a prominent part. His own religious standpoint — extremely low Anglican [3] — gave him sympathy with the Dissenters' viewpoint. But he urged the inexpediency of action while the House of Commons was likely to be hopelessly divided about it. His argument prevailed. On this committee he may have served *ex officio*. Nevertheless his argument was exactly that of Walpole himself and its success achieved Walpole's political purpose at the time. Moreover, he might afterwards have to preside over discussion of the problem in the House of Commons.

[1] *Parl. Hist.*, XXVIII, 506; also John Nichols, *Literary Anecdotes of the Eighteenth Century* (1812–15), II, 414. The Speaker also received £1,000 equipment money for each Parliament, 200 ounces of plate, a claret allowance, a stationery allowance, an official residence, and one Chair for each Parliament over which he presided.

[2] For examples see below.

[3] He calls himself 'A Church Puritan', *Onslow MSS*, p. 497.

It is not easy to draw a dividing line between committees of a national and uncontroversial nature (on which Shaw Lefevre himself would consent to serve and those which served the interest of a ministry. The committee of the Cabinet to meet the Dissenters seems to straddle any line. The committee of the Privy Council (set up in August 1733 and working until 1738) to discuss the Crown's assumption of rights in the soil in the Bahamas was of a non-partisan character. The Lord Chancellor, the Lord President, the Lord Chamberlain, Earl Godolphin, the Earl of Halifax, Lord Harrington, Lord Delaware, Horatio Walpole, Sir Charles Wager, the Chancellor of the Exchequer, and the Speaker served on it.[1] Yet it is interesting that the Barbados residents sent advance copies of their petition to two men, to Sir Robert Walpole as head of the executive and to Arthur Onslow as the head of the Commons branch of the legislature.[2] It was this respect for the Speaker as leader of the House which Walpole echoed in telling George II that he could not decide upon the date for the end of the session until he had consulted 'our governor'.[3]

The Bahamas were not the only colonial territory whose problems Onslow considered as a member of a Privy Council committee. In January 1738 he sat in a special committee to hear the appeal of the Georgia Trustees against a decision of the Board of Trade. But though apparently this was a simple case of a special judicial tribunal for which the Speaker was qualified by his office, his legal background, and his integrity, it did in fact involve matters of controversy with which Onslow had been closely concerned. At some periods Onslow had been an unofficial parliamentary agent of the Georgia Trustees.[4] Law, national interest, and politics were so intermingled that Onslow had to walk delicately. Even though

[1] *Commons Journals*, XXIII, 199-201.

[2] *Egmont Diary*, I, 149.

[3] *Ibid.* I, 176.

[4] In this respect his position was like that of Jekyll, Master of the Rolls, who also served on the committee but in 1733 had presented the petition of the Georgia Trustees.

his reputation shielded him against accusations of impropriety, Egmont (an enthusiast for Georgia) came to think of him as a false friend who was secretly in league with Walpole against the Trustees and had managed the whole affair to the advantage of the Ministry.[1]

Nevertheless these Privy Council committees may be regarded as administrative rather than political assignments. On the other extreme are discussions in which Onslow helped to concert action which later had violent political results on the floor of the House over which he presided. The affair of the judges' salaries in 1758 comes somewhere between. Onslow had always sympathized with that part of the Leicester House argument which stressed the need for greater naval strength. Pitt, even when he broke with Leicester House and was working with Newcastle, also put emphasis on this. But impressment for the Navy brought up the question of the use of Habeas Corpus on behalf of those impressed. In March 1758 Pratt brought in a Habeas Corpus Bill to make the issue of the writ compulsory. On this the opinion of the judges was taken. Then Hardwicke in the House of Lords effected the rejection of the Bill without a division.[2] The proposal, under discussion at the same time, to raise the judges' salaries was, according to Horace Walpole, characterized by Pitt as the payment of a fee for giving an opinion against Pratt. Ministers were doubtful whether they should proceed with it. On 27 April 1758 a meeting was called to meet in the Speaker's House. Legge, the Chancellor of the Exchequer, was the convener : Pratt (Pitt's mouthpiece) refused to attend. Onslow had been in favour both of Pratt's Bill and of the raising of the salaries. Now, however, he tried to frighten Legge with talk of a contested budget 'getting off from what he said though he professes in words to adhere'. Onslow proposed to drop the Bill, to leave the judges with the one year's advance that had been made to them, and to promote measures to

[1] *Egmont Diary*, III, 107.

[2] P. C. Yorke, *Life of Hardwicke* (Cambridge, 1913), III, 17.

prevent their taking presents (of sheep and so on) while on circuit.[1] Onslow, speaking with authority about the temper of the House and backed by the knowledge of Pitt's feelings, prevailed : his views became government policy.

Onslow's strength, when it came to an argument, was that he spoke not as a group leader but as the guardian deity of the independent members of the House. His contacts (in guiding private Bill legislation and advising on procedure) with all members made him the best informed member of the House. Respect for his character made his consequence grow with the passing of time. He exerted this strength in the aftermath of Walpole's Excise Bill in 1733.

When Walpole gave up the Bill, Pulteney and Wyndham asked for a committee to consider abuses in the Customs. It was a skilful move. For one of the arguments for the Excise Bill had been the disorders in Customs' collection. The committee would appear to be an attempt to find an alternative answer to the problem. But it would keep alive the anti-Walpole agitation and explore his system of patronage. Walpole's argument might thus be used to destroy him. The moment was propitious not only because of the Excise campaign but because at this very time reports were received on scandals concerning the Charitable Corporations and the York building funds. In the Lords an investigation was begun into what had happened to the South Sea Bubble accounts over the last decade.[2]

Walpole was bound to assent to the appointment of the committee on frauds in the Customs. On 23 April he held a Cockpit meeting (on the usual lines for whipping up his supporters before each session). 263 members came. Egmont, it is noteworthy, refused because he wished to avoid appearing to prejudge the issue. No such scruple troubled Onslow. From the way in which his appearance at Cockpits is noticed — when it happens to be — it may probably be assumed that

[1] *Ibid.* III, 55.

[2] *Parl. Hist.*, IX, 1-10, 13, 79, 91, and Hervey, *op. cit.* I, 184.

his attendance was quite normal.[1] He not only attended but he was a leading speaker announcing the plan agreed upon by the ministry. The opposition, he said, were plotting against the constitution and the royal family. They were under the influence of Bolingbroke. The only defence of good men was to agree in advance upon a list of names, men who would keep the enquiry on trivial matters and prevent a general indictment of the king's servants. This speech needed only emphasis from Pelham and the Attorney-General. The advice was taken. The ministerial forces carried the whole of their list by a majority of 85 on the following day. The situation was saved.[2]

Onslow's defence against our criticism that he had helped a party manœuvre may be inferred from his life and from his recollections. Opposition for the sake of winning power 'to force the Crown and distress the administration in Parliament' would 'debase and corrupt the minds of men who use it'. 'Concerted opposition could only be justified when the constitution is in danger from the settled plan of the administration.' There was no such 'settled plan' in this case for Walpole had given up his Excise Bill. The Speaker's task was to take 'the middle track between these two extremes', 'the path that honest and wise men will take and the true character of a Parliament man'. He believed that he was avoiding party for 'parties are usually factions and the chief business of factions is to annoy one another'.[3] He might appear to be a champion of the Walpole administration — on 6 February 1734 he even spoke in Committee of the House to urge the need for a larger army[4] — but in his own eyes he was simply regulating the balance of the constitution.

The opposition presumably would not have agreed that they were factious. But there was no open attack upon the Speaker. There was talk of opposing his re-election to the

[1] An example is H. Fox's Cockpit to discuss subsidies in 1755 — see below.
[2] See *Egmont Diary*, I, 365.
[3] *Onslow MSS.*, pp. 458-69.
[4] *Egmont Diary*, II, 24.

Chair. It was expected that Sandys would be put up by Morpeth.[1] But the aim seems to have been the traditional one of testing the strength of ministerial and opposition forces in an untried Parliament [2] rather than to vent resentment. In the event the idea was dropped and Onslow was re-elected unanimously. From a modern point of view it is more surprising that no adverse notice was taken of the Speaker's acceptance of the office of Treasurer of the Navy in 1734.[3] It was a reward for faithful service in his first Parliament, service as the official watchdog of the constitution.

In his second Parliament in the Chair Onslow continued to feel that Walpole represented sound Whig principles but he was increasingly concerned that the Walpole government was deaf to the warnings of its critics. His prejudices and his interest in the Georgia scheme made him wish for a more active policy against Spain on the high seas. In 1738 he delivered as usual a speech on presenting money bills to the Crown. In it, however, his voice sounded more like that of the opposition than of the ministry. He justified the grant of £3¾ million for the armed forces on the ground that the number of seamen must be doubled because 'to suffer the Spaniards to rummage our ships is to give them a right to the Sovereignty of those Seas as . . . was never allowed by any of your Majesty's predecessors'.[4] This theme was present again in his presenting speech on 29 April 1740 — with an added note which could have been taken offensively. £4 million had been voted 'not only with cheerfulness but with unanimity . . . from the assurance they have that it will be expended for the great and necessary purposes for which it is granted' — these purposes being a more profitable sea war and consequent gains in trade.[5] Onslow's views may — if

1 Hist. MSS. Comm., *Earl of Carlisle*, p. 143.

2 Everyone agreed that Onslow would win but the Court believed his majority would be 100 while the opposition hoped to reduce it to 50.

3 In the place of Lord Torrington who became Vice-Treasurer of Ireland.

4 *Parl. Hist.*, X, 867, 868.

5 *Ibid.* XI, 599.

we may trust the reports — even have affected his conduct of debate, for in that of 8 March 1739 he made no move to check violence in attacking the Spanish convention: even more at variance with his usual strictness was his allowing Pitt to appeal to the Prince of Wales (who was in the Gallery) on behalf of the opposition — 'Sir, I know who hears me and for that reason I speak'.[1]

George Lyttelton, at that time still a 'patriot' of the opposition kind, had good reason to dedicate his 'Letter to a Member of Parliament from his friend in the Country' (1739) to Arthur Onslow.[2] For his pamphlet argues that members are elected not for interests but to speak for the nation: the nation felt resentment against Spain but could only express it effectively by uniting under the Crown. Onslow seems to have echoed all this except the implied rejection of Walpole. He wanted to press Walpole on, not to destroy him. On 4 March 1741 he spoke in committee on the Seamen's Bill in favour of naval expansion but contended that the government really agreed with him — and he denied that they were responsible for seamen being defrauded of their pay.[3] In later stages of the Bill he intervened from the Chair to protect Walpole from Barnard's procedural fault-finding and pacified the House when a row blew up about Walpole's attitude to merchants.[4] The Speaker openly condemned Wyndham's behaviour in seceding from Parliament in 1739 in protest against Walpole's majority. 'There never was such behaviour as this' the Speaker is reported to have interrupted a debate on 23 March 1739 to declare . . . 'since the Great Rebellion: that he wanted an opportunity to declare . . . his detestation of it . . . that this session destroyed the rule of Parliament on which all government depended, which is that the minority should yield to the majority.'[5] He might thunder, but the

[1] *Parl. Hist.*, X, 1284.

[2] A. J. Phillimore, *Memoirs and Correspondence of George, Lord Lyttelton* (1845), I, 187.

[3] *Parl. Hist.*, XII, 48.

[4] *Ibid.* XII, 126-215.

[5] *Egmont Diary*, III, 43.

opposition felt that he sympathized with them as to policy if not about persons. Chesterfield wrote that the Speaker had 'by a certain decency of behaviour . . . made himself many personal friends in the minority' and he discouraged Doddington from contesting his re-election to the Chair.[1]

Onslow was unopposed for the Speakership in the new Parliament of 1742. Walpole after his fall expected that the Speaker would go all the way with his rivals: 'popularity', said Horace Walpole, 'was his great aim, impartiality his professed means . . . partiality to whatever was popular his real means of acquiring it'.[2] But the Walpoles soon were to realize that he was 'tough and steady when pushed to an extremity and he would sometimes see that extremity as soon in trifles as in materials'. A secret committee to investigate the affairs of the late ministry was decided upon. It could well have been the prelude to a parliamentary prosecution, an impeachment. Onslow thought such prosecutions (he was writing of the South Sea Bubble period) brought out 'the arts of power and of faction, of party resentment and of personal pique of great men against one another'. He thought parliamentary criticism should be sufficient to prevent abuses of public trust.[3] Walpole was punished for any failings by his loss of power and had been 'the best man to live with and live under of any great man I ever knew'.[4] There was apparently no preparation for the ballot for the Secret Committee as there had been in 1733. There was a tie for the last two places on the committee between William Finch, Sir Henry Liddell, the Hon. John Talbot, and Hume Campbell. Hume Campbell was perhaps less equal than the others because one of his votes had a spelling mistake. The Speaker then gave his casting vote. He did not choose one member of each opposing viewpoint. He put Liddell and Talbot on the

[1] Phillimore, I, 188.

[2] Horace Walpole, *Memoirs of the last ten years of the reign of George II* (ed. Henry Fox, 3rd Lord Holland, London, 1822), I, 112.

[3] *Onslow MSS.* pp. 506, 507.

[4] *Ibid.* p. 473.

committee and both were reckoned as friendly to the fallen minister, and be able to 'stop any iniquitous proceedings'.[1]

Onslow acted not from friendship alone. He believed himself once again to be charged to act as a judge who guards the constitution: his position differed from that of a judge only in that he had usually to achieve equity by political action and by concerting measures with the parties to a dispute. This time he had only had to declare his views. It was effective. Thomas Prowse, an anti-Walpole man on the committee, wrote to Doddington that he began to despair of a prosecution of Walpole because some of its members had been put there to obstruct and frustrate their work.[2] It was not only effective, it was resented. For once, it appears, Onslow had failed to convince everyone that he acted only out of constitutional duty. It was alleged that he had acted as a client of Walpole, making a return for the salary he enjoyed as Treasurer of the Navy. Without delay Onslow resigned the Treasureship.[3] What he had won after the choice of one secret committee he abandoned after the choice of another.[4] But he resigned these profits not from any theoretical belief that he should avoid dependence on the Crown: rather he resigned so that he might be free to serve the Crown in his special way, to free his hands and remain active as the custodian of constitutional correctness.

[1] *Parl. Hist.*, XII, 589, and Horace Walpole, *Letters* (ed. Toynbee, Oxford, 1903–25), I, 206.

[2] This was 26 July 1742. Hist. MSS. Comm., *Various Collections*, VI, *Eyre Matcham MSS.*, 16, 17.

[3] The reasons for this resignation are noticed by Porritt (*op. cit.*) and by Laundy (*op. cit.*) but glancingly. They are darkly hinted at in a debate in 1780 when Rigby defended Mr. Cornwall, by saying that Onslow was a placeman also. 'Why Mr. Onslow lost that place . . . he would talk over . . . in private' (*Parl. Hist.*, XXI, 805). The story was set out in detail by Montagu in a speech in 1790 (*Ibid.* XXVIII, 515 H.). By comparing Montagu's speech with Horace Walpole's account (*op. cit.* I. 208) the story becomes quite clear.

[4] Onslow was succeeded in the Speakership by a friend, Mr. Clutterbuck, who had seconded him for the Speakership and who was also a friend of Pelham. Horace Walpole thought it all a political trick (*op. cit.* I, 209 n.).

Later generations certainly believed that at this point Onslow set up a standard of independence of the Crown and of party. But this is to make assumptions about the meaning of party. For Onslow the word meant a combination for factious or illegitimate or tyrannical purposes. It could never mean combination for the preservation of Whig ministries, or of the Hanoverians, or of legitimate enterprises (such as the Georgia colonization), or of the decencies due to a former minister. He paid a forfeit because for once he had failed to convince others that he was acting from the highest motives of duty. Two divergent impulses were thus imparted to this office: on the one hand towards active political work and on the other to a striving for independence which would eventually entail inactivity.

Onslow had emphasized his independence of spirit: he was able therefore to continue to be an active element in political life without serious hindrance. George Grenville called the Speakership a part of the ministry but he added that it was outside the main fury of controversy.[1] The period immediately after Walpole's fall was not Onslow's happiest. Horace Walpole believed that he rejoiced in the political eclipse of Lord Granville (baronet) because he was anxious to see all strong ministers disappear and leave him all powerful. It is probable that he was pleased to see Granville go, but only because he regarded the Pelhams as the better representatives of that moderate Whiggism in which he always felt confidence. His link with those who wanted a stronger naval policy was retained, however. In May 1745 his presenting speech dwelt on the need to use the larger sums voted for defence on naval defence. He showed where his sympathies lay when Henry Pelham, supported by Fox, produced a plan for reducing the Navy by 2,000 men. On a motion about the Navy being made by Barrington (14 April 1749), the Speaker, from the Chair, intervened to give the House advice about the proper

[1] *Onslow MSS.*, p. 516. George Grenville had ambitions to be Speaker and seems to have accepted a leading rôle in administration as a second best.

way of granting money to the Navy. He recommended them to take the matter up in a Committee of Supply.[1] Onslow, again, had not only approved of the Commons' decision to set up a special committee to discuss failures in the Mediterranean, he had also emphasised their demand for more punishments by court martial.[2]

This pre-occupation with the Navy went along with another concern, that for the militia.[3] Here again his interests were more like those of Pitt than of the Pelhams. Nevertheless the Pelhams could rely on his seeing the need for a regular army, even a hired army, and could depend upon his sternness against anyone who, in a spirit of faction, might try to rouse popular feeling against those who did what was necessary. On 16 November 1743 when Pitt opposed the maintenance of Hanoverian troops Onslow came down from the gallery or from 'Solomon's porch' in which the Speaker normally sat watching Committee proceedings[4] to vote for the government view against this opposition. In December 1743 he was quick and harsh in rebuking Pitt for breaking the rules in a denunciation of foreign levies.[5] At the end of this session he shared with Carteret the distinction of receiving letters which threatened violence if the Hanoverian troops should be brought over to England that winter.[6] But though a necessity, the use of foreign troops was always, to a country gentleman like Onslow, regrettable. In the mid 1750s the Speaker was making no secret of his dislike of subsidies to foreign powers —'Mr. Onslow has preserved his chastity while the band of chosen youths, while every Pulteney, Pitt, and Lyttelton, have

[1] Earl of Ilchester, *Henry Fox, 1st Lord Holland* (1920), I, 163, and *Parl. Hist.*, XIV, 554. Pitt and Newcastle agreed with Onslow at this time: Henry Pelham and Fox were on the other side.

[2] *Parl. Hist.*, XIII, 1303-7.

[3] His belittling the standing army by comparison with the militia involved him in a quarrel with some young officers in an inn. Horace Walpole, *op. cit.* III, 123.

[4] See Hatsell, *op. cit.* II, 196, 197.

[5] *Parl. Hist.*, XIII, 142. He had a tussle with Stanley, who took Pitt's view, in the next session also (*ibid.* XIII, 464).

[6] *Parl. Hist.*, XIII, 388.

fallen around him', recorded Horace Walpole.[1] In a presenting speech in 1756 he once more contrasted the zeal of the people of England for the Navy with their reluctance to find money for foreign subsidies or for the employment of foreign troops.[2]

Thus in the period between the fall of Walpole and the death of Henry Pelham Speaker Onslow continued to play his double rôle, the voice of the independent gentry in ministerial councils, and the guarantor of the legitimate claims of government in the suspicious House of Commons. His authority increased naturally enough simply with the passage of time. Every ruling on procedure, each exposition of tradition, all successful interventions to restore order in debate, added to his consequence. He was actively concerned in every Private Bill and in the reign of George II, in which there were 1,447 Public Acts, there were 1,244 Private Acts.[3] The Speaker had to rule — no easy matter — which Bills were private and which public. Once they were taken as private he had to advise the movers, select members for a preliminary committee, and, because many of them were of no interest to the majority of members, he had also in his own person to be the watchdog of the general public interest, calling the attention of the House to any odd features or dangerous proposals. This legislation was the Speaker's special province.[4] But much of the time of the House was concerned with quasi-judicial rather than legislative work. Members heard witnesses as a stage in Private Bill legislation, but they heard them also in connection with the investigation of disputed elections. The House regularly became a court, if an irregular one, to prosecute those who dared, in defiance of Standing

[1] September 1755. H. Walpole, *op. cit.* III, 409, 350.

[2] *Parl. Hist.*, XV, 770. This speech was quoted by Grey in 1794 as an example of the good old view.

[3] W. C. Townsend, *History of the House of Commons . . . 1688–1832* (1843–4) II, 380.

[4] For evidence of this see Hatsell, *op. cit.* (*passim*) and O. C. Williams, *The Historical Development of Private Bill Procedure and Standing Orders in the House of Commons* (London, 1948–9).

Orders, to report the debates. On all such occasions debate was eclipsed by the need for having one spokesman. This spokesman, this president who acted in the name of the whole House, had necessarily to be the Speaker. So the multiplicity of such cases could only increase Onslow's prestige in the eyes of all members. His allocutions — as that to the much harried Alexander Murray[1] in 1751 were heard with awe by his fellow members. Some might jest, in private, about his pomposity. But the rotund phrasing of his addresses was part of his method of building up his authority with which he associated that of the House of Commons.

By the 1750s the Speaker had buttressed his emotional ascendancy with administrative machinery. From the beginning of Onslow's Speakership he had answered to the House for the officials of the House. He supervised their fees and took responsibility for their actions, though he did not appoint them, as any Minister answers for his Civil Servants.[2] To the young John Hatsell, appointed as Clerk assistant in 1760, he said, 'The Clerk has appointed you to be his Clerk Assistant, but now you are appointed you are the Clerk of the House, you are my Clerk'.[3] So the Sergeant at Arms, though appointed by the Crown and holding office on the same terms as a judge, was the Speaker's chief police officer. The messengers were his subordinate agents,[4] as were Housekeepers, Doorkeepers, and so on. All these officials received fees, on a table fixed by Onslow, for such things as hearings at the bar, holding prisoners, or the hearings on a private Bill. Though the House had no power to inflict fines, its extortion of fees,

[1] Murray was imprisoned by the House for disorderly threats at a Westminster election followed by attempts, which were construed as breaches of privilege, to get a Habeas Corpus and so to appeal from the Speaker to the judges.

[2] As an example *Parl. Hist.*, VIII, 121, 122. See also O. C. Williams, 'Officers of the House of Commons', *Blackwood's Magazine*, March 1909, p. 321.

[3] Hatsell (1st ed.) 2, 191.

[4] They were paid fees not just by the distance they had to go but with regard to whether the journey was 'on the stones' (*i.e.* on the streets which had been paved by the early eighteenth century) or not.

as poor Robert Raikes of the *Gloucester Journal* remarked when he was accused of printing reports of debates,[1] amounted to a financial punishment.

At the head of this civil service, which had not expanded into the five chief offices, Public Bills, Journals, Committee, Private Bills, and Fees, was the Clerk. He was like the permanent secretary under his parliamentary chief, the Speaker. The Clerks for most of Onslow's time were Nicholas Hardinge (1731–48) and Jeremiah Dyson (1748–62). Both, it is noteworthy, subsequently went into Parliament and both acquired minor office, Hardinge as a Lord of the Treasury and Dyson as Secretary of the Treasury. Both made their contributions to the Onslow tradition of the House. Dyson purchased his Clerkship for £6,000 but he appointed Hatsell to succeed him without charge and so began a new convention. Hardinge was responsible for putting the *Journals* into order and for arranging their first printing. In 1742 it was discovered that the 26½ million words written by Clerks since the time of Edward VI were becoming mildewed and illegible in the small dark room by the chimney. It was decided to print a thousand copies of 23 volumes at £600 a volume. The clerk was to be recompensed for the loss of fees he had hitherto received for searching the *Journals*. The Speaker appointed Samuel Richardson (the author of *Pamela*) as the printer under the supervision of a Clerk of the Journals.[2] From this time on all members were free to follow Onslow's advice to seek answers to problems in searching the *Journals*. Though this, in the end, raised up amateur experts on procedure to challenge the Speaker, the effect in Onslow's lifetime was further to increase the staff and the dignity with which he was surrounded.

When Onslow consulted privately with members or

[1] *Commons Journals*, XXI, 119, and Michael MacDonagh, *The Reporters' Gallery* (1913), p. 115.

[2] Nichols, *Literary Anecdotes*, IV, 580 : *Commons Journals*, XXIV, 262–266.

appeared in committee, he carried round him the consequence which accrued from his growing judicial and administrative authority. When he called a line of conduct 'factious' it was not to be treated as the hackneyed abuse of politics but as the pronouncement of a constitutional pontiff. He stressed this himself in his speech in committee on the Regency Bill in May 1751 — he did not expect to sway them but to inform them of danger. . . . 'I have nothing to ask and consequently whilst our constitution is preserved I have nothing to fear.'[1] The Regency Bill was brought in, on the death of the Prince of Wales, to prevent the Duke of Cumberland's being sole regent. Henry Fox, as an associate of the Duke, was thereby separated from the Pelhams. Pitt was suspected of favouring the Bill in an effort to curry favour with the Princess of Wales.[2] Speaker Onslow attended a ministerial meeting intended to organize support for the Bill and made clear that he did not like it. No one, indeed, says Coxe, was more conspicuous in opposition to it.[3] Pelham had no justification for his surprise when Onslow attacked it in committee. Onslow's argument was that monarchy may be limited but it cannot be divided. A Regency council with the Princess and the Duke on it would lead to intrigue. From such intrigue a factious and tyrannical minister would rise to destroy the constitution. The threat of praemunire against those who might wish to alter the arrangements afterwards was a weapon aimed at the freedom of members of Parliament. The Attorney-General, Dudley Ryder, answered him politely, conceding that his opinion had great weight. But on this occasion his protest was over-ruled. He turned his main energies for a while to the organization of proceedings against the Sheriffs for their insolence in the Westminster Election.[4]

[1] *Parl. Hist.*, XIV, 1017-23 : cf. also Horace Walpole, *George II*, I, 110 foll., and Horace Walpole, *Letters* (ed. Toynbee), III, 57.

[2] Ilchester, *op. cit.* I, 162, 163.

[3] W. Coxe, *Memoirs of the Pelham Administration* (1829), II, 169-72.

[4] Parliamentary tactics for this were agreed at a meeting in the Speaker's house. H. Walpole, *George II*, I, 181.

In 1753 the Speaker is twice recorded as speaking in committee. The first occasion was very formal and unpolitical: it was on the Hans Sloane Bequest and the care of the Harleian manuscripts.[1] The second was more contentious. Inspired by Hardwicke, the administration brought forward a Marriage Bill in May 1753 to end the disreputable system of 'Fleet' Marriages. Henry Fox bitterly opposed this and turned opposition to the Bill into an assault on Hardwicke's ambition and power. Onslow had a great respect for Hardwicke both as a lawyer and as a politician close to Newcastle. In later years he was to urge Hardwicke's inclusion in ministries and even his being given the directing part in them. Nevertheless Onslow argued on 28 May with some vehemence against the clause in the Bill which annulled marriages entered into contrary to its provisions. Unfortunate women might find their marriages void after they had become pregnant.[2] So strongly did he feel the injustice of the proposal that he gave the Attorney-General the lie direct.[3] In the House of Lords Hardwicke answered Onslow mildly, maintaining that he was misled: he reserved his fury for Fox, accusing him of screening his personal motives behind allegations of caste feeling among the nobility.

The interest of these two unsuccessful interventions of the Speaker in controversial debate is that they brought him closer in sympathy to Henry Fox. The rivalry between Pitt and Fox was building up inside the Pelhamite broad-bottomed administration.[4] For Fox, as the pupil of Walpole, Onslow might be expected to have sympathy: on the other hand —

[1] He later (1761) became a trustee of the British Museum. Nichols, *Illustrations of Literary History* (1817–58), III, 492. Unpolitical also was his speech about his exemption from taxes. Hist. MSS. Comm., *Round MSS.*, 296.

[2] Yorke, *Life of Hardwicke*, II, 64, and H. Walpole, *George II*, I, 342. When Mr. Grierson was convicted of solemnizing marriages contrary to the law 1,400 marriages became void and of these 900 had resulted in (or conceivably resulted from) pregnancy.

[3] Horace Walpole, *Letters* (ed. Toynbee), III, 162.

[4] Fox was Secretary at War 1746 to 1754 and Pitt was Paymaster of the Forces from 1746 to 1755.

as has been instanced above — Pitt's appeal to the xenophobic and naval prejudices of the independent (or opposition) members was not without answer in the Speaker's heart. Argument about the militia rumbled on during these years. In December 1755 Charles Townshend introduced a new Militia Bill. Onslow greatly assisted the passage of the Bill, as amended by Pitt, through the Commons, despite the fact that the administration had slackened in advocacy of it.[1] It was rejected by the Lords. It was not until Pitt was playing a leading part in the administration that, in 1757, a new Militia Act was passed. By that time the opposition had ceased to regard the militia as a bulwark of liberty. As it was made more efficient militarily it became more like a regular army: it was now called an example of Whig tyranny.[2] Onslow's share in the passage of the Militia Act exposed him to insult in the streets of Guildford: a troop of the Blues had to be sent to protect his house, Ember Court.[3]

The death of Henry Pelham in 1754 could only increase the rivalry between Pitt and Fox, as they jostled one another for the position of partner of Newcastle and leader of the House of Commons. Onslow's divided sympathies did not force him into inactivity. When the Bill to enable Scottish Sheriffs depute to hold office by the king's pleasure rather than for life was before the House (March 1755) the Speaker was greatly stirred. In committee on the Bill he 'uttered one of his pompous pathetics couched in short sentences' for his Whig spirit groaned under this exertion of the power of an administration over the judiciary.[4] Henry Fox laughed at his fears and derided him discreetly. Pitt sprang to his feet to rebuke Fox for 'levity on this great principle'. The only pleasure, he went on, he had had from the debate was to hear an authoritative expression of two great principles of the

[1] Horace Walpole, *George II*, I, 451.

[2] See Horace Walpole, *George II*, II, 232; and Yorke, *Life of Hardwicke*, II, 266, note 4.

[3] Horace Walpole, *Letters*, IV, 102.

[4] Horace Walpole, *George II*, I, 379.

constitution: first, that the judicature ought to be free of executive control and second that no effort should be spared to make the king's hands as strong as possible. He ended by putting Onslow's views in an epigram, that liberty was the truest loyalty. Fox could not be bothered to play up to the Speaker in this way. He thought the fuss unnecessary and that there was a difference between honouring the fire of liberty and its smoke. Newcastle, however, feared the weight that the Speaker might carry with back-benchers. He asked Webb, the secretary to the Treasury, to convince Fox that this matter, even if it had originally been but a Scottish cabal, was now serious. Eventually the Attorney-General yielded to a compromise in order to conciliate the Speaker.

Onslow, in spite of this brush, seems to have regarded Fox as a sounder constitutionalist than Pitt. He thought Fox did right to refuse the lead in the Commons under Newcastle without the necessary authority. He thought this humiliating.[1] When Pitt tried to embarrass the ministry by opposing a grant of £120,000 to zealous individuals in America it was evidence, in Onslow's eyes, that, notwithstanding his enthusiasm for the Navy, he was acting more in faction than in pride of the colonies. 'The Speaker (not apt to be explicit) says I — H. Fox — had a complete conquest and that if Mr. Pitt go's on as he has these three last days, and do's not provide better matter to make his fine speeches upon, he will soon grow as insignificant as any man who ever sat in that House.'[2]

As leader of the House, Fox wrote the circular letter in the autumn of 1755 to summon 'my friends' to the Cockpit meeting before the first day's debate. The absence of Pitt, Legge, the Grenvilles, the Townshends marked their hostility. Onslow, however, attended. He had, as Speaker, his duty to make preparations for the session with the ministers of the Crown. But he attended to put his mind alongside theirs, not to take orders. Fox's main theme was the necessities for subsidies as set out in the king's speech. In this there

[1] Ilchester, *Henry Fox*, I, 210. [2] *Ibid.* 313.

was the phrase — 'to disappoint such designs . . . as there is reason to think have been formed against my Kingdoms and dominions'. Onslow objected to this and had doubts about the whole of Fox's speech. He said he must understand the word dominions as British dominions or else the speech would be in breach of the Act of Settlement. He added that he had so far not been able to make up his mind on the issue of the subsidies. He gave notice that he therefore reserved his right to act as might seem best when the Bill reached the committee stage and he could speak and vote.[1] Hillsborough at once announced that when he moved the address he would make clear that by dominions, British dominions were intended. As an interpreter of the Constitution, Onslow was as unquestioned in a government party meeting as in the House of Commons.

The moving of the address by Hillsborough was marked by disorder.[2] 'Poor Arthur was mad and spoke ten times to order', said Horace Walpole. It marked the opening of eighteen months of political upheaval. At the end of it Pitt, forced out of office in November 1755, was back (April 1757) as Newcastle's masterful partner in a war-winning ministry: Fox had sunk into a secondary position by a failure of nerve — or by lack of ambition — in 1756. In this successful conquest of power by Pitt the Militia Bill had been one part of the offensive. The support of Onslow for this Bill, demonstrated in presenting speeches and in conversation with members of Parliament, was an important element in Pitt's hold over the Commons. For Onslow had always been in day-to-day touch with members both obscure and important — as, for example, with Sir William Browne who wanted to reform the coinage,[3] with Lord Carlisle who wanted to reconcile the king and the Prince of Wales,[4] with Sir Gilbert Heathcote who wanted to know how to draft a

[1] Ilchester, *Henry Fox*, I, 283. [2] *Parl. Hist.*, XV, 536, note.

[3] Nichols, *Literary Anecdotes*, III, 328.

[4] Hist. MSS. Comm., *Earl of Carlisle*, p. 179.

Bill, with Ravensworth who feared the rebound of his charges of Jacobitism against Murray,[1] as well as with ministers about the programme of the session. He took a mock-modest delight in the frequent sight of 'statesmen's equipages at my humble door'.[2] On the victory of Pitt he continued to wish that rash spirit might be balanced by other talents, wishing to see Hardwicke given a share of power.[3]

When on 18 March 1761 Arthur Onslow retired from the Chair it was the end of an era in the House of Commons: his conception of the Speakership was never successfully demonstrated again. 'When I began my duty here,' he said, 'I set out with a resolution, and promise to the House, to be impartial in everything, and to show respect to everybody. The first I know I have done, it is the only merit I can assume.'[4] This aspect, impartiality, was uncritically assumed by others also to be the simple key to Onslow's success. In seeking candidates to replace him the names bandied around — Prowse, Morton, Rushout, even George Grenville — were those of men noted for their learning and independence. It seemed that any good-hearted country gentleman with legal education could carry on Onslow's work. But in fact there were three elements in Onslow's triumph: first, his single-minded devotion to the House of Commons which made him deaf to the temptations of power; second, his faith in a general will of Parliament which could be called into self-consciousness by an active leader who divined and expressed it in his own activity, an activity which might involve co-operating first with one group and then with another; finally there was his own character, which was forceful and self-assured.

The unfortunate Sir John Cust who succeeded him in the

[1] H. Walpole, *George II*, I, 270. [2] Yorke, *Life of Hardwicke*, II, 393.

[3] *Ibid.* II, 371, note. The esteem was mutual: in 1763 it was on Hardwicke's advice that the government sought to get the ex-Speaker's views on how to handle the Wilkes affair. *Ibid.* III, 467, 492. Newcastle, after his fall, discussed the possibility of the ex-Speaker's using his influence in Parliament to get him restored to office. *Ibid.* 446.

[4] *Parl. Hist.*, XV, 1014.

Chair from 1761 to 1770 was no less impartial than Onslow. But he was deceived by his predecessor's success into believing that it was enough to sit in the Chair and show no favour. His inactivity made these years a deplorable period in Parliament. Debates were disorderly and excessively long. Cust either gave the House no advice or saw his rulings defied. When Burke was reproached by Stanley on 9 March 1769 with having accused Cust of being a party in the debate, he very justly replied that his grievance was not that the Chair took part in the debate but that the Speaker had not entered into it.[1] Cust's inactivity allowed the Wilkes disputes to wreck the machinery of the House of Commons. If he had been willing to take part in discussions outside the House, to make clear to ministers and to opposition what his own view of the constitution was, he might then have intervened, whether in the Chair or in Committee, with effect. On the issues of constitutional interpretation raised by Wilkes or by America, Onslow would have had his own view. They were issues more divisive than those of the previous half-century. They were issues which aroused party feelings but as yet there were no parties in a proper sense to absorb and decide them. The result was chaos. Had there been a tradition of party government, then programmes would have been organized and the issues settled in a regular battle between two opposed opinions in Parliament. But instead there was only Onslow's idea of a basic agreement between all men of patriotic good-will superimposed upon faction and self-seeking. It is significant that the idea of party (in any modern sense) seems to have arisen in Rockingham's unfortunate ministry of 1766. For Rockingham's friends acted in the old spirit, seeking stability in making a government which should be as inclusive as possible. The resulting compromises were unattractive and unworkable. The Rockingham group concluded that they had been betrayed. Their remedy was to

[1] *Sir Henry Cavendish's Debates in the House of Commons . . . 1768–71*, ed. J. Wright (1841–3).

take power in future only with a band of friends who were used to working together and who could trust one another, a 'party' government. It was a solution adumbrated in theory but impossible to put into practice either in the conditions of 1782 or of 1783 or in 1806. No one group on a narrow bottom was strong enough to stand. Coalition was a prerequisite for power. Nevertheless, the conclusion, so alien to Onslow's age, that opinion organized for unity was the best basis for government came into existence for the first time during Cust's Speakership.

Sir John Cust himself, impartial but ineffective, was killed by the Speakership. His fatal intestinal disorders, it was said, were the result of the days and nights spent sitting without respite in the Chair.[1] In choosing his successor ministers correctly judged that there was need to emphasize another side of Onslow's tradition, its vigorous leadership. Sir Fletcher Norton, who was chosen, was an exceptionally fierce lawyer in a period of rough legal careerists. He had earned the nickname 'Sir Bull-face Double fee' in the Courts. In the House of Commons he had distinguished himself by the vigour with which he had led the ministerial members against John Wilkes. With the supine Cust in the Chair he had declared, with greater accuracy than tact, that as a constitutional lawyer he would attach as much importance to the opinion of the House on the legality of General Warrants as he would to that of a lot of drunken Covent Garden porters.[2] Norton was a lawyer on the make. His career up to 1770 had been impeded by the rivalry of Charles Yorke. He accepted the Chair as a stop-gap until he could make good a claim to become Lord Chancellor.

The ministry hoped to get a clear lead from the Speaker on the constitutional questions which had bedevilled debate

[1] There was no deputy Speaker until the nineteenth century so that the Speaker could not leave the Chair without suspending the debate. Debates going aimlessly on until dawn were thus a physical torture to the Speaker.

[2] *Parl. Hist.*, XV, 1403.

for the past decade. Norton obliged. He was quick to rule, to speak in committee, and to use his authority with independent members. In 1771, for instance, he persuaded the Privy Council to issue a proclamation against the printers of parliamentary debates. He then led the House of Commons through debate, investigation, and punishment of the offenders[1]. It might seem that with Lord North coaxing the independent members (as Walpole had done) and with Norton rebuking any factious opposition (as Onslow had done) the former unity of spirit in the House might be restored. But two factors prevented any such return to a golden age. The first was that as the American dispute came to a crisis members were deeply divided in opinion. The minority who supported American claims would not admit — did not feel in their hearts — that they were factious. They could not be shamed as Onslow had shamed irresponsible critics of Walpole or Pelham. There was, indeed, no longer an agreed middle way which a Speaker could embody and express in stately sentences. The emotions of party (though not the mechanism) had replaced the agreement of an earlier epoch. The second cause, aggravating the first, was Norton's reputation. When he very justly condemned Sir William Meredith for obstructive pedantry [2] in 1770 his ruling was resisted in the House : Junius commented on his 'usual prostituted affrontery. . . . We were not surprised at the decision : but he hesitated and blushed at his own baseness, and every man was astonished.' [3] Norton was too ambitious to be accepted as a pundit.

The attempt to re-impart vigour to the Speakership collapsed in 1777. In his presenting speech with a money bill in May of that year the Speaker . . .

'. . . to the world's surprise
Advis'd his sovereign to be wise', [4]

[1] *Cavendish Debates*, II, 382. [2] *Ibid.* I, 459–70.
[3] *The Letters of Junius* (ed. C. W. Everett, 1927), p. 168.
[4] Malcolm Macgregor [Revd. Wm. Mason], 'Ode to Sir F. N. affixed to an Epistle to Dr. Shebbeare' (2nd ed., 1777).

that is, he told the king that the grants of the Commons were 'great beyond example, great beyond your Majesty's highest expense'.[1] This was taken as a declaration that the Speaker had joined with the opposition to the government. Reproaches eventually drew from him his motive. He was using the prestige of the Chair to force the government to promote him or to take the unpleasant consequences of his ill-temper. The outcome was that he was not re-elected in 1780. Norton's energy had proved as calamitous as Cust's indolence. It was impossible to find a man who combined limited ambitions with great abilities. But even Onslow, one must suspect, could not have survived unchallenged in authority if he had been active in the 1770s. He would, it is clear, have been anti-American. Would Edmund Burke have suffered even Onslow to tell him that he was erring and straying from the path of the true Parliament man ?

The Onslow Speakership could not be revived. Some later Speakers, it is true, approached more nearly to it than had Cust or Norton. But there could no longer be a high priest of the constitutional balance once the idea that there are two sides — two equally loyal and patriotic sides — to every political question became accepted. Not that this acceptance was general for a long time after 1760. The pluralist view of politics, that unity is produced out of conflict, not out of uniformity, was slower to develop than nineteenth-century historians believed. The argument between the Junto and Bolingbroke at the beginning of the century was not of a party kind, in this sense : it was a conflict for power which could only end in the destruction of one side or the other. The dispute between Harley and Walpole was not really about issues at all : it was a personal struggle between men who were really agreed on issues : yet, such was the tradition of politics, it too had to end in permanent victory and could not be allowed to enliven political life with recurrent debate. It was not until the

[1] *Parl. Hist.* XIX, 213, and note.

1760s that there were arguments on which men could take sides according to their temperament. Even after this in the 1780s there seemed a chance that these partial views might be smothered in a general will of all the politically conscious classes.

Onslow threw himself into political discussion in order to restrain partisans from going to extremes. It was the easier for him to find the proper point of balance in an age when legislation was infrequent and therefore the emphasis was upon preserving an ideal system. But the element of balance and moderation was, so to speak, built into the practice of party when it came to be acknowledged and respectable in England. The battle of opposed temperaments organized in the House of Commons made the machine work so long as both sides implicitly recognized what they had in common. The loyal opposition, of its own motion, drew back from unconstitutional courses. Once this was so the Speaker might safely retreat into the neutral eminence of Shaw Lefevre. At most he had, by a pained silence standing in his place or by a few brief words of reproach, to remind members from time to time of the principles on which their own party game operated. It is significant that when Mr. Speaker Brand did feel obliged to assume a great responsibility and a more active rôle it was because a party, the Irish party, did not feel this sense of constitutional self-limitation and control.[1]

The Speakership of Arthur Onslow was thus not above party but an indication that there was no party in the true sense. His active participation in the battle to preserve liberty might well be thought a more useful example for some modern one-party parliamentary régimes than the sterile neutrality of Shaw Lefevre is likely to prove. But for the Onslow conception in action there is no need to look back to the eighteenth

[1] See the report of Brand's explanation to his constituents in G. H. Jennings, *Anecdotal History of the British Parliament* (4th ed., London, 1899), p. 605. Under Speaker Peel the Speaker's initiative was reinforced by Standing Orders of the House.

century. In the United States of America the Speakers of the House of Representatives have always felt free to manipulate and control politicians in the interest of the constitution as they from their high position could see it. By gaining the confidence of members, by managing committees, they have been politically powerful and governments have been obliged to conciliate them. The need for such involvement in the details of politics arises no doubt from the comparative weakness of party considered as a means of government in the United States. But the Speakership of Czar Reed (with his private 'Cabinet'), of 'Uncle Joe' Cannon, and of Mr. McCormick may claim a descent from Arthur Onslow as legitimate as that of Sir Harry Hylton-Foster.

6

A. F. McC. Madden

THE IMPERIAL MACHINERY OF THE YOUNGER PITT

ON 11 December 1783 it was rumoured that George III had authorized Lord Temple to indicate to any peer the royal disapprobation and enmity towards those who might vote for Fox's India Bill: a week later, after the rejection of the measure in the Lords, he dismissed the Fox-North coalition and offered to William Pitt the First Lordship of the Treasury which this time the young man did not refuse. Eighteen years and six weeks later it became known that at a *levée* George had burst out angrily that he would reckon any man his personal enemy who proposed a measure of Catholic emancipation for Ireland: forthwith the ailing Pitt penned a letter to the king assuring him that, if after reconsideration he was refused full royal confidence for a 'full latitude on the principle', he would feel compelled to resign. Choosing to consider this as final, George III sent for Addington, and the war Cabinet of Pitt, Dundas, Grenville and the rest resigned.[1] So it was that one threat of royal displeasure had ushered Pitt into power while another bowed him out.

These events are familiar. What has perhaps been more rarely noticed is the part played by overseas problems in shaping Pitt's career. It was India which gave the king the opportunity to rid himself of Fox and North and to secure as his chief minister the alternative he had long desired, the

[1] See K. G. Feiling, *The second Tory party, 1714–1832* (1951), pp. 156–7, 221–3.

son of the great Chatham. It was Ireland which alerted the king's conscience about his coronation oath — which, incidentally, had never troubled him, even in the face of anti-popery mobs, over the Quebec Act in 1774; it was Ireland which forced him to replace Pitt's administration by Addington's. Furthermore, in a period remarkable for its 'scarcity of memorable legislation',[1] the trilogy of statutes settling the government of India, Canada, and Ireland for half a century or longer should necessarily bulk large. However, until recently, the contribution which Pitt and his colleagues made in founding a second British Empire has been insufficiently considered and largely overlooked.[2] Scant attention has been paid to the close supervision, the intimate exchange of intelligence, and the unique coherence which the triumvirate of Pitt, Dundas, and Grenville gave temporarily to the metropolitan management of overseas affairs; or perhaps more particularly and permanently to the influence they had in the development of colonial administration and machinery, and in the evolution of professional departments from the protoplasm of patronage, amateurism, king's friends, and clan loyalties.

Pitt had been chosen by the king as an alternative both to Fox and to North:[3] an advocate of moderate reform as well as a friend of the king, but a man committed neither to faction nor to courtly influence and possessed of a popular name. George III had hoped in February and again in March for young Pitt to save him from the Fox-North coalition, but he had refused. The king was clearly annoyed, but he

[1] J. S. Watson, *The Reign of George III* (Oxford, 1960), p. 302.

[2] V. T. Harlow, *The founding of the second British Empire* (1952), 2 vols. For the subject and some of the material of this essay I must acknowledge my debt to Professor Harlow. Among his papers at his death were notes for a talk on the triumvirate to a college society in Hilary Term, 1959. These he had intended to work up into a contribution for the *English Historical Review*. The transcripts of his material which I have used are now in Rhodes House Library (MSS. Br. Emp. S.123-206).

[3] A. Aspinall, 'The Cabinet Council, 1783–1835', *Proceedings of British Academy*, XXXVIII (1952), p. 225.

disciplined his irritation, for Pitt still seemed the safest bet. As George had written to Temple, 'I hope many months will not elapse before the Grenvilles, the Pitts and other men of abilities and character will relieve me from a situation that nothing but the supposition that no other means remained . . . would have compelled me to submit to'.[1] For their part Pitt and his Grenville cousins were happy to wait. If they were assuredly becoming indispensable to the agonized king, they were in a strong position. They could preserve freedom of action. They could be true to themselves, advocating moderate reform 'whenever there is a reasonable prospect of success', and opposed to any recovery by the Crown of 'that influence which had been already taken from it'.[2] While they would not press their principles awkwardly or unreasonably and would not object to Crown support, they would not let royal influence dominate their administration.

But when Pitt took office in December 1783 his colleagues were hardly a reforming ministry and they were patently dependent on Crown influence. Moreover, both in debating power and in administrative capacity his team was undoubtedly weak. Only Dundas had such abilities and Grenville was not given office. How far this administration fell short of his goal Pitt well knew. For him it was the Delectable Mountains, not the Celestial City : a step towards that reunion of the Whigs for which he had been working ever since Shelburne's defeat. In an attempt to come to an arrangement with Portland and Fox he held off from the election which the king was pressing on him. Gambling on Portland's obstinacy and Pitt's pride George III had to bide his time with patient courtesy and sweet reasonableness for the 'angry boy', as Sheridan had called him. Pitt indignantly refused the rôle which Portland offered : he was no returning prodigal, but a leader seeking support from fellow Whigs. So Pitt's dream

[1] *Correspondence of George III* (ed. J. Fortescue), VI, 330.

[2] Hist. MSS. Comm., *13th rept.*, App. III : Fortescue Papers (Dropmore MSS.), I, 217.

of succeeding his father at the head of a reunited Whig administration faded. To him the alternative seemed to require the establishment of a personal ascendancy with talent and ability which would command general support in many quarters inside and outside Parliament. For half a dozen years he was the only member of the Cabinet who was in the Commons.[1] He could nevertheless dominate the House, but he came to see that his position would be more assured if he put administration first and sought the strength that the employment of the best 'men of business' available would give. From Jenkinson and from some of the stable group of king's friends, as Namier has indicated,[2] stemmed the permanent and professional civil servants. From the failure of Pitt's attempt to reunite the Whigs came this new concept of his personal government, and in the course of time from the men and methods he used to broaden the base of that government and to quicken its head, modern administration, as Feiling has suggested,[3] may be said to proceed.

Three estimates worked out by John Robinson in late December 1783[4] had shown convincingly that a proper deployment of royal influence, assisted by the unpopularity of the Fox-North coalition, could win a general election for Pitt and could bring him back with a majority of approximately 180: an estimate which, though slightly in excess of the actual victory in 1784, was respectable enough by the standards of latter-day psephologists. There was undoubtedly a hard core of Chatham or Shelburne Whigs and personal adherents to Pitt; but whenever prejudice or self-interest lined up with loyalty to the king against the ideas of his first minister, the many independents and king's friends were able to reduce,

[1] J. S. Watson, *op. cit.* p. 273.

[2] In his unpublished Ford Lectures (1934); see Miss L. S. Sutherland's note in L. Namier, *Crossroads of power* (1962); and E. T. Williams, 'The Cabinet in the eighteenth century', *History*, XXII (1937), 242 foll.

[3] K. G. Feiling, *A History of England* (1950), p. 726.

[4] See W. T. Laprade, 'Parliamentary papers of John Robinson, 1774–84', *Trans. Royal Hist. Soc.*, XXIII (1922), 65–118.

and often to obliterate, the government's large majority. By restraint and tact and by trusting the known political and personal factors to produce the result he desired, George III had escaped the peril of a Whig reunion. Pitt evidently believed that his own ability and reputation would suffice to carry a measure of moderate reform, provided the king agreed to stand neutral. He believed in parliamentary reform not only for its own sake as a worthy national cause but as a means of reducing his dependence upon royal support. The king realized this and when the test came in March 1785 he indulged neither in neutrality nor in open enmity but in quiet disapproval.[1] That was (as he well knew) quite enough, and despite Pitt's oratory and moderation his motion for reform was lost.[2] Pitt had been taught the limits within which he could manœuvre. He had had a lesson in the facts of political life. He had also learnt from the king's example the rewards that could derive from cautious and painstaking management.

Until the painful experiences of the spring of 1785 Pitt had believed that, with the talisman of his surname, his intelligence, his sincerity, and his oratory could sweep a heterogeneous ministry and a raggle-taggle following into the enlightened courses which he planned and that under his discipline and ascendancy they would bring down the citadel of influence and reaction. But when he realized that he had over-rated his own magnetism and under-rated the power of prejudice and self interest, he began cautiously to consolidate his personal position anew. This he attempted by a twofold process — partly by adapting policy to suit the prevailing climate of opinion, but more particularly by weeding out recalcitrant and inefficient ministers and concentrating effective administration in the hands of an inner hand-picked junta ; sometimes (as we shall see) the policy was affected by the persons.

[1] Cf. Windsor, Royal Archives, George III to Sydney, 19 Mar. 1785 : 6 P.M. and P.R.O. 30/8/331 (Pitt Papers), George III to Pitt, 20 Mar. 1785 : 8 A.M. [2] *Parl. Hist.*, XXV, 475.

Observation of the king's own methods had shown him that the art of politics demanded an infinite capacity for taking pains ; a meticulous study of the subtle cross-currents of opinion among individuals and clans and of the routine details of management. He must woo and persuade as well as lead ; but, if he was to govern, he must create an efficient and reliable body of administrators. It was these methods, aided by the repercussions first of the French Revolution and then of war, which gained for him that national leadership he craved. But he knew that his rule was always subject, of course, to the condition that he did not require his followers to put obedience to himself above loyalty to the royal wishes. The Regency crisis in 1788 with its threat of dismissal by the Prince of Wales and the steady drift of the Commons towards the Regent's bandwagon were further sharp reminders that Pitt's position as leader was still by grace and favour of the king. And so on that basis his rôle as the king's servant continued — until 1801.

If the king's will constituted one limitation upon Pitt, the personalities of his trusted colleagues could themselves cause him to adapt his personal policies to prevailing opinion. The fate of Pitt's plan for Anglo-Irish reciprocity in 1785 illustrated this. Pitt had proposed a scheme for partnership between the two countries in which an autonomous Ireland would be admitted into the British economy on equal terms and would in return provide a voluntary contribution to the general defence costs of the Empire which governments in London had been seeking from America and Ireland for twenty years. Though the correspondence between Pitt and Rutland, the Lord Lieutenant,[1] revealed the difficulty of such a conditional agreement being accepted in either country, Pitt (as with parliamentary reform) appears still to have had confidence that by logic he could convince the serried ranks of British commercial interests that they had nothing to fear from Anglo-Irish free trade. When the outcry in Britain against

[1] See *Pitt-Rutland Correspondence* (Edinburgh, 1890), *passim*.

the eleven Irish resolutions[1] became insistent and politically disastrous he turned to the astute and trustworthy intelligence of one of his new advisers, Charles Jenkinson. Jenkinson's caution and expertise saved Pitt politically; but his influence in redrafting the resolutions so mangled Pitt's original plan that they were instantly and indignantly rejected by the Irish Parliament.[2] Pitt's grand design failed; but his frustration did not rankle, for a year later Jenkinson was created Baron Hawkesbury and appointed Chancellor of the Duchy of Lancaster. Pitt had chosen Jenkinson as his own right-hand man in trade matters. At the new Committee of the Privy Council for Trade his efficiency and enormous capacity for methodical hard work rapidly made him the virtual dictator of British commercial policy overseas. Though he killed the Anglo-Irish treaty as he had dished the Shelburne-Pitt scheme for Anglo-American reciprocity and as he was to thwart the scheme for Anglo-Dutch commercial co-operation in the Far East, Hawkesbury had made himself indispensable to Pitt and Pitt was prepared to pay the price in policy direction in order to retain the services of a first-class man of business. Part of that price too, as it was of keeping Dundas, was the acceptance of their opposition to the abolition of the slave trade.

The Regency crisis further stimulated the consolidation of administration. When George III recovered his sanity he wrote that he would avoid 'a pressure of business' and 'only keep that superintending eye which can be effected without labour or fatigue'.[3] This was, indeed, written when the king was still barely convalescent and it has been doubted whether in fact the king did retire so dramatically from the arena as he implied. What seems likely is that his interest was less consistent and reliable, that he did not continue his previous detailed direction of departmental business, and that his temper

[1] P.R.O., Home Office MSS., 100/16. ff. 16-21: printed in V. Harlow and F. Madden, *British Colonial Developments*, 1774–1834 (1953), pp. 252-5.

[2] See H. Grattan, *Life*, vol. III, 258-65.

[3] P.R.O. 30/8/103 (Pitt Papers), George III to Pitt, 23 Feb. 1789.

was more unpredictable. Though his mind could be as clear and as decisive as ever, an emotional outburst was never far from the surface. The king was more difficult to work with; and, though the partial vacuum created by the king's fitful superintendence helped ministers to develop into a co-ordinated administrative team instead of a congress of almost autonomous heads of departments as they had been under North, the king seemed to restrict that process by yoking Pitt with Thurlow in a frustrating dualism: his chief minister and his Lord Chancellor were his consoling 'blessings' and he desired their cordial conference at an early stage on important matters so that their opinions might be 'mutually formed'.[1] The king's insistence on this dual control may be explained less by any strong liking for Thurlow than by his regard for the Lords as a sure second line of defence as and when the dykes broke in the Commons, as they had over Fox's India Bill. For George III the Lord Chancellor was second in importance only to the First Lord of the Treasury in preserving the authority of the king's government. In that dual control Pitt had, of course, for a further period no option but to acquiesce.

But meanwhile the process of strengthening the administrative junta continued: the weeding out of the inefficient and their replacement by the 'men of business'. In June 1789 Pitt got rid of Lord Sydney, who as Secretary of State for the Home department had proved in home and colonial affairs to be inadequate and unimaginative: the price paid was a viscountcy and a pension of £2,500 a year. He was succeeded by W. W. Grenville, proud indeed but energetic, scholarly, and inventive: within weeks he was tackling the problem of Canada, preparing a new constitutional settlement which he hoped, by assimilating a colonial constitution more closely to the Westminster model, would prevent another secession from the Empire. The following year, in order to equip himself with a loyal spokesman in the Lords, Pitt raised

[1] P.R.O. 30/8/103, George III to Pitt, 21 April 1789.

Grenville to the peerage; but the expedient did not work well. Thurlow, ignored and by-passed by Grenville, was stung to such persistent sneers at government measures that in June 1792 Pitt felt constrained to face the king with an ultimatum: George must choose between his First Lord and his Lord Chancellor. With reluctance but without hesitation the king chose Pitt, and Thurlow disappeared from the political scene. In the meantime (April 1791) the prickly and ineffective Duke of Leeds had also been removed. He was superseded at the Foreign Office by Grenville and Henry Dundas took charge of home and colonial affairs.

So by gradual steps the effective government of the country was concentrated in the hands of the triumvirate. Pitt at the Treasury fostered a buoyant economy with new financial and fiscal measures, built up the strength of the Navy and (with far less sureness of touch) supervised foreign policy. Dundas, that genial soldier of political fortune, carried a heavy load: he managed Scottish affairs, was virtually Secretary of State for India and alternated with Grenville as secretary for home, colonial, and Irish affairs till July 1794. Then to accommodate the Portland Whigs, Dundas was moved to the new Secretaryship of State for War and the Duke of Portland took charge of the Home Office. Dundas had long been angling for a secretaryship and had no objection at all to relinquishing home affairs if he could concentrate on the wider strategy of overseas problems. But Portland was inadequately briefed on what was contemplated, and Pitt had to persuade Dundas to surrender specifically colonial affairs to Portland, though his influence in general imperial matters remained considerable.[1] Even on the eve of Pitt's resignation in 1801, in drafting the plan for 'the strongest Government ever known in this country',[2] Dundas was still seeking an adjustment of responsibilities between the Secretaries of State which would have restored the conduct of war to the Home Office and

[1] C. Matheson, *Henry Dundas* (1933), pp. 202–5.

[2] See K. G. Feiling, *The second Tory party*, Appendix III, pp. 399–400.

combined the Presidency of the Committee for Trade with a Secretaryship for the Colonies. For this latter joint post he suggested Lord Hawkesbury, the laconic, hard-working, prototype civil servant who had made himself an expert in overseas trade. Somewhat unambitiously he thought of himself at the India department as a second choice to Lord Cornwallis. Though there were proposals subsequently for a combination of colonial and India affairs under a single minister, Dundas himself did not revive that idea.

For a period then there had been effective supervision of overseas affairs from the centre. For years Pitt, Dundas, and Grenville worked and almost lived together. The Cabinet gradually became an executive committee. It was also, in Mr. Watson's words, 'a sounding board rather than a place for discussion'.[1] Often enough Pitt had already decided policy with Grenville or Dundas and had, moreover, calculated timing, presentation, and management of tactics. There were occasional strains between Dundas and Grenville. The members of triumvirate were not always of one mind, nor were they committed to blind support of Pitt's policies. Pitt might rely on their advice most heavily, but even Dundas and Grenville were not invariably consulted. Grenville wrote to Pitt in October 1794 that before another Cabinet meeting took place on relations with Prussia, it would be 'very desirable' if they could have 'discussed this point a little amongst ourselves'.[2] They provided an efficient nucleus of power to which able men of business were drawn : George Rose with his ability in finance and management and William Eden with his knowledge of trade and diplomacy. Cornwallis was employed with distinction in India and Ireland ; and Wellesley was groomed by way of the Treasury and the Board of Control for the governor-generalship of India. So too were the *kindergarten* — Canning, Huskisson, and the young Jenkinson — trained in these administrative methods for high office

[1] J. S. Watson, *op. cit.* p. 301.
[2] J. H. Rose, *Pitt and Napoleon* (1912), p. 260.

later: an ideal of a ministry which would be recalled nostalgically by Peel in conversation with Gladstone half a century later.[1]

The close character of their teamwork can perhaps be best demonstrated by reference to the functions and methods of two of the administrative boards they created: the Committee for Trade and the Board of Control. On 5 March 1784 an Order in Council established a special Committee of the Privy Council for Trade, including Jenkinson, Dundas, and Grenville among its members, and three days later it undertook the task for which it had been created: a full-scale enquiry into Anglo-American trade in the new context of American independence and on the pretext of a petition from the West India Committee. It was Jenkinson who shaped the report of 31 May[2] which largely governed British commercial policy towards America until Grenville and Jay negotiated the Treaty of 1794. In August 1786 Pitt reconstituted the Committee of *ex officio*, as well as specifically nominated, members as a permanent instrument for Trade with Jenkinson (now Lord Hawkesbury) as President, Grenville as his deputy, and Grey Elliott and George Chalmers[3] as their right-hand men. Hawkesbury devoted himself to this work almost exclusively and he rapidly became the ministerial spokesman for all commercial and manufacturing interests. Under him the Board exercised an influence and power which greatly exceeded that of most, if not all its predecessors. On any issue evidence was taken from the merchants, shippers, and industrialists concerned: a policy decision was taken and (when necessary) a draft Order in Council was prepared forthwith.

The way in which this body was used as an instrument of policy by the inner ring of ministers may be well illustrated

[1] J. Morley, *Life of W. E. Gladstone* (1903 ed.), I, 297.

[2] P.R.O. Board of Trade MSS., 5/1, pp. 229-54. See also his Report of 28 Jan. 1791, an extract from which is printed in V. Harlow and F. Madden, *op. cit.* pp. 269-71.

[3] G. A. Cockcroft, *The public life of George Chalmers* (1939).

by its minutes during the negotiations for the Anglo-French commercial treaty. Between 4 September and 14 November 1786 no less than eighteen meetings of the Board were devoted to this subject and on *every* occasion those present included Pitt, Grenville and Hawkesbury and usually Carmarthen, the Foreign Secretary, and Joseph Yorke. This was indeed, it may be urged, a matter of exceptional importance, but here is a list of those attending during an average month when only routine business was transacted — March 1787 :

3 March	Hawkesbury, Grenville, Pitt
8 March	Hawkesbury, Grenville, Yorke
9 March	Hawkesbury, Grenville, Pitt, Carmarthen
10 March	Hawkesbury, Grenville, Pitt
17 March	Hawkesbury, Grenville, Pitt
19 March	Hawkesbury, Grenville, Pitt, Mr. Speaker, the Archbishop of Canterbury [1]
21 March	Hawkesbury, Grenville, Pitt
24 March	Hawkesbury, Grenville, Pitt
26 March	Hawkesbury, Grenville, Pitt
27 March	Hawkesbury, Grenville, Pitt
28 March	Hawkesbury, Grenville, Pitt
29 March	Hawkesbury, Grenville, Yorke.[2]

After 1788 Pitt still attended frequently but more irregularly. Grenville was fairly regular in his appearances. Dundas turned up when matters concerning India and the Far East were under discussion. The supervision they gave was, indeed, close and even intimate ; but Hawkesbury had become, in effect, the managing director of British overseas trading enterprises. He it was who devised the measures calculated to modify the navigation system in order to meet the new situation created by the secession of the American colonies. He fought a long and largely successful battle to exclude American shipping from the British West Indies and strove to replace American provisions for the Caribbean by Canadian and Irish foodstuffs.

[1] Ecclesiastical problems in Quebec were being discussed.
[2] These details come from the minutes in P.R.O., Board of Trade MSS, 5.

He sought to secure the old British imperial monopoly, in the new circumstances of increasing manufacturing potential, by legitimizing privateering and developing a free port system in the West Indies as a means of breaking into the monopoly of the Spanish American empire with cheap British goods :[1] a technique of value later against Napoleon's continental system. He strove to seek a vent for British manufactures into the American Middle West either by a thrust south of the Great Lakes or by a trade treaty with an independent Vermont. To satisfy the growing demands of the Lancashire mills he encouraged experiments in cotton-growing in the British West Indies and in West Africa. To render British consumers independent of foreign whale oil he helped the Southern Whale Fishery to develop one of the consequential legacies of Captain Cook's voyages. Sometimes, indeed, the vigour and the rich variety of expedient and opportunity shown by individual traders and the risks taken by his colleagues caused him anxiety that the fabric of the old mercantilist system might be destroyed.[2] But his department, conservative as it was, lacked nothing in imagination and initiative and was fertile and far seeing in its methods of preserving that system in changing circumstances.

The impress of another personality, that of Henry Dundas, was equally strong upon that other instrument of overseas policy, the Board of Control.[3] The attendance showed the same consistent core :[4] Dundas and Grenville as president and vice-president, Mulgrave as military adviser, and Walsingham. Pitt's attendance was frequent but more irregular than at the Committee for Trade. In Indian affairs Dundas was

[1] F. Armytage, *The free port system in the British West Indies* (1952).

[2] C. B. Fergusson, 'The colonial policy of the first Earl of Liverpool' (unpublished Oxford thesis, 1952). These themes are illustrated by extracts in V. Harlow and F. Madden, *op. cit.* pp. 11-64, 246-80, 317-32, 367-80, 386-7.

[3] Sir W. Foster, 'The India Board', *Trans. R. Hist. Soc.*, 1917.

[4] The first volume of the minutes (8 Sept. 1784 to 22 June 1793) could be used to demonstrate similar regularity of the main personnel (Commonwealth Relations Office, India Office MSS., series II, vol. 1).

managing director, but in this (as in other matters) he was working in the closest personal co-operation and daily discussion with Pitt and Grenville. While giving his firm support to Lord Cornwallis in his work of administrative reorganization in India, Dundas imposed his authority upon the Court of Directors of the East India Company (even in matters of trade policy and patronage which by the Act of 1784 were exclusively Company concerns) and had begun to convert the Court into something akin to a sub-department of government.[1] It was a stiff and acrimonious fight which made him, and to some extent Pitt too, unpopular in Leadenhall Street and among the 'nabobs' in Parliament. It was Dundas, moreover, who developed a wider-ranging policy of 'informal' commercial empire in the Far East: in part by seeking co-operation with the Dutch, in part (in association with Grenville) by applying diplomatic pressure to secure strategic bases and *entrepôts* at Trincomalee, Rhio, and the Cape, and in part by negotiating new markets in China for British goods and furs from the North Western Coast of America. The incident at Nootka Sound, which brought Britain to the brink of war in 1790, was no mere outburst of a rootless jingoism on Pitt's part, but a facet of a world-wide commercial strategy.[2]

The administrative detail of Hawkesbury's Committee for Trade and Dundas' Board of Control well illustrates the nature and extent of Cabinet integration which Pitt desired to achieve. In the drafting of legislation — Pitt's India Act, Pitt's Navigation Act, or Pitt's Canada Act — the triumvirate were deeply and intimately concerned with the detail, though the prime responsibility rested with one or another of Pitt's trusted advisers. It was Dundas who made the India Act, Hawkesbury the Navigation Act, and Grenville the Canada Act. The considerable amount of letters and memoranda existing among the Pitt, the Dundas, and the Grenville papers,

[1] C. H. Philips, *The East India Company* (1961 ed.), chapter III.
[2] For examples see V. Harlow and F. Madden, *op. cit.* pp. 11-64.

however, are witnesses to their exchange of ideas and the extent of their knowledge. Did not Pitt shut himself away with Dundas for ten days at Wimbledon to master the detail of the Bengal revenues?[1] The minutes of the Committee for Trade and the Board of Control further substantiate this impression of detailed interest.

The character of the overseas policies pursued by Pitt and his colleagues was remarkable both for its combination of old and new principles and for its practical adaptation of methods and machinery to the new circumstances. Within their limits they were coming to terms with the facts of empire, reshaping principles, accepting differences, and taking fore-thought to prevent secession, as, for example, by the offer to Ireland of an eighteenth-century form of 'dominion status': a device similar to that of equal partnership between two legislatures which had been conceived in the agony of the American revolt by Madison, Franklin, and Jefferson, in order to avoid their ultimate treason. Pitt's administration provides a case study in the appreciation of some of the complexities in imperial responsibility and of the need for the parent state to shoulder more supervision and management. Some solution had to be found intermediate between the expensive (and impossible) bold stroke of direct government and the total disengagement of disappointed imperialism.

Of course they did not find it: they had to move experimentally and with circumspection. They feared both to do too little and to do too much. They must grasp the nettle of the wayward East India Company; they must clear up its irresponsible corruptions and make it into a national rather than a sectional asset.[2] On the basis of Dundas' draft Bill, the India Act had been passed in 1784: a compromise because of the facts of political life and of the want of precedent to guide them. The proposed powers of the Governor-

[1] R. Pares, *King George III and the politicians* (Oxford, 1953), p. 161.

[2] See L. S. Sutherland, *The East India Company in eighteenth century politics* (Oxford, 1952).

General were sacrificed temporarily to stifle the cry of personal tyranny ; but the need for such an overriding power had been shown by Hastings' painful experiences with his Council,[1] and two years later Dundas was able to restore it as an indispensable condition of Cornwallis's appointment. Likewise, Dundas's advocacy of a third Secretaryship was given up and the government's supervision was put into commission as the Board of Control ; but in practice as long as Dundas was there as President of the Board, he was virtually Secretary of State for India. So they set in motion the machinery of a dual control linking the Company with the Crown and the Cabinet : a device made easier by the co-operation and understanding of the king and his chief minister.

For Canada, Grenville's nostrum was assimilation 'as convenient and agreeable as may be' to the equipoise of the British constitution : to balance the concession of representative institutions by strengthening the Governor and building up his Council as an imitation aristocracy.[2] But again it accepted the facts. Grenville noted that there would inevitably be 'differences arising from the manner of the people and from the present situation of the Province'. Moreover, his Canada Act conceded equal rights of representation and franchise to alien Catholics, as Pitt wished to do for the Irish. Similarly too in drafting instructions for the new colonies — San Domingo, Martinique, St. Lucia, and Guadeloupe — Hawkesbury had accepted their differences.[3] He had taken care to win alien inhabitants by recognizing their local laws and institutions rather than to provoke their exodus or revolt. He was also at pains to free the Governor from local impediment, in order to act as the agent, legislative and executive,

[1] K. G. Feiling, *Warren Hastings* (1954), chapters XI-XIII, XVIII.

[2] Grenville to Dorchester, 20 Oct. 1789 ; printed in W. P. M. Kennedy, *Statutes, treaties and documents of the Canadian Constitution* (1930 ed.), pp. 185-8.

[3] C.O. 319/4. The instructions for San Domingo are printed in V. Harlow and F. Madden, *op. cit.* pp. 83-8. Pencil notes on the copy indicate that they were used for draft instructions elsewhere. The original draft by Hawkesbury was found by Dr. D. Murray in Brit. Mus. Add. MSS. 38353/130.

of the metropolitan government. And Dundas borrowed his draft for similar instructions to the Governors of the Cape and of Ceylon. As yet it is no more than a practical solution of a wartime problem ; not a prototype for a new form of colonial government.

But it was still fundamentally a ledger book empire : indeed perhaps more so, for ships, ocean routes, naval bases, and *entrepôts* were evidently more profitable than dominions. Hence their impulse to refashion and rationalize mercantilist principles ; to buttress the commercial system ; to expand into the Far East, the South Pacific, and North Western America ; to penetrate the close monopolies of rival mercantilist powers, Holland or Spain ; and to liberate their colonial subjects, detach their loyalty, and to attract their trade. This was a task, under Pitt's encouragement, primarily for Dundas and Hawkesbury, but also for Grenville, both in private discussion and correspondence and in the Committee for Trade and the Board of Control.

Where Pitt failed, however, to secure the same coherence and administrative clarity was in the conduct of colonial affairs themselves.[1] This was, as we have seen, partly the consequence of misconception of, and imprecision in, Pitt's terms with Portland in 1794, for Portland refused to forgo his interest in colonial patronage. But traditionally too colonial affairs had been dealt with by the Crown's servants in the ordinary routine with, and in the same ledgers as, domestic affairs. The Secretaries of State shared duties, seals, fees, and repository. Moreover, colonial problems, unlike those of trade, had been matters for a department rather than a board. Only belatedly in the history of the first British Empire had there been a separate American department, and this had been abolished along with the Board of Trade by

[1] The most recent researches among the sketchy and confused materials dealing with the origins of the Colonial Office have been by Dr. D. M. Young in *The Colonial Office in the early nineteenth century* (1961) and Dr. D. J. Murray in his unpublished Oxford thesis, 'The Colonial Office and the plantation colonies 1801–34' (1963).

Burke's Act of 1782.[1] Whereas the duties of the Board were undertaken for a while by committees of the Privy Council, and then in 1784 by the special committee to deal with the West Indian petition, in August 1786 the new permanent Committee for Trade, part official, part nominated, was virtually the old Board, with the same functions as its predecessor, under a new guise.[2] But since the American department had also been swept away by economical reform, colonial business was carried on primarily by the Home department, though other bodies (such as the Customs, the Treasury, and Admiralty) had their own officials in the colonies and their own separate lines of correspondence. For four years many colonial matters were dealt with in the Home Office by the same clerks who had handled them under the third Secretary and who were now forming a special Plantations Bureau under Elliott.[3] When the permanent Committee for Trade was established with its three under-secretaries, six clerks, two messengers, and 'one necessary woman', Elliott's departure was the pretext for merging colonial work into the general routine of the office, so that the same clerks dealt with domestic, Irish, and Canadian correspondence as it turned up. Elliott had often been summoned to attend the temporary special Committee on American trade ; but the Plantations Bureau had also prepared commissions and instructions, examined colonial laws, prepared colonial estimates and supervised colonial governments,[4] and these became matters for the Home Office personnel. Such co-ordination and policy making as

[1] M. M. Spector, *The American department of the British Government, 1768–1782* (1940).

[2] P.R.O., Privy Council MSS. 1/61/5. See A. L. Lingelbach, 'The Inception of the British Board of Trade', *American Hist. Review*, XXX, 701-28.

[3] Hawkesbury corresponded directly with Colonial officials but he tended to become more concerned with trade than with the plantations, especially when colonial despatches ceased to be communicated to the Cabinet. H. T. Manning, *British Colonial Government after the American revolution 1782–1820* (1933), pp. 30, 84-5.

[4] *Parl. Papers*, 1st XII. Select Committee on Finance, 16th Report, Appendix L.

was achieved came from the triumvirate and from the minister's personal under-secretary: the suggestion that an under-secretary should be a permanent official was rejected in 1786 on the grounds that close confidential personal relations must exist between him and the minister.[1] After 1794 when the third Secretaryship of State was established to deal with War and Dundas went off to the Horse Guards, then to Parliament Street, and finally to 14 Downing Street (for over half a century the home of the Colonial Office), governors continued to correspond both with him and with Portland at the Home department. Even after 1801 when somewhat casually — perhaps to effect a fairer division of patronage[2] — colonial business was transferred to the War Office,[3] probably only one additional clerk was added to the establishment in Downing Street: Adam Gordon who had tended to deal with colonial matters earlier at the Home Office.[4] Had the Treaty of Amiens proved lasting, the third Secretary might well have become primarily concerned with the Colonies, but in the event he found his energies were engrossed by the French wars; and colonial business came to be considered predominantly from the standpoint of defence or commercial strategy or to be dealt with by the under-secretary or by clerks writing despatches from general basic notes. The joint establishment for War and the Colonies in 1801 consisted of the Secretary of State, his under-secretary, eight copying clerks, 'two office keepers', one précis writer, one interpreter, the customary woman — and Adam Gordon. From the ramshackle Restoration House in Downing Street with Thames water in the basement these officials managed to defeat Boney

[1] *Parl. Papers*, 1st XII, 309. See also Liverpool's comment on the confidential under-secretary quoted in A. Aspinall, *op. cit.* p. 173, n. 6.

[2] G. P. Pellew, *Henry Addington* (1847), I, 400-12.

[3] P.R.O., Colonial Office MSS. 323/176. Pelham to Hobart, 12 Aug. 1801.

[4] There are some doubts here. Dr. Murray makes it clear that Gordon had been at the Home Office; Dr. Young seems to imply that he had already moved to the War Office. It is possible that he followed Dundas in his migration in 1794.

and to gain a new empire in a 'fit of absence of mind'. They were also pioneering the transformation of a simple personal executive department into a diversified professional bureaucracy : one largely unexplored dimension of the development of Cabinet government.

Pitt then in his first ministry achieved some notable success in integrating a policy-making machine in the realm of overseas affairs ; but painstaking as his work had been it had fallen short of his intention. Moreover, the respective positions, the interdependence, of the king and his chief minister made it brittle. Though it pointed the way to new facets of responsible government, individual, collective, departmental, it did not alter the constitutional position of the king's servants, Pitt, Dundas, Grenville — they were still at the disposition of His Majesty who was free to dismiss them, one or all, and to call in others for which he could provide the working majority. Though the ministerial machine had become more homogeneous under their direction, it could still break into fragments when it came into collision with the royal conscience and oath : especially when the king had an alternative chief minister who was not Fox. But the construction and operation of such a machine under the direction of one head for a critical period of years had established a precedent, an ideal, and a usage of solidarity which could not fail to have its effect in the evolution of the conventions of the Cabinet system. Although personalities, policies, and circumstances would delay the return to Cabinet integration, and although the absence of Pitt would remove a centralizing force, the members of his *kindergarten* would carry their devotion to the business of administration into other, later ministries.

Pitt had wished to become a national leader at the head of a reunited Whig party. When that hope failed, he struggled with some success to avoid becoming a king's minister in the mould of Lord North. He became a national leader in his own right but only because fear of Jacobinism and invasion brought his own views and those of the king and the electorate into substantial agreement. This was not the sort of leadership he had desired in his youth. His hold over his heterogeneous following in the Commons was always precarious until fear stiffened them. He did not create his own party, whether Whig or Tory. By harvesting intelligence of the detail of business and politics within a small dependable circle of able men he had been able to concentrate power and to add such cubits to his stature as he was able. In the sphere of overseas policy at least such a co-ordination was not attained once more for another generation. Even then India was regarded as a distinct and separate trust, and imperial problems, wider and more complex than in Pitt's day, could not be the intimate concern of the prime minister, home secretary, and foreign secretary as India, Quebec, Ireland, East and West Indies, China, and the Pacific had been at the turn of the eighteenth century.

brought his own views and those of the King and the Cabinet into substantial agreement. This was not the sort of leadership he had desired in his youth. His hold over his heterogeneous following in the Commons was always precarious until fear solidified them. He did not create his own party, whether Whig or Tory. By harnessing the machinery of the detail of business and policies within a small dependable circle of able men he had been able to concentrate power and to add such talents to his service as he was able. In the sphere of overseas policy at least such a co-ordination was not attained once more for another generation. Even then India was regarded as a distinct and separate issue, and imperial problems, while far more complex than in Pitt's day, could not be the intimate concern of the prime minister, home secretary, and war secretary as India, Quebec, Ireland, East and West Indies, China, and the Pacific had been at the turn of the eighteenth century.

7

E. G. Collieu

LORD BROUGHAM AND THE CONSERVATIVES

BROUGHAM'S House of Commons and ministerial career was associated exclusively with the Whigs, but he was not a Whig by birth, adoption, or conviction. For that matter, neither was he a Tory. Socially, he was an outsider in the aristocratic system of his day ; temperamentally, he was individualistic to the point of idiosyncrasy ; intellectually, he was a man of original political genius, beyond partisanship or predictability ; and the causes which he most consistently espoused for nearly three-quarters of a century — the promotion of education, and of law reform, and the abolition of slavery — provided few party shibboleths. Very conscious of his great physical and mental powers, he carved out his own career in law and politics, employing any and every instrument for the purpose that came to hand. In the fraternity of the Law, he mixed with all sorts and conditions of men ; while, outside it, he could readily form attachments with men as various as the Duke of Wellington, the radical 'Tear 'em' Roebuck, or the socialist Owen, who at one time interested him in spiritualism. In the circumstances, it is not surprising that Brougham should have been actively associated with the Whigs for a quarter of a century, before he passed a similar period in association with the Conservatives — nor that both, in the end, brought him disappointment.

When Brougham first came to London early in the century, he relied upon Wilberforce to secure Pitt's interest for him. When Pitt was not forthcoming, Brougham turned to the Whigs, who were instrumental in providing him with fame and frustration in roughly equal measure. By 1830 he was ready and willing to join the government of Peel and Wellington ; but, while the former kept him dangling, the latter made no offer, and later in the year Brougham agreed to enter Grey's government as Lord Chancellor — a condition which, by removing him to the House of Lords, ensured his eventual destruction as a political force of the first magnitude. The end came in 1835, when Melbourne declined to re-employ him, and put the Great Seal into commission for a year, before promoting Scarlett as Lord Cottenham to the Woolsack in 1836. *The Times* now set up his obituary in type ; but if Brougham realized that his ministerial career was for ever closed, he did not admit the fact. For the next two decades he volunteered his services to the Conservatives, whether leading the opposition to Whig governments or making himself, during Wellington's decline, an unofficial and unsolicited Conservative leader in the Lords on behalf of the Peel whom he disliked and distrusted. Since Brougham was fated to pass this last stage of his career in the wilderness, it is easy to dismiss him as a political Ishmael, and most of his biographers have devoted comparatively little attention to this phase.[1] But he did not regard himself as a spent force and, especially after the political convulsion of 1845–6, he was more than ever eager to fish in the waters which he helped to trouble. Something of his own version of events, and of the part which he sought to play in them at this time, has survived, and it is with one particular rendering of his account that this essay is concerned.

At no time did politics engage the whole of Brougham's time and attention, and even in politics his interest was divided,

[1] The most important secondary authorities on Brougham are J. B. Atlay, *The Victorian Chancellors* (1906) ; A. Aspinall, *Lord Brougham and the Whig Party* (1927) ; G. T. Garratt, *Lord Brougham* (1935) ; F. Hawes, *Henry Brougham* (1957) ; C. W. New, *The Life of Henry Brougham to 1830* (1961).

since he gave to French political life hardly less attention than to affairs in England. So far did this carry him that, after the February revolution of 1848, he made an abortive application for French citizenship. His second home was at Cannes where, in the Château Eleanor-Louise, named after the daughter ('the dear and lost person for whom it was built and made') whose early death in 1839 had inflicted upon him his deepest personal loss, he wintered every year, between parliamentary sessions. Throughout life, Brougham's pen was as vigorous and inexhaustible as his tongue, and his prolonged sojourns in France helped to swell his copious daily correspondence with a very wide circle of relations, friends, and acquaintances who were the recipients of his racy, erratically punctuated, and nigh illegible missives of news, gossip, and observation. His letters to one particular correspondent during the 'forties have survived almost complete, and possess a special significance because they were, in the nature of things, wholly disinterested, and they artlessly portray the writer as he saw himself and his own part in events. They form the substance of this essay, in so far as they deal with the English political scene.[1]

In February 1839 the Scottish judicial bench was more than once severely criticized by members of the House of Commons on the grounds that many of its members were rendered incapable of effectively discharging their duties by deafness, physical decrepitude, or senile decay.[2] The Lord President of the Court of Session, Lord Granton, was one of the judges so criticized, and after they had been defended by Brougham at the end of a Scottish appeal case in the House of Lords on 4 March,[3] he wrote a letter of thanks to Brougham, and thus opened a correspondence which ended only with his death a dozen years later. The two men were not personally

[1] The letters are in the possession of Laurence Middleton, Esq., to whom I gratefully acknowledge the permission given for their use. All quotations from correspondence in this essay are from them.

[2] *Hansard*, 3rd Ser., XLV, 314-35, 471-94, 875-81.

[3] *Ibid*. XLVI, 145-69. For Charles Hope, Lord Granton, see *D.N.B.* XXVII, 312.

acquainted at the time, but Brougham had long admired his correspondent professionally, and would appear to have made him his model in forensic and political oratory. When Granton died in 1851, Brougham wrote to his eldest son, the Lord Justice Clerk,[1] 'My admiration was of sixty years and the brilliant qualities which then dazzled me were afterwards fully equalled, in my more experienced estimation, by the other extraordinary merits of his firm and honourable character, which commanded veneration'. Brougham freely acknowledged his debt, and paid tribute, to his master in this correspondence. In his first letter, 14 March 1839, he wrote: 'It was from your lips that I first heard what eloquence was, your noble speech in Capt. Johnstone and Drummond's Case 1793 having awaked in me a sixth sense, as well as in Horner who sate by me in Court, and I have ever since looked up to you as my master in the art I have practised'. He again recalled the occasion in a letter, in 1848,

I would fain send you a collection of my speeches, published five years ago, because tho' of little value, it is due to you. I may assure you as I have said 100s of times to others, that my first practical idea of what real Eloquence was, I derived from what I shall never forget, your inimitable speeches, and the second rather than the first in Drummond v. Capt. Johnstone's case. . . . I at once acceded afterwards to our old friend Malcolm Laing's[2] criticism (in company with Clerk and Gillies and J. Allen) 'If C. H. had been transferred to the English Parliament, he would have been a finer speaker than Pitt'.

Brougham, born in 1778, was junior to his correspondent by fifteen years, and still displayed the verve and energy of a man another fifteen years younger than he was. This correspondence confirms the impression which was left on John Bright when he noted in his diary for 9 April 1854, 'He is a wonderful man for his years — and seems almost as young

[1] Rt. Hon. John Hope, 1794–1858. *D.N.B.* XXVII, 324.

[2] Malcolm Laing, 1762–1818. *D.N.B.* XXXI, 404. He would appear not to have profited from the example, his success at the bar being impeded by a poor delivery and harsh accent.

and active as at any time for 20 years past'.[1] In these letters, the enquiries after his correspondent's health, and his frequent reassurances on the subject, lead Brougham to give a clear picture of his own condition as he approached and passed his seventieth year : good health and high spirits he still possessed in abundance. He found his family history reassuring.

As my good mother lived to 89 [he wrote in the winter of 1844] . . . and my Grandmother lived to 97 . . . and never ailed till the week she died in 1807, I naturally have great trust in the longevity of persons who have temperate habits, and, what I believe, conduces to length of days, a firm mind, so that I don't much regard your 81½. So with my dear friend Lord Grey, exactly the same age, though he has been suffering under two evils, blindness and great pain, for above a year and a half, but he is of a long lived race, and Sir James Mansfield, a little contrary to my abovesaid maxim about temperance, used to say, legally, that long life depended more upon the *original term* than the behaviour of the tenant.

But, this example notwithstanding, Brougham preferred to practise a measure of austerity.

The receipt [he wrote in July 1848] falls well in with my usual morning discipline of ¼ hour's general flesh brush which for 25 years and upwards I have successfully persevered in. . . . Have you persevered in being a water drinker, as you were some years ago ? Lord Eldon cautioned me against it, saying he should have been dead had he left off his wine, viz. nearer 2 than 1 bottle of port a day. My allowance is ¼ of that and generally less.

In view of this record and his precautions, it was the more unlucky for Brougham that the excitement of the February Revolution of 1848 in Paris found him seriously ill at Cannes.

I have been confined [he wrote a few days after the event] for three weeks and one of them entirely to my bed (a thing by God's blessing before unknown to me) and I have only been downstairs since all the dreadful events happened. (It was a very bad quinsey such as the doctor and surgeon had never seen).

[1] *The Diaries of John Bright* (1930), p. 168.

Although Brougham had suffered from severe illness earlier in life,[1] it is possible that the unexpected and unusual severity of this malady had a disturbing effect upon him, and contributed to the curious state of mind in which he decided to apply, abortively, for French citizenship at this time. But soon enough, he was well again, and was boasting in October 1849, in a letter written from Tholonais,

I came here yesterday having left Paris on Sunday and travelled all night three times so that I believe I am made of iron, for my legs swelled the second night and got well the third. This at 71 is doing well and I am really thankful for it. I had it is true a very fine travelling carriage with a bed, but I did not use it the first night at all and very little the second.

The repeated references to France and things French serve to remind us that Brougham's interest in the politics of the July Monarchy and the Second Republic was as keen as his preoccupation with the English political scene, and that he aspired to be influential in both. The early years of this correspondence are concerned almost wholly with French politics — a fact which is perhaps partly attributable to a Liberal kinsman of Lord Granton's having later suppressed those letters which animadverted on Gladstone. An antipathy towards the latter was only to be expected in Brougham, and the one unfavourable reference which survives here is also the first which introduces English politics into the correspondence. On 4 February 1845 Gladstone explained to the House of Commons the reasons for his resignation on the Maynooth issue, and Brougham reported :

Our opening [of the new session] went off quite well. Gladstone's explanation, like that of some Shakespeare's commentaries, went off so badly that every body said the matter was scarce intelligible, in consequence, and Peel had to explain after him. My friend Aberdeen told him (G) 'Why go out ? Only two or three have read your book and they dont comprehend it', which is more true than

[1] For evidence of illness in middle life, see New, *op. cit.* pp. 161, 263-4, 324-5.

pleasant. G. is in perfect amity with the ministers, that is he loves them as well as an *outgoing* man can love *instaying* ones.

There was little else of domestic interest in the session which held Brougham's attention, though when Peel published his budget ten days later, on 14 February, the fact was noted: 'Peel's budget two months before the usual time is compared to a 7 months child, but may have (income tax) as long a life as Geo. 3 had in the like circumstances'.

Within twelve months, however, the scene was transformed, and Brougham had begun his last serious attempt to regain a position of influence in party politics.

The opportunity to exert his influence did not immediately arise, and to begin with Brougham viewed the scene with a degree of detachment.

So here, at this hour [he wrote after 27 January 1846] is Peel on his legs sweeping away all protection whatever, and proposing — and wisely he is to put in the front of his battle — the repeal of all protection for callico men, the Cobdens and others, I hear are in a gloomy state, having fallen into their own snare. The Land is to be very handsomely counted. Meanwhile, the Whigs easily get up intrigues with the land party and in the end outvote P. But then they are no nearer office, for office they cannot take if P. were out, and the Q. sent for them. P's position is impregnable, as the French say *imprenable*, which literally means that no one can take it. But between ourselves I do somewhat lament P. doing this turn and so giving credit to the vile mob-brawlers. Famine there is none nor any at all likely. I wish he had stood a little more firm and done the thing at a calmer moment. I was happy to find he highly approved my speech on this topic,[1] and I only wish he *act likewise*.

By the following month the position had not materially changed, in Brougham's view.

The Protectionists are wisely prolonging the debate. It will now not be over till Friday, if then, and that vote only puts the speaker out of the chair. The Committee will then debate the Resolution

[1] In a speech in the House of Lords on 22 January 1846, Brougham had said that he regarded the actions and behaviour of the Anti-Corn Law League as legal, but unconstitutional. See *Hansard*, 3rd Ser., LXXXIII, 29-42.

and then report it and then the Bill may be brought in. So in our House we shall not have it before Easter. The Protectionists rely so confidently on having the Country with them and the age of the Parlt. is so advanced, that I should not wonder if the Bill were lost in our House. Were these Protectionists to see it must pass next year they would let it pass now to have done with it. My calculation of numbers rather lowers than rises. Not more than 70 if so much.

By the end of June, however, the Bill had passed both Houses, the government had resigned, and the Whigs were, after all, able to form an administration. This last fact distressed Brougham even more than the split in the Conservative party, the reunion of which he regarded as the first step towards turning out the Whigs ; and he now actively entered into the campaign to gain both objectives.

The new Govt. [he wrote in early August] is as unlike a Govt. as any thing in heaven above, or earth beneath, as can well be imagined. There exists no commandment therefore to prevent people of any sort from worshipping them. They themselves avow that they are of a temporary existence. But they rapaciously take the chapter of accidents and hope to get some strength, I see not how or from where, and at all events they make sure of the places, ribbons etc. that fall during the summer.

The rent which Peel's unfortunate measure (unfortunate at least in his way of carrying it) made in the Great Conservative party is closing by degrees. Lyndhurst and I have been labouring with some success in this, and a dinner I gave of the chiefs of both sections last Sunday did good service to the cause of good govt. as opposed to mob-govt. and job-govt. Still many of our friends hold that next summer would be better and safer for dissolving than this. Hence a dread of driving the Ministers to the wall on Sugar, or any thing else, as this, say these calculators, would make them dissolve. But sounder judgements hold this cheap and we (of course you suppose I reckon myself among the latter) we say that the Whigs will dissolve if and when it suits their own calculations and not wait for any beating, or any thing else.

Considering Slave Trade (that is importing sugars free from *all* colonies) to be far too important a question to be sacrificed to any tactics and moreover very well convinced that no cry of *cheap sugar* on which J. Russell may wish to dissolve can ever be strong enough to overcome a cry of *No Slave Trade*, I gave my notice for Friday, meaning to blow my trumpet then before the Commons debate, should I find the Conservatives etc. shrinking or cold on the sugar question. If I find my alarm false, I can put off my oration. We shall beat the Govt. in the Lords ; in the Commons it is doubtful, for Peel and Graham are full of Free Trade. The excellent Chief Justice (Denman), though a Whig, writes me the strongest exhortations to persevere and defeat a measure, which he says, is 'meant to make England an accomplice in the African Slave Trade'.[1]

The first battle of the campaign, fought on the sugar issue, was quickly lost, and Brougham's disappointment now found expression in censure, so far muted, on Peel, as well as upon the Whigs. Mutual distrust and dislike had long existed in both men, and Brougham was soon to find that Peel's attitude towards him was shared by nearly all the leading, official Conservatives. Meanwhile, the relaxation afforded by a visit to Aston Hall enabled him to review the situation at length on 17 August.

I was prevented from performing my promise of writing from London, by extreme pressure of business judicial and political. But having come here yesterday to my old and valued friend J. Watt's magnificent residence (where I am surrounded by the pictures, marbles, books, MSS and models of the great man, his father,[2] who has changed the face of the world more than any man ever did) I have a quiet hour to communicate with your Lordship, on the present unexampled and *absurd* aspect of our affairs.

First I really do think, however disinterested it was and even in some respects noble, yet Peel's whole proceedings have been unexampled for absolute folly. What could be more uncalled for than

[1] The Bill, however, eventually passed, to become the Sugar Duties Act of 1846 (9 and 10 Vict., cap. 63) which provided for the gradual equalization of duties on all foreign and colonial sugar. Complete equality between free and slave-grown sugars was not achieved until 1854.

[2] James Watt (1736–1819), engineer, scientist, and inventor, among other things, of the improved steam-engine. His son, also James Watt (1769–1848), was responsible for the first steamship to leave a British port, in 1817. Brougham's well-known enthusiasm for mechanical invention and improvement led T. L. Peacock to satirize the Society for the Diffusion of Useful Knowledge as The Steam Intellect Society.

his panic and forcing the Corn Law Repeal this year rather than another year, and though I rejoiced as a friend of the measure, yet I was bound to say I did not. I disapproved the manner of doing it entirely. Indeed had he *unbuttoned* himself (but that he never does) and written half a dozen letters to his chief supporters in each shire giving them notice and speaking civilly to each, tho' they might all have voted against him, it would have been without any quarrel at all. Now the breach is almost impossible to heal. Next comes his resigning and leaving all who had stood by him in the lurch. Hence *those* are angrier than even the Protectionists, and justly in my opinion. Then his closing speech on Cobden and last and worst of all his Slave Trade inconceivable and incredible duplicity [?]! So many capital errors crowded into so small a space ! Again he has been thwarting all Lyndhurst's efforts and mine to reunite the two fragments of the party! *However he will fail in that!*

I found in town much remains of bad personal and spiteful feeling, in every way. The Protection men feared to divide lest they should turn out the Govt. The Peel men (a small handful) voted for the Slave Trade encouragement bill, for the sake of spiting the Protectionists. The Govt. are more loud and spiteful in their abuse of Peel than of all others beside, so he gets mighty little credit for his help, and yet that help alone enabled these wretched incapables to weather the Session.

The Protection men at my instigation screwed their courage up to take the risk of J[ohn] R[ussell] and Co. resigning on losing their execrable Bill. But the Peel men turned the scale and we had no sufficient attendance.

Debating we had in perfection. Stanley spoke admirably. I did my best and destroyed some base creatures by the way. Denman was honest and intrepid and pronounced severe, even awful sentence on his Whig friends ; but they by a low trick prevented him from speaking with his accustomed effect. Bp. Wilberforce made an admirable speech, Bp. Blomfield an excellent one. In short, we settled the matter, and the Protests are invaluable for the country and the Gen. Election. But we have let the Bill pass, *for the present*, I trust not for more. Oct[obe]r is said and I believe truly, to be fixed for Dissolution.

Never, to be sure was seen such a wretched Govt. It is in a minority of 90 if all its enemies, who all hate and scorn it, join on any one question. Its calculation is that the elections give them 12 or at most 18, leaving the majority against them still 56 or 68. With all its ultra-Whig friends it has already quarrelled. In its own bosom it has a viper, Grey, who will sting it to death. All this is vile enough, and all this it feels. Hence the fury with which my late speech was received: especially my quotation from Tacitus, *Maneat quaeso duretque gentibus*. For it is true and it is a picture.[1]

Meanwhile our fear is that whatever Govt. succeeds them will be weakened exceedingly by this late affair of Corn Law and c. and we cannot afford a weak govt.

In a postscript he added his information on current expert calculations upon the results of an autumn election. 'The Prots rely on B. Holmes. The Peelites on Bonham. I omitted to mention Bonham's (*i.e.* Peel's) calculation of his probable loss at a Gen. Election, 55 to 60. But B. Holmes says 75 to 80. The former give Govt. a gain of 13, the latter of 18.'[2]

By the time Brougham repaired to France in the early autumn, it was clear there would be no general election in 1846. If the government was weak, the opposition was even weaker, and now began to appear likely to remain so. It had become apparent that Lyndhurst had failed to draw the two Conservative factions together, and where Lyndhurst failed, Brougham was unlikely to succeed. Peel and Wellington had shown no live interest in Lyndhurst's overtures; Stanley, when approached by him, had referred him to Bentinck who in turn referred him back to Stanley. Moreover, there now occurred a serious quarrel between Lyndhurst and Bentinck

[1] See *Germania*, § 33: maneat, quaeso, duretque gentibus, si non amor nostri, at certe odium sui, quando urgentibus imperii fatis nihil iam praestare fortuna maius potest quam hostium discordiam. The debate is reported in *Hansard*, 3rd Ser., LXXXVIII (13 Aug. 1846), where the Protests of the dissentient peers are at 674-7. Grey was the third Earl Grey (1802–94) who had succeeded to the title in 1845. Relations between him and Brougham had been seriously strained in earlier years. It was his objection to Palmerston which Russell had made an excuse for not forming a government in 1845. Now, as Secretary of State for the Colonies, he was largely responsible for the Sugar Duties Act of 1846.

[2] Billy Holmes was William Holmes who had first become a M.P. in 1808, and who died in 1851. He was for many years a Tory whip in the House of Commons. For Bonham, Peel's political man of business, see N. Gash, 'F. R. Bonham: Conservative "Political Secretary", 1832–47' in *English Historical Review*, LXIII (1948).

which damaged the future prospects of co-operation in this quarter. Towards the end of the session, Bentinck, in an effort to inflame opinion against the late government by a number of personal charges of jobbery, was hardly less successful in inflaming it against himself.[1] Lyndhurst and Ripon were included in this attack, and Brougham was implicated. Between Brougham and Lyndhurst there existed a warm and deep personal attachment, which ended only with the latter's death in 1863, and even if Brougham had not been personally concerned, he would have condemned Bentinck's maladroit performance. Disraeli was so dismayed by it that he dissociated himself from it, and made no reference to the unfortunate manœuvre in his biography of Bentinck. In the circumstances, it is of interest to read Brougham's explanation of one of the issues, as given in his letter of 23 September.

Affairs are still in an unsatisfactory condition. The folly of George Bentinck has been most mischievous. Anything so absurd as his attack on Lynd[hurs]t and Ripon (whose late corruption [?] however is foolish) I never have yet seen. The facts were within my personal knowledge both as to being and professing absolutely fictions, without shadow of foundation. But had they all been as true as they were false, what then? Had not Lyndhurst a perfect right to ask Ripon to appoint Dr. Pollock a Judge, if he was quite fit for the place, and to appoint Parry a Commissioner in his room (or in C. Phillips room) if he, Parry, was fit? No one can question the fitness of both Pollock and Parry and had I been Lynd[hurs]t I would have said 'I promised Pollock to make way for my private secretary Parry, both being fit men, and I defy you all to object'. I should then have added, as was the truth, that the whole was a mere falsehood. He named seven for the vacant place in India all fit men, and Ripon without communicating with L. chose Pollock. Then the folly of G. Bentinck in saying I had my sop, for I had got the place for C. Phillips! It happens that I never supposed that C. P.

[1] See Atlay, *op. cit.* I, 150-1; Martin, *Life of Lyndhurst*, 422-4; Monypenny and Buckle, *Life of Disraeli*, III, chap. 1; and *Hansard*, 3rd Ser., LXXXVIII, 810, for Disraeli's attitude. Lyndhurst refused to accept Bentinck's account of the matter, as given by him in the House of Commons on 21 August. Lyndhurst had been Lord Chancellor, for the third time, 1841–6. Ripon had been President of the Board of Control for Indian Affairs, 1843–6.

would prefer 1500 a year in London to 1800 in Liverpool, a much cheaper place, so I had asked the Indian place for Jackson, whom I never saw but as a counsel for 12 years practising before me in all the Indian cases. Ripon however had already given Pollock the place before I recommended Jackson and then C.P. sent to say he was ready to come to town to succeed Pollock. So that all the story is a fiction. As for the living, I know about that too, for our people here begged me to ask Nocton of Lyndhurst for the Rector of Brougham parish, and my answer was that I would do no such thing for I know Ripon's house adjoins the church at Nocton and it is (said I) to my particular knowledge the invariable rule in such cases to let the owner of the place name his parson. I always acted on this rule and so did Eldon and therefore I did not interfere, any more than if the place was full. Thus you see my evidence puts an end to this silly story altogether ; and I may add, if it had not been so, a chancellor appointing a colleague's friend to a living and in return asking that colleague to appoint a *fit* man an Indian judge, is really a very ordinary and very harmless occurrence were it all true. . . . I shall give you a letter from Walmer where I sleep before crossing to Boulogne.

This next letter, when it came, had little to add in the matter of news.

I fear my London or Cinque Ports letters will be as barren as my Westmoreland one for though I slept at Holland House on Sunday and came here yesterday and saw Peel for a minute in passing through, I really found nothing stirring. The split in the party, thanks to G. Bentinck, is far from healed, but there prevails more sense — a good deal more than before — and it will heal though slowly. Meantime the Whigs reckon upon it as all they have to comfort them while they hardly know most to dread Parliament remaining or being dissolved, the Conservatives have large funds and plenty of zeal and candidates happen when it may.

I find [he added] the excellent Duke [of Wellington] in very particular force. I never saw him better. He is one of the most delightful of men to discuss any subject with, great or little, military or civil, for no head is like his and then he is so candid and kindly that you can really canvass things in every view.

Not the least of Brougham's weaknesses as a political manipulator sprang from his absence of several months in the year abroad. On his return from France after the New Year, he picked up the story where it had left off, but could not conceal the deterioration in his hopes for the situation. In 1847 the Irish famine was more nearly complete than in either of the two previous years, and Bentinck chose this issue for a major political initiative which is described at length by Disraeli in chapter XX of his biography of Bentinck. No move could have commended itself less than did this to Brougham, who habitually regarded the Irish as lying outside the ordinary considerations of politics and almost of humanity. He therefore rejected all temptation to employ the Irish crisis as a stick with which to attack the government, and so dissociated himself, on a major issue, from the Conservative opposition. In condemning any parliamentary strategy which relied upon Irish support, his instinct was sound ; Melbourne had suffered from such reliance a dozen years before, and Gladstone was to suffer the same disadvantage forty years later. But on this occasion, Brougham's criticism of Bentinck's measure extended to its author, whom he wished to see discredited with it.

As he sat 'hearing endless counsel in one of *four* cases in the nature of impeachment of judges (Colonial)' in the Privy Council on 11 February, he scribbled his first report on the session of 1847 :

> Tonight comes on G[eorge] B[entinck]'s famous Motion and if he, aided by the *beggar-robbers*, carries his bill the Govt. must go out. But how can the Conservatives succeed ? For assuredly J. Bull, patient animal as he is, will not bear G. Bentinck and Disraeli to be ministerial chiefs, how well soever he may be disposed to have my friend Stanley at the head. Unhappily the squabbles and split so fatally and so imprudently caused by Peel's unaccountable proceeding last session is still subsisting and time is wanting to end it. . . . The Govt expect, I find, to throw out G.B.'s bill. It will save much embarrassment, if they do.

In the event, the second reading was postponed by a day, though without effect upon the final outcome. On 13 February he was able to report reassuringly

The G.B. debate goes on at least till Tuesday, when this volunteer Ch. of the Exch. will be defeated. He is deserted by the jobbing Irish, whose *shameless* and *false* conduct was the theme of universal disgust when they imprudently came forward on Thursday and avowed their plans (*lie plot*) to be to support J. Russell as long as they could get any money out of him and then to take G. Bentinck and get more. . . . The more G.B. is lowered the better chance is there of the Conservatives shaking together. But he is really a very clever and honest though empty and indiscreet chap.

With its Irish policy vindicated against the alternative proposed by the opposition, the government survived the session, at the end of which Parliament was dissolved. The General Election brought it less strength than could be wished, but also brought little satisfaction to Brougham. Before all the results were in, he wrote on 9 August :

The Elections are queer things altogether. As for Edinburgh, it has fallen in my estimation 50 per ct. Macaulay's defeat by free-church and Co is too bad. He may not be a great statesman or first-rate debater, but he is a most brilliant speaker, and his honest frankness and refusal to *toad-eat* the mob of fanatics demand every praise. I only wished he had spoken more out about paying the Irish priests.

Roebuck's defeat by Connel and false humanity at Bath is also a great blot on the people. Whatever we may say of his extreme opinions, his honesty and courage are above all praise. He attacked the Irish jobbers in a mass, and was all but murdered by them. He also muzzled old O'Connel for the last three years of his discreditable life, by attacking his combined *Mendicity* and *Mendacity*. O. dreaded him more than he did his pope and his confessor, which is saying a good deal.[1]

Well, I have gone carefully over the returns down to the last day, Saturday 7th, and I have had Billy Holmes's help, who is the whipper-in of the Protection party. We together make out that Peel has 54, and that the Govt are in a minority of 1, if all the

[1] J. A. Roebuck Q.C. (1801–79), known as 'Tear 'em', had been M.P. for Bath 1832–7 and 1841–7, his very independent radicalism losing him the seat on both occasions. He re-entered Parliament in 1849. 'Connel', whose name is here misspelt by Brougham, was Daniel O'Connell, the 'Liberator' who died this year.

protection and Peel join together. They will be, however, in a much greater minority, probably of 20 or 25, when all the Counties are returned ; for hitherto they have been more in the Boros, and there are 50 or 55 County returns to come.

When I speak of the Govt. forces, I assume all to be theirs that are not Prot[ection] or Peel. I wish them joy of such *support* as they may expect from Hume, Wakly, G. Thompson, F. O'Connor, O'Gorman Mahon etc. etc. These allies will worry them to death.[1]

The Parliament which sat from 1847 to 1852 was the last in which Brougham was politically active, and it brought him a large measure of personal and political disappointment. The Whig government survived almost the whole of its length, thanks to Peelite support, the Conservative schism remained largely unhealed, while the Protectionists, led by Stanley, offered no viable alternative government. In his sustained vendetta against the Whigs, Brougham possessed a nuisance value only, and this diminished in effectiveness as the sessions passed. His failure to reassert himself politically, so long patent to others, at last became clear to himself. But, however unpropitious the outlook, he did not easily abandon the fight, for which he prepared himself when the new Parliament was unexpectedly summoned for an autumn session in 1847. He hastily returned from France and wrote to explain, from his town house in Grafton Street on 23 November :

I had intended to write from Cannes and mention how matters looked in France, when the sudden meeting of Parlt. came upon me

[1] Hume was Joseph Hume (1777–1855), a leading Radical M.P. for thirty years, now re-elected for Montrose. Wakly was Thomas Wakly (1795–1862), M.P. for Finsbury, 1835–52, a radical reformer in matters of public health. G. Thompson must be a reference to Thomas Perronet Thompson (1783–1869), now radical M.P. for Bradford, perhaps here confused, by a slip of the pen, with his namesake George Thompson (1804–78), supporter of parliamentary reform, of abolition of the Corn Laws and of Slavery, who was not an M.P. F. O'Connor was the Chartist leader, just elected for Nottingham. The O'Gorman Mahon was C. J. P. Mahon (1800–91), the Irish nationalist, who had just been elected for Ennis ; in the course of a long and adventurous life, he had prompted O'Connell to stand for County Clare in 1828, was himself elected for it in 1879, and lived to repudiate the leadership of Parnell in 1890.

like a thunderclap. It was (as the Govt. tell me) only resolved upon in the greatest haste, and was as great a surprise to them as to me. At first I resolved to be selfish and stay where I was and I really feel that I do a very patriotic and a very foolish thing too in coming away from Summer to Winter, for nothing can be conceived more useless than one coming to Parlt. in a state of things which makes it impossible to do any good, or do otherwise than let matters take their course. . . .

I find parties here in a state of compleat dislocation, and of course nothing of a *party* nature will be attempted. Indeed all men of all classes must wish to help the country out of its great difficulties without much examining into their causes. The Money market and Ireland are the main ones, and the govt. will endeavour to prevent any other matters being brought forward. But as the govt. is weaker than water and the Commons are the most nondescript body ever collected, they will probably have to do as every body pleases and not as they please themselves.

One thing I devoutly hope will be done. I mean, some stop put to the horrible state of things in Ireland, where life is certainly less secure (and landed property too) than in any country calling itself civilised. Indeed in no savage country is there less security. Some notion is gone abroad that the Govt don't mean to ask for more powers but only for more troops. If so it can only be because they joined in throwing out the Arms Bill of 1846 (which they had called for themselves) with the design of throwing out Peel. Possibly the recollection of this may make them afraid of doing their duty now by requiring some such measure.

At the first opportunity, Brougham returned to Cannes, and was detained there by illness when the year of revolutions began with the overthrow of the Orleans monarchy at the end of February 1848. The state of the continent and of France almost completely monopolized Brougham's correspondence with Lord Granton for the next twelve months or more, whether he was in England or abroad. Back in England in April 1848 he was able to dismiss the last demonstration of the Chartists there as an irrelevant trifle :

'The utter flooring of sedition and chartism here is highly satisfactory, but who can believe we were in the very least danger from these bullies? The utmost that could have happened was their own severe punishment by the troops.'

Although his preoccupation with continental affairs remained, Brougham was ready by the beginning of 1849 to resume an active interest in home politics. On 3 January he wrote from Stuttgart: 'I go tomorrow and hope D.V. to be at Paris 9th, London 22 or 23, and 1 February I shall give my friend Palm[erston] one lecture on his foreign policy and that presumptuous ass Cobden another on his budget which is as false as it is foolish.'

The session of 1849 was, indeed, to present Brougham with his most favourable opportunities of defeating, and perhaps overthrowing, the government in the House of Lords. The opposition there to both the Navigation Bill and the Canada Rebellion Losses Bill in the early summer, with which he was actively associated, came near to success, and the final failure was in each case the more disappointing. And no such opportunity was to be presented to Brougham again.[1]

It was, therefore, in dejection that Brougham wrote on 25 June

We have had sad work in our House since I last wrote. Navigation Law Repeal, by a majority of absent Lords, we having majority in the House. Canada Bill brought in by Rebels, now ministers there, to give other Rebels, their accomplices, compensation for losses in creating their rebellion; this motion of mine carried last week by a majority of 9 present, negatived by 3 including proxies, but Lucan and Polworth chose to go to Brighton with 4 proxies in their pockets, else I was sure of victory. All this is sad enough.

[1] The House of Lords debate on the third reading of the Navigation Bill, on 12 June, is in *Hansard*, 3rd Ser. CVI, and Brougham's speech at 22-5. The existence of the government depended on its passage, which was secured only by a handful of proxies. Broughton, *Recollections*, records Russell as expecting Brougham's opposition because he hoped to be Stanley's Chancellor. The Canada Rebellion Losses Bill was debated in the House of Lords on 19 June when two hostile resolutions of Brougham's were lost by a majority of only 3 votes. The voting in the division on these was: Contents — Present, 54; Proxies, 42; total 96. Not Contents — Present 46; Proxies 53; total 99. See *Hansard*, 3rd Ser., CVI, 450-548, with Brougham's spech at 450-83.

Lyndhurst came down with a speech in his very best manner and Plain John made so brutal an attack on him as disgusted all the House and *the Govt. quite as much as us.* So that his Plain-John-ship was literally roared down by cries from all sides. I assure you his execution of this vile attack was if possible more despicable than the design. In short it was like an act of suicide and the party not injured but benefited by it was Lyndhurst.[1]

The narrow failure of 1849 was as near as Brougham came to defeating or unseating the ministry, and thereafter the effectiveness of his opposition declined. There was a limit to what could be achieved in the Lords, and he exercised no influence in the Commons, where the main battle had to be fought. In the Commons, the strategy of the opposition remained poor, in his opinion, and the Conservative split still remained open. The new session of 1850 offered no hope, as he wrote on 7 February :

This Session has opened most dully for all, for the Protection party most fatally. Their folly in having an amendment (and such an amendment) was incredible.[2] They had a clear game and sure to win had they made their attack on Grey and his colonial administration. But it really seems as if they did not wish to unseat the Ministers, not being ready to take their places. This indeed forms the only hope of these imbecile Ministers ; but this must sooner or later end, for I don't believe the Conservatives can much longer bear their present exclusion *with a majority* in Parlt. and in the Country.

One of the chief difficulties confronting Brougham at this time, as in his earlier years, had been the attitude of Peel. Peel had always had the measure of Brougham's temperamental and political weaknesses, and had latterly been the main support of the ministry in the House of Commons. After his accidental death in the summer, Brougham reviewed the

[1] 'Plain John' was the nickname of John Campbell, first Baron Campbell (1779–1861), who had become Chancellor of the Duchy of Lancaster in 1846. Even Brougham's good-natured tolerance could not extend to Campbell, who reciprocated his dislike.

[2] The amendment to the Address was on agricultural distress and for the *relief* of the agricultural industry.

situation in a long letter on 2 August, into which flowed twenty years' accumulation of disappointment and personal dislike :

The death of Peel has been a melancholy event and owing to the manner of it has exerted a degree of zeal in favour of P. which never could have existed had he died after a month or two's illness without any accident. Hence he has been very much overpraised and his great defects overlooked : for instance, his fear of *responsibility* and resolution, selfishly as well as timidly, to leave friends and even relatives in the lurch, witness his treatment of poor Bonham some years ago, in the Railway scrape of no moment into which he had got. I once asked him, as head of a Society which he much approved, to subscribe as Chancellor and Judges had done to continue a most valuable work (Biographical Dictionary) which we were forced to give up for lack of funds. Baring had given £300, D. of Devonshire as much and many others. We were still 2000 short and applied to Peel. I had myself advanced 1500 being a pauper. P. said he could not as it would make him *answerable for the opinions* contained in the Book! So that if I subscribe to enable a poor author to bring out his book I make myself answerable for all he writes! The D of Wellington never liked him and thought himself ill used by him, in 1846. He told Lynd[hurs]t t'other day he disapproved the meeting for a Monument. But (I suppose because the Queen asked him) he attended and moved the first resolution. P. himself was decidedly against the Exhibition. But Albert got into it and the Queen sent for Peel and asked the favour of his pulling him through. P. did so and devoted 3 weeks all day to this labour. . . .

Peel's death is fatal to the present most imbecile Govt. They already bitterly feel it. He kept people quiet, he also advised the Govt. and kept them out of scrapes, such as the Jewish scrape they are now in. Above all his death removes the chief bar to a reunion of the sections of the conservative Party. This will surely be seen next Session, perhaps sooner.

The most favourable opportunity in this session for achieving the defeat of the government had arisen over the Don Pacifico scandal, and it is interesting to be told in this letter that prudent electoral considerations rather than Palmerston's oratory on the theme 'Civis Romanus sum' had then saved the day for it.

Palmerston after being beaten in the Lords had a momentary success in the Commons, not that any one approved his abominable proceedings all over Europe, but wiser men detected [detested ?] the expenses of a General Election. Then came his dinner at the Radical Club, and so great a failure is not on record.

Not a single Minister except P. himself, not even a subaltern except Att[orne]y and Sol[icitor] General, and the rest a mob of obscure and unknown radicals. Palm[erston] went away after dinner and a man told the Sol. Gen. 'You are the greatest rascal that ever held an office'. Immediately a fight took place and some say the Police were called in. I am not certain either way. Cockburn, Sol. Gen. is such a man as no minister dares put on the Bench, though after Jervis, C. J. Com[mon] Pleas all things are possible.

The letter closes with a characteristic postscript which goes far to explain why Brougham seldom failed to be liked even when he was not trusted. 'Notwithstanding I differ so much with my old colleague Lord Palm[erston]. I dine with him next Saturday as usual.' [1]

If Peel's death was a loss to the government, it contributed no positive strength to the opposition in the House of Commons. Bentinck had died in the autumn of 1848, but Brougham appears not to have regarded Disraeli as a serious political figure who could assume the leadership ; and no alternative was presented. Lord John Manners, who had lost his seat in 1847, was returned at a by-election in 1850, but was quickly dismissed as a light-weight, as Brougham wrote on 1 September : 'J. Manners is an excellent man, but *quite Puseyite*. However, independently of that *twist* he would not do to lead, and as your Lordship observes this is a great difficulty, else Peel's death was most useful to the Conservatives.' Always hostile to religious sectarianism, Brougham was the more put

[1] The 'Jewish scrape' refers to Don Pacifico. The defeat of the government on this issue was achieved on 18 June by a majority of 37 in the House of Lords where, comments Herbert Paul, *A History of Modern England*, I, 172, 'Lord Brougham, who was always afraid of offending Lord Palmerston, added nothing to the strength of the attack'. The dinner at the Reform Club is described, more decorously, by H. C. F. Bell, in *Lord Palmerston* (1936), II, 30-1.

out by the Prime Minister's adroit exploitation of 'Papal Aggression' at this point, and the consequent distraction from political and party issues. Returning earlier than usual from France this winter, he reported on 28 December 1850,

On my arrival in England I find all is No Popery, and I have not often seen such disgraceful scenes as some of the meetings present. However, the folly and impatience of the Pope and of his ambitious but blundering Cardinal are undeniable and it is only of the *excess* in the publick feeling that one complains. The same remark applies to certain Ministerial proceedings.

I saw [he went on] during the day I was in London quite enough to prove to me that it will be necessary for the Govt. to act on Law matters without regarding either the clamours of the Bar or of the Press, or of the Multitude. The Ch[ancello]r is wholly of my mind and if he had the same influence that some Ch[ancello]rs I knew (not the last) [1] possessed, all would be safe. I hope all is safe.

During 1850, as the political situation continued to offer little hope of change, Brougham had become increasingly active again on a subject which had always moved him, legal and judicial reform. It was a sphere in which he was more fruitfully employed, and it occupied an increasing space in his correspondence at this time. The collapse of his political hopes, which had now worn thin to vanishing point, was complete when, early in the session of 1851, the government was reduced to a gesture of resignation, of which the opposition was able to take no advantage.

Things are indeed in a sad situation [he confessed on 4 March 1851] and any thing like a strong government seems now quite impossible. The Protectionist party have distinctly confessed that they cannot form a government. Nor can they unless by dissolving Parlt. they acquire such force and get rid of part at least of their protection principles, as will enable them to obtain the help of sufficient supporters to carry on the business in both Houses, but especially in the Commons for it is there that their staff is so compleatly deficient. And really a dissolution in the present fever of

[1] Lord Truro had succeeded Lord Cottenham as Lord Chancellor in the summer of 1850.

No-Popery in this country and pro-popery in Ireland would be a frightful calamity. In 1831 however certain folks ran that risk which other folks have not run now. I feel as grateful to them for not running it, as they would have been to me had I declined it in 1831. There is nothing to be done without risks and sometimes great risks are more safe to run than doing nothing. But with my own feelings and opinions, both as to Protection and as to No-Popery, I feel truly grateful for the self-denial of those who have preferred running no risks at all, a self-denial which some of their own party may not be so thankful for as I am. . . . Altogether the prospect of affairs is gloomy, for a very feeble Government always leads to mischief by tempting many to urge them on in directions in which they should not walk, and one apprehends injudicious concessions as the price of safety or of support.

Thus it was that the last letter, as it proved to be, in this correspondence, written at Brougham on 30 July 1851, dealt only with legal and judicial matters, to the exclusion of politics, as had the first in 1839.

Lord Granton died in the autumn of 1851. Thereafter, Brougham continued to correspond with his son, the Lord Justice Clerk, until the latter died in 1858 ; and then, for another ten years, until his own death in 1868, with Louisa Octavia Hope, Lord Granton's daughter, who had for many years acted as her father's secretary, and who preserved his correspondence. This last she lent to Lord Penzance, in 1870, when he contemplated writing a life of Brougham.[1] In a covering letter, dated 20 July 1870, she wrote,

. . . Remember that I have a most beautiful declaration of Ld. Brougham's christian faith to me in his own hand Feby 1867, if any Biography of him does not do him justice in this respect and if I am still alive I shall send it to you to publish. Otherwise I consider such things too sacred. And I have *many* letters from him expressing his horror of secularism and the Broad Church semi-catholicism of

[1] James Plaisted Wilde, first Baron Penzance (1816–99), brother of the first Lord Truro. Both had been well known to Brougham at the Bar. Penzance was at this time a judge in the court of Probate and Divorce. He later undertook the duties of judge under the Public Worship Regulation Act of 1874, when he came to be regarded as a hammer of the Ritualists.

the day. Bye the bye I can't find his Letters to my father ab[ou]t '*Glad.*' (*i.e.* Gladstone) not knowing how both to please the Free Kirk and the Puseyites. It was rich. I suspect Edward Baxter M.P. (my sheriff-nephew's brother-in-law) of suppressing them for the credit of his chief, when my nephew gave them to him to read!

These Letters to my father are on public topics chiefly. But if another aspect of Ld. Brougham's character was wanted, his opinions upon scepticism, spiritualism and many other 'ism', I am not sure that his 90 Letters to me would not be in one sense as valuable. And to shew his wonderful memory about such trifles as my concerns, and his kindheartedness in exerting himself with Government about my nephews, dunning Dukes and officials of all kinds most perseveringly.

To be sanguine is a necessity for the reformer, and Brougham was often over-sanguine, expecting too much from the enterprises to which he put his hand. He more than once appears so in this correspondence, during his political decline. But this source of weakness was also the source of a yet greater strength, and it is not as a subject for pathos that he invites sympathy. Above all, his defects of temperament, which were very real and very great, were more than counterbalanced by a generous disposition and a warm heart, which he could rarely conceal or stifle off-stage.

8

Robert Blake

THE RISE OF DISRAELI

In an essay in honour of Sir Keith Feiling it is agreeable to be able to begin with a scene in Oxford. Perhaps the moment when Disraeli can be said to have 'arrived' was when on 9 June 1853 he received an honorary D.C.L. from the newly installed Chancellor, his political leader, the fourteenth Earl of Derby. It is true that this was less of an accolade from the University than from Derby personally, for then, as now, the Chancellor could nominate his own list for his first Encaenia, and by long-established usage it was never queried. However, Disraeli's honour went down well, anyway with the young. He was greeted with prolonged cheers in the Sheldonian Theatre, and that evening, after he had dined at the Christ Church Gaudy, a throng of undergraduates assembled in Tom Quad despite the rain to applaud him on his way back to the gate. As he reached 'Mercury' someone called out, 'Speak'. Disraeli paused. 'Gentlemen,' he said, 'within these classic walls I dare not presume to attempt to thank you ! But, believe this, never will I forget your generous kindness.' [1]

The enthusiasm which he had inspired made a deep impression on him and on his wife too. Twelve years later at a house party in Raby Castle she sat next to the future Lord Rosebery then just down from Eton. He told her he was going up to Oxford. 'Oh yes, I love Oxford,' she said, and added with that engaging touch of dottiness seldom absent from her utterances, 'they are all so fond of Mr. Dizzy there, they all

[1] Sir William Fraser, *Disraeli and his Day* (1891), p. 355.

applaud him so. . . . He was made a D.T.C.L. or something of the sort.'[1]

During the sixteen months before June 1853 Disraeli had achieved an important transition. His public image was at last changing from that of a reckless piratical adventurer. He had not yet become a serious statesman. Perhaps this always eluded him, for, as he himself at the close of his career told a member of the Fourth Party, 'I was never respectable'.[2] But he was on the way to becoming an accepted 'character', one of the personalities of English public life, whom everyone knew about, whom cartoonists caricatured, whom writers biographized. Oxford can be regarded as setting a seal upon his new status. The year 1852 was his *annus mirabilis*. He had been for ten months Chancellor of the Exchequer and Leader of the House of Commons, a man who had never before held office of even the humblest description, a man for whom six years earlier few people would have predicted much beyond a certain reputation as an eccentric literary back-bencher, a better novelist but lesser politician than, say, Bulwer Lytton.

In its first number for 1853 the *Edinburgh Review* accorded him the honour of what would now be called a 'profile':[3] it was a forty-page character sketch. He could not expect very favourable treatment from the intellectual organ of the Whig party, but the anonymous author at least gave him credit for becoming a celebrity. 'What individual from February 1852 to January 1853 has most occupied the pens, tongues and ears of Englishmen?' he asked, and answered, 'the Right Honourable Benjamin Disraeli, late Chancellor of the Exchequer is indisputably the man.' The article continued:

His appointment to this post was one of the most startling domestic events which has occurred in our time. People seemed never tired of talking and speculating on it, with its recondite

[1] R. R. James, *Rosebery* (1963), p. 43, quoting Rosebery's journal.

[2] W. S. Churchill, *Lord Randolph Churchill* (new ed. 1951), p. 131.

[3] 'Mr. Disraeli: his Character and Career', XCVII, 420-61.

causes and its problematical results. He at once became an inexhaustible topic of animated discussion in society. His portrait was painted by one fashionable artist ; his bust was taken in marble, *aere perennius*, by another ; what were called likenesses of him appeared in illustrated newspapers by the dozen ; and, above all, he was placed in Madame Tussaud's repository — that British Valhalla in which it is difficult for a civilian to gain a niche without being hanged. He glittered in the political horizon as a star of the first magnitude ; and every glass was turned on him the more eagerly because it was impossible to discover and hazardous to predict whether he would turn out a planet, a fixed star, a comet, or a mere vapoury exhalation, or will o' the wisp, raised by an overheated atmosphere from a rank and unwholesome soil.

It does not require much further reading of the article to discover what answer the *Edinburgh Review* gave to this last question. The journal went on to quote Pope's well-known couplet :

> The thing we know is neither rich nor rare
> But wonder how the devil it got there.

How did Disraeli get there ? To answer the question we must be careful of avoiding two extreme interpretations of his early career. On the one hand there is the generally accepted modern version that he triumphed only by extraordinary talents overcoming natural barriers in the form of alien extraction, humble birth, and personal prejudice, which would have baffled anyone but a genius. On the other hand there was the view expressed by many contemporaries, not merely political opponents, that the disadvantages under which he laboured were self-imposed rather than external, and that in any case his ascent was due as much to good luck and the incalculable accidents of politics as to any great genius on his part. It is the thesis of this essay that the truth, though lying between these opposites, is rather nearer the contemporary view than is generally conceded today.

In the first place Disraeli's origins were not as obscure as all that. His grandfather was a Sephardic Jew who emigrated from Italy (Cento, near Ferrara) to England in 1748. He was a straw-hat merchant and later graduated to the Stock Exchange. When he died in 1816 at the age of 86 he left £35,000. His only son, Isaac, Disraeli's father, was born in 1766. He was heir to a substantial fortune from his maternal grandmother and on her death in 1791 when he was 25 he became independent of his father, and settled down to the life of a learned literary man of comfortable private means. He spent most of his days working in the British Museum and his most famous work was *The Curiosities of Literature*, a fascinating anthology of anecdotes, character sketches, observations, written in a drily elegant style. He was a friend of Scott, Byron, Croker, and John Murray. In 1802 he married Maria Basevi, like him of prosperous Italian Sephardic Jewish origin. There were four children : a daughter Sarah born at the end of 1802, and three sons of whom Benjamin was the eldest, born in London on 21 December 1804. He was devoted to his father and his sister but never seems to have felt for, or inspired in, his mother much affection. Nor did he get on particularly well with his brothers though he did his best to procure jobs for them. He detested the Basevis.

Disraeli thus came from a family of prosperous middle to upper-middle class circumstances, with a father who moved, not indeed in the *beau monde* but in the respectable Tory literary circle constituted by the world of *The Quarterly Review*, and who was a well-known character in London. True his name and appearance were foreign and the family suffered under the disability of being Jewish. But it is important not to overstate that disability. There was not in England the racial anti-semitism to be found in many parts of Europe. England was a tolerant country. The disability lay in the fact that, along with all who would not subscribe to the formularies of the Church of England, including Papists, Methodists, Quakers, and Unitarians, Jews were barred from office and membership of Parliament — Jews by religion that is to say. Fortunately, however, in 1817 Isaac quarrelled with the local Synagogue for trying in effect to dun him for what he regarded as an excessively heavy subscription. He was a sceptic in any case and had conformed only to please his father who was now dead. He withdrew from the Jewish community and had all his children baptized as Christians of the Church of England.

Disraeli did not go to either a public school or a university. He was educated at a modest establishment in Epping Forest and then became articled to a solicitor. Too much should not be made of this. It is true that nearly every nineteenth-century prime minister went to either Eton or Harrow and then to Oxford or Cambridge (the most notable exception being Lord John Russell who, faithful to the family tradition of eccentricity, attended Westminster and Edinburgh). But it seems to have been only an accident that Disraeli did not go to Winchester. Both his brothers did — and — appropriately — ended up as civil servants.[1] The first and only Wykehamist prime minister was Addington. It is odd to think that Disraeli might have been the second. As for the university, after Disraeli decided to give up the Law when he was only 19, 'My father made a feeble effort for Oxford but the hour of adventure had arrived. I was unmanageable.'

In 1829 Isaac left London and became tenant of Bradenham Manor, a beautiful redbrick Queen Anne house near High Wycombe. He lived there performing the ordinary functions of a country squire. He preserved pheasants, and invited people to shoot. His children called him 'the Governor'. In the 1830s the house provided a comfortable *pied-à-terre* for Benjamin, to which he could invite his grand friends after the London season was over. His sister was engaged to the son of a rich landowning family, William Meredith, who died tragically of smallpox before their marriage while travelling with Disraeli in Egypt. One of Disraeli's brothers farmed the home farm. The other was in barrister's chambers in London.

[1] James Disraeli was Robert Lowe's fag and was wont to say, 'No one knew what a bully was until he knew *him*'. Hughenden Papers, Box 26, A/X/A, Note by Disraeli, undated but *c.* 1863.

The family took their place in Buckinghamshire county society. They were on familiar terms with landed gentry such as the Dashwoods of West Wycombe, the Carringtons of Missenden, the Norrises of Hughenden.[1] Early in the 1830s Benjamin struck up a friendship with Lord Chandos, the future Duke of Buckingham, and, though a man of exceptional silliness, the leading grandee of the county. It is significant that in August 1836 when he was only 31, Disraeli, in spite of his notoriously debt-ridden, turbulent, irregular mode of life was sworn in as a Justice of the Peace. 'It is really nonsense', wrote the Duke of Argyll in his autobiography, 'to talk of a man in such a position as a mere "Jew boy" who by the force of nothing but extraordinary genius attained to the leadership of a great party. The only impediments in his way were not any want of external advantages but his own often grotesque and unintelligible opinions.'[2]

No doubt the Duke was going rather too far here. Even if Disraeli's want of external advantages has been over-stressed the fact remains that his birth and upbringing were different from that of any other nineteenth-century prime minister. He certainly had some external handicaps to overcome, but the Duke was shrewd enough in noting that part of his difficulty was self-imposed. Moreover, grotesque opinions were not the only trouble. Disraeli's reckless and apparently unscrupulous behaviour as a young man constituted an obstacle to his ascent, such as would have hindered anyone whatever his social origins. A brief survey of his early life will show what is meant.

At the end of 1824 he decided to abandon the Law and make his fortune on the stock exchange. This was 'the hour of adventure'. He lost heavily, and in the hope of arresting the fall in his South American mining shares wrote in 1825

[1] Hughenden Papers, Box 7, A/I/B, containing Sarah Disraeli's letters to her brother gives a good picture of life at Bradenham in the 1830s.

[2] George Douglas, Duke of Argyll, *Autobiography and Memoirs* (1906), I, 280.

three anonymous pamphlets puffing the merits of some of these rickety and fraudulent companies. It may have been an appropriate beginning for an able exponent of the art of fiction but it is a strange literary debut for a future chancellor of the exchequer. He continued to lose money, but — a tribute to his extraordinary persuasiveness — managed, still not yet of age, to induce his father's hard-headed Scotch friend and publisher, John Murray, to launch a Tory daily paper as a rival to *The Times* and promised to put up one-quarter of the money. The whole affair was hopelessly botched, there was no editor appointed till the last minute, finance and printing arrangements were chaotic. There was a collapse on the stock exchange in December 1825. He was unable to produce the money. *The Representative*, as it was called, ceased publication after five months in May 1826 losing John Murray some £26,000. Of course this was Murray's fault as well as Disraeli's, but his young protégé promptly made matters worse by writing an absurd novel, *Vivian Grey*, in which the whole story of the fiasco, transposed from journalism into politics, was told in thin disguise and Murray caricatured as a tipsy nincompoop.[1] A violent quarrel followed and Disraeli was henceforth regarded as an incorrigible scoundrel in the world of Murray, Croker, Lockhart, and *The Quarterly Review*. That great organ of Conservatism contrived to avoid even mentioning his name until 1848.

Not surprisingly, he then had a nervous breakdown. It lasted from 1826 to 1828. But he brightened up, wrote a second novel, *The Young Duke*, if possible even more extravagant and affected than *Vivian Grey*, and, on the strength of an advance from the publisher who was not John Murray,

[1] The full measure of the offence given can only be appreciated by reading the original version of the novel. The 1853 edition on which nearly all subsequent ones are based was much altered by the author, whole scenes and episodes being excised. Monypenny errs (W. F. Monypenny and G. E. Buckle, *The Life of Benjamin Disraeli*, 1910–20, I, 75) in depicting Murray as hypersensitive. He had every cause for annoyance.

he went on his celebrated journey to the Mediterranean and the Near East where he blossomed out as a fop of the first order, wore a sort of fancy dress wherever he went, and astounded the British garrison and diplomatic colonies that he visited. His companions were his sister's fiancé, the virtuous Meredith, and a singularly unvirtuous youth by the name of James Clay. Clay was handsome and debauched, and he and Disraeli together explored the more dubious pleasures of the Orient.[1] On Meredith's death Disraeli at once returned to England. *En route* he struck up a friendship with Henry Stanley, a younger grandson of the twelfth Earl of Derby and brother of Edward the future fourteenth Earl and Prime Minister. In circumstances still not wholly clear Disraeli managed to arouse the suspicion that he had on his return lured the young man to a 'hell' in St. James's Street, kept by a money-lender to whom Disraeli was in debt.[2] Although the charge was almost certainly false, and was not believed by most of the Stanley family, it was believed by Edward, the only one who mattered politically. This was a piece of bad luck perhaps. Or would the moralist regard it as an occupational hazard of the sort of life Disraeli led? At all events he had been seriously damaged in yet another influential quarter.

Disraeli evidently had no idea at the time that his actions had been thus misconstrued. It was with complete confidence that early in 1832 he took lodgings in Duke Street, determined to assault simultaneously the heights of politics, society, and

[1] The evidence is a letter from Clay which could not be printed unexpurgated even in this enlightened era. Later Clay became a Liberal M.P. and one of the country's greatest experts on whist. There is some interesting confidential correspondence between him and Disraeli at the time of the Reform Act of 1867.

[2] The letters referring to this episode have disappeared from Disraeli's papers but a memorandum exists by his solicitor, Sir Philip Rose, Hughenden Papers, Box. 27. Monypenny makes only a passing allusion to the matter. Rose's memorandum was printed in full by C. L. Cline in his article 'Disraeli and Peel's 1841 Cabinet', *Journal of Modern History*, vol. XI, 1939, 509. The Derby Papers show that Henry Stanley later became a complete ne'er-do-well, ending his life as a remittance man in France.

literature. In all three ventures he was much assisted by Bulwer Lytton with whom he had struck up a sort of pen-friendship a year or two earlier and who must at this time have seemed the *beau ideal* to a man of Disraeli's character and aspirations. He began with a set-back, being blackballed for the Athenæum as Lytton had warned him would probably happen.[1] But he attributed this to the malice of Croker, and proceeded to set his sights at 'the best club in the world'. The problem was on which side to stand for Parliament. His family tradition, in so far as there was any, inclined to the Tories, and his ill-fated attempt at political journalism had been in the Tory interest. But the prospects for the party seemed very dark in 1832 when the Reformers were carrying all before them. Lytton, who was a Reformer, tried to persuade the Whigs to endorse Disraeli as a candidate at a by-election in High Wycombe—probably the last ever to be held on the old franchise.[2] He did not succeed, but Disraeli was determined to try his luck all the same and stood as an independent Radical against Colonel Grey, the Prime Minister's son. 'Toryism is worn out', he told a friend, 'and I cannot condescend to be a Whig.'[3] Whether he would have said the same thing if Lytton had been successful may perhaps be doubted. He lost, and in spite of repeated attempts there and elsewhere during the next three years completely failed to make headway as a Radical. He did, however, manage to acquire the friendship of an important if slightly dubious political figure, the Tory ex-Lord Chancellor, Lyndhurst, to whom he acted as an informal private secretary.

Much ink has been spent in trying to discover a consistent thread in his political utterances at this time and to link his

[1] Hughenden Papers, Box 104, B/XX/Ly/9: Lytton to Disraeli, undated. 'I think there is some chance of your not coming in because you have written books people have talked about. Had you compiled some obscure quarto which nobody had read you would have been sure of success.'

[2] Hughenden Papers, Box 104, B/XX/Ly/13: Bulwer to Disraeli, 17 June 1832.

[3] Monypenny and Buckle, *op. cit.* I, 211.

views then with his opinions later. It is wasted. He gave the answer himself, sending without comment to his sister a newspaper cutting which alleged that when asked to say on what he intended to stand he replied, 'On my head'.[1] The truth was that like many ambitious young men he wanted above all else to get in. Greville drily summed up the situation when told by Lord Lyndhurst in December 1834 that Disraeli was uncertain whether to seek the parliamentary aid of Lord Chandos or Lord Durham: 'he must be a mighty impartial personage'.[2]

Perhaps one consistent element can be distinguished in Disraeli's political creed at this time. He was — anyway after Lytton's rebuff — always a staunch anti-Whig. No doubt this was partly caused by the political balance at High Wycombe, the scene of three out of his four unsuccessful attempts to win a seat. The sitting members were both Whigs, and for some reason the Tories never put up a candidate. Disraeli thus thought in terms of a Tory-Radical alliance, a union of extremes against the centre, at a very early stage in his career. Again and again during the long years of opposition from 1846 to 1868 he tried to persuade his leader to pursue a similar course on a national scale, but Derby, an ex-Whig, would not play that game. Possibly the situation at Wycombe also inspired the clever but fantastical anti-Whig theory of history which Disraeli first adumbrated during the 1830s. In the election of 1835 after failing first to secure Lord Durham's support for a safe Radical borough and secondly Lord George Bentinck's for a safe Tory one,[3] he stood yet again as a Radical for Wycombe. But this time, thanks to the support of his patron Lord Lyndhurst, he was financed to the tune of £500

[1] Ralph Disraeli (ed.), *Lord Beaconsfield's Correspondence with his Sister, 1832–52* (1886), pp. 18–19.

[2] Lytton Strachey and Roger Fulford (ed.), *The Greville Memoirs* (1938), III, 117.

[3] Monypenny's theory that he was converted to Toryism by the Tamworth Manifesto cannot hold water. The overture to Bentinck was made before Peel had even returned from Rome.

from the Tory election fund.[1] He did not get in, but as soon as the election was over he took the plunge, put his name down for the Carlton — and was not blackballed — and became official Tory candidate for a by-election at Taunton. Once again he lost and in the course of the struggle made himself somewhat ridiculous by his famous quarrel with O'Connell. But he was now a definite Tory and his candidature had the party's backing.

He did not confine himself at this time to politics. There was Society and literature in which to make his mark. In the latter he was unsuccessful. *Contarini Fleming*, *The Rise of Iskander*, and *Alroy* all fell flat. Indeed the author admitted of *Alroy* that its first chapter made just as good sense if it was read backwards. He then essayed epic poetry, a genre to which his muse was ill suited, and the *Revolutionary Epick* was a total failure.

As for society it is clear that he made some advance though it is hard to say how much. Our chief source is the sparkling series of letters that he wrote to his adoring sister but one can never be sure how far these corresponded with reality. Certainly under the auspices of Bulwer Lytton he became a conspicuous figure in the slightly raffish salons over which such people as Lady Blessington and Mrs. Norton presided. His flamboyant dress, his epigrams and witticisms, his good looks and the charm which he could exercise if he wished made him well known, if not always well liked, and his earlier novels had given him some *réclame* in that world. He was taken up by D'Orsay, the arch-dandy of the era, and in 1833 he commenced a liaison with a married woman of title thus following the correct routine for a fashionable young man. The episode may, however, have done him more harm than one might have expected in an age of such lax morality.

Disraeli's mistress was Henrietta Sykes,[2] wife of a foolish

[1] Norman Gash, *Politics in the Age of Peel* (1953), p. 436.

[2] The only historian to give an account of this episode, which is almost entirely suppressed by Monypenny, is B. R. Jerman, *The Young Disraeli* (Princeton, 1960).

spendthrift, valetudinarian baronet called Sir Francis Sykes. The affair was facilitated by the acquiescence of her husband. Sir Francis had recently become the lover of a Mrs. Bolton, who was the wife of Disraeli's doctor and who had earlier been Disraeli's mistress for a short while. For a time all four lived in the same house near Southend, but this was too much of a strain. The baronet departed on a prolonged tour of the continent, while Disraeli lived openly with Henrietta at her husband's house in Park Lane. The affair in itself not unduly damaging, now began to become more so, and it became a good deal worse when gossip reported that Disraeli had introduced her to Lyndhurst who was a notorious roué (said to be the original of Gilbert's 'highly susceptible Chancellor' in *Iolanthe*) in order to further his own political career. What really happened is far from clear, but in fact Henrietta knew Lyndhurst quite independently, and, although she certainly went on a holiday with him in France in 1835, there is no proof that Disraeli approved or encouraged it. But the trio did come down on two occasions to stay at Bradenham, to the great scandal of the county — an act, so Disraeli's solicitor, Sir Philip Rose, was told forty years later, 'which could never be forgotten and which all Disraeli's subsequent career could never obliterate'. The affair ended in 1836 when Henrietta became the mistress of the then well-known painter, Daniel Maclise.

Throughout these years and indeed for long after, Disraeli was embarrassed by an ever-increasing burden of debt. It originated with his speculations in 1824/5 but it increased enormously thanks to his wild extravagance and reckless methods of raising money. He was in frequent danger of arrest, and is even said to have hidden on one occasion in a well at Bradenham to escape the attention of the Sheriff's Officer. In December 1836 he had to attend a county Conservative dinner. 'I have been requested to move the principal toast, "the House of Lords"', he wrote to his solicitor. 'I trust there is no danger of my being nabbed, as this would be a fatal *contretemps*, inasmuch as in all probability I am addressing my future constituents.' Echoes of these early financial embarrassments were to trouble him as late as 1849[1] after he had become leader of his party in the House of Commons.

A lot has been written about the Jewish side of Disraeli's character and career. He became intensely interested in it himself, to the point of becoming something of a bore on the subject, and no doubt it should not be under-estimated. But racial and national stereotypes are of doubtful value, and, in any case, Disraeli was not at all typical of the Jews who were coming to the top of the tree in his day. They tended to be silent, prudent, high-principled men who acquired vast wealth, became Masters of Hounds and bought up the Vale of Aylesbury. Their quintessential figure was Disraeli's friend Baron Rothschild, who on grounds of pure principle stood again and again for Parliament until at last the bar on Jews was removed and then, having got there, sat for fifteen years without uttering a word.

Perhaps if stereotypes are to be introduced at all, the Italian side of Disraeli is worth considering. He was proud, vain, flamboyant, generous, emotional, quarrelsome, extravagant, theatrical, and addicted to conspiracy and backstairs intrigue. His great object in his early days was to be someone, to cut a dash, make an impression, 'far figura', as the Italians say. These qualities are not peculiar to Italy. Byron, for example, possessed nearly all of them, and indeed in Byron's character and career we can find the clue to much of the young Disraeli's conduct. Of course he never actually met Byron, but his father had done so and had been highly praised by the great man. Disraeli was fascinated by every detail of Byron's career. He had himself rowed by Byron's boatman on the Lake of Geneva in 1826, and after his tour of the East he managed to acquire for the Bradenham *ménage* Byron's former gondolier, an Italian, Battista Falcieri, known as 'Tita', who remained

[1] Hughenden Papers, Box 17, A/V/A/20, 21.

as Isaac's butler and factotum till the latter died in 1847. He even wrote a novel '*Venetia*' based on Byron's life. It is very bad.

What is amazing about Disraeli during the time when he seemed to be imposing on himself almost every disadvantage was his confidence that he would win in the end. He was avowedly and intensely ambitious. His object was to get to 'the top of the greasy pole'. As early as 1833 he astounded Melbourne whom he met at Mrs. Norton's by declaring that he intended to be Prime Minister. The Home Secretary surveying this dandiacal young coxcomb could scarcely believe his ears. 'You must put all these foolish notions out of your head; they won't do at all', he said.[1] Disraeli's extraordinary ambition and immense determination cannot be explained by any simple event. No one really knows what it was that drove him on, whether it was some sort of aspersion cast on him as a boy for his alien appearance and creed, whether it was a desire to prove himself to a mother who never seems to have much liked him and to have doubted his genius, or whether it was sheer egotism, love of the limelight, desire to be the centre of attention. He rightly believed in his own capacity as a speaker. 'I could floor them all', he told his sister after listening to a debate in the House. He certainly did not strive for a parliamentary career in order to promote some great cause or principle. 'We came here for fame', he said to Bright many years later.

There can be no doubt that, although he was in his youth much better known as a novelist than a politician, politics was always his main objective. His novels are for the most part absurd extravaganzas, though very readable and redeemed by a certain gaiety, vitality, and a sheer outrageousness which holds the reader's attention. The best of them, *Coningsby* and *Sybil*, are vehicles for his paradoxical political opinions. They will always be read. So too will *Lothair* and *Endymion*

[1] W. M. Torrens, *Memoirs of . . . Viscount Melbourne* (new ed. 1890), p. 275.

if only for the oddity of being written late in life by an ex-Prime Minister. But Parliament was his real passion. In the last thirty-four years of his life, although he had plenty of leisure, being nearly always in opposition, he only wrote two novels. From 1831 onwards or even earlier he lived for politics, and his early failures gave him an acute sense of frustration. When he was old and famous he took Lady Derby for a walk from Hughenden towards Bradenham which had long gone into other hands. 'It was there that I passed my miserable youth', he told her. 'Why miserable?' 'I was devoured by ambition I did not see any means of gratifying.' [1]

From 1837 things began to look up. He was elected to Parliament as Tory M.P. for Maidstone. True he was shouted down by the Irish members in revenge for O'Connell during his maiden speech, but it was so bad — Peel we are told 'quite screamed with laughter' [2] — that this was a stroke of luck, for he acquired a certain sympathy, and the worst parts were never heard. Then his wealthy colleague for Maidstone, Wyndham Lewis, died leaving a life interest in a London house and £5,000 a year to his widow. She was twelve years older than Disraeli but he decided to marry her. There is no question but that he did it for money, although it may be true, as she used jokingly to aver, that 'Dizzy married me for my money, but he would do so again for love'. She paid some £13,000 towards his debts, and the curious can discover among Disraeli's papers a complete list of the contents of her house which were pledged in 1843 — one can only hope with her assent — as security for the renewal of an immense loan from one of his creditors.[3] Despite this unpromising start the marriage was a great success, and even Gladstone conceded that Disraeli's behaviour towards his wife was admirable and

[1] Quoted Wilfrid Meynell, *The Man Disraeli* (1927), p. 30.

[2] James Pope-Hennessy, *Monkcton Milnes*, I (1949), 100, quoting a letter of Milnes. There is some conflict of evidence here, for a contemporary parliamentary reporter describes Peel as applauding Disraeli. Perhaps he laughed and cheered at different times during this curious performance.

[3] Hughenden Papers, Box 17, A/V/D.

above criticism. As for Disraeli, returning after a triumph in the House of Commons in 1867 he found that she was up and waiting for him with a bottle of champagne and a pie from Fortnum and Mason. After consuming half the pie and all the champagne, he gave her his highest praise. 'Why, my dear, you are more like a mistress than a wife.'[1]

In 1841 Peel at last turned the Whigs out, and the Tories came back with a majority of 90. Disraeli confidently expected office, not the Cabinet but some under-secretaryship as a first step in the ladder. Peel ignored him, and returned a cold answer when he wrote in somewhat abject terms asking for a post.[2] It has been said that Peel intended to give him office but was deterred ; as some allege, by Stanley (the episode of the 'Hell' and his younger brother), or, as others claim, by Bonham and the party wire-pullers, or, as yet others maintain, by the notoriety of the Lyndhurst–Henrietta imbroglio. Peel may have been aware of all or any of these objections, although the evidence is thin. But it seems clear that Disraeli never had a chance. There is no mention at all of him in Peel's papers in this context,[3] and Peel's principles in constructing his government would appear to have excluded Disraeli from the running simply because he had so many stronger claims to consider. If Disraeli had made a really startling impact on the House in 1837–41 possibly Peel would have chosen him but there is no evidence, apart from Disraeli's own, that he had made any such impression. His exclusion, however natural, was none the less fraught with consequences for the future of the Conservative party and the whole course of nineteenth-century politics. For Disraeli was bitterly dis-

[1] T. E. Kebbel, *Lord Beaconsfield and Other Tory Memories* (1907), p. 40.

[2] Monypenny and Buckle, *op. cit.* II, 118-20.

[3] The only reference that does appear is a letter from Bonham, the chief party manager, attributing to Disraeli a pseudonymous letter in *The Times* attacking Peel's plan to re-elect the Speaker of the previous Parliament, Peel Papers, British Museum, Add. MS. 40486, f. 7 : Bonham to Peel, 2 August 1841. Disraeli repudiated the charge (*ibid.* f. 119 : Disraeli to Peel, 17 August). I am indebted to Dr. Kitson Clerk for drawing my attention to this point.

appointed. He did not at once move into open hostility but his whole attitude gradually changed. Had he been, say, a Secretary to the Admiralty or a Lord of the Treasury, it seems unlikely that he would have taken up the cause of Young England, that curious translation of the Oxford movement by Cambridge from religion into politics ; or that he would, have propounded first in *Coningsby* then in *Sybil* his ingenious, persuasive, but fallacious theory of English history which depicted Whiggism and official Conservatism alike as perversions from some mysterious undefined, perhaps indefinable, natural order ; or that he would have resigned office for the sake of the Corn Laws.

It was early in 1845 that Disraeli came out in open rebellion against Peel. There had been no obvious change in Peel's policy, nor on the other hand did rebellion offer any obvious hope of success, for Peel's position looked safe enough and the Corn Law question lay in the future. Disraeli was probably actuated by his old desire to cut a figure, by a certain sense of vengeance, and above all by the feeling that the last hope of promotion had gone. Time was against him. He was 40, old for first entry into office in those days. Ahead of him in the official hierarchy was a whole group of able hard-working younger men, Gladstone, Sidney Herbert, Cardwell, Canning, Lincoln, Dalhousie ; all in office, all born between 1807 and 1813, all Oxonians, mostly products of Eton and Christ Church. He could not hope to overtake them if party politics proceeded on their normal course. Nothing was now to be lost by attacking Peel and in doing so he discovered an important fact. For the first time it was beginning to be true that he 'could floor them all'. His witty acid remarks delivered with a countenance as inexpressive as an antique mask appealed to those who had begun to resent a certain smugness on the part of the Prime Minister. Disraeli at last began to have the ear of the House.

And now his luck changed. In the autumn the Irish famine determined Peel to repeal the Corn Laws. Here was an issue on which a really large — no one could say how large — section of the Conservative Party was likely to rebel. Moreover, Peel handled the situation badly, was over-confident, and presumed too much on his prestige with the party. When Parliament opened on 22 January, one of the great days of Disraeli's life, Peel endeavoured to play down the whole business as if it was a mere detail. He spoke long and boringly and he was followed by Lord John Russell with equal length and tedium. It looked as if the House would disperse without further discussion that afternoon, and a general impression might have been given that no great opposition existed to Peel's proposals. At that moment Disraeli, who does not seem to have concerted his action with anyone else, leapt to his feet and made a devastating personal onslaught upon Peel, carefully prepared no doubt but not the less effective for that. It was one of those rare occasions when a speech may have changed the course of political history, by focussing and expressing the dumb, incoherent resentment of the Tory backbench squires. No doubt there would have been some opposition to Peel even if Disraeli had not existed. There was, for example, the Anti-League,[1] and there was Lord George Bentinck. Nor would it be right to say that Disraeli *led* the opposition during 1846. It was Bentinck, King of the Turf, son of a duke, grandson of one prime minister and nephew of another who did that. The squires of old England would not have taken orders from Disraeli at that time. He was Bentinck's adjutant and counsellor, not his equal. Disraeli's own account of their relationship in his *Lord George Bentinck* has been criticized for being over-modest and self-deprecatory, but in fact it seems far nearer the truth than the popular notion that Bentinck was a mere puppet.

What Disraeli could and did provide were the fireworks,

[1] See Mary Lawson-Tancred, 'The Anti League and the Corn Law Crisis of 1846', *Historical Journal*, 1960, iii, no. 2, for an account of this body, which did much to provide the organizational basis on which Bentinck and Disraeli built up the parliamentary opposition to Peel.

the display, the parliamentary show which a largely inarticulate opposition needed if its morale was to be kept up and its vengeance pursued to the bitter end. Here he was unsurpassed. Peel, accustomed to the respectful attention of the House, had never encountered anything quite like the mocking invective of which Disraeli was a master. He could not cope with it. Forty-five years later Morley asked Gladstone what Disraeli's famous attacks were really like. 'Mr. G. said Disraeli's performances were quite as wonderful as report makes them. Peel altogether helpless in reply. Dealt with them with a kind of righteous dullness.'[1] Only on one occasion did Peel score in this strange duel and even then far less effectively than he might have done. He asked why, if Disraeli had always had such a low opinion of his leader, was he willing to serve under him in 1841. With a degree of folly explicable only by panic Disraeli in a personal statement denied having ever asked for office. His reply apparently carried little conviction, but for reasons that are still obscure Peel did not nail down the lie by reading out Disraeli's letter. This was a piece of luck. Such an exposure might well have been ruinous.

The story of the way in which Peel was driven from office, and the Conservative party split from top to bottom, is well known. Less clearly recognized is the nature of the cleavage. Its significance was that almost every man of intellectual ability, administrative experience, and parliamentary repute followed Peel. The list given above of those who were ahead of Disraeli such as Gladstone, Herbert, Cardwell etc., all supported the repeal of the Corn Laws. Suddenly and overnight, Disraeli, who a few months earlier had no prospects of promotion whatever, found himself with only a single person, Bentinck, between himself and the almost inevitable reversion to the leadership of the Conservative Party in the House of Commons. Not the leadership of the party as a whole. That was and remained for over twenty years firmly in the hands of Stanley, the future fourteenth Earl of Derby, who had

[1] John Morley, *Life of Gladstone* (1903), III, 465.

already been called up to the House of Lords and who was the only man of importance to resign from Peel's cabinet. Then in September 1848 Bentinck suddenly fell dead while walking alone on the Welbeck estate. Disraeli, as the Duke of Argyll puts it, became 'by this strange event . . . the only piece upon the board on that side of politics that was above the level of a pawn. . . . He was like a subaltern in a great battle where every single superior officer was killed or wounded.'[1]

Disraeli was genuinely shocked at Bentinck's death. He was devoted to his leader, and there was never anything cold-blooded or calculating about him. But in fact Bentinck's death came opportunely for his career ; late enough for Bentinck to have made the arrangements which committed his brothers to financing the purchase of Hughenden and setting up Disraeli as a country gentleman ; soon enough for there to be no viable alternative to Disraeli's succession as leader. If there had been, Stanley would certainly have exploited it. As things were he had no option but to accept as colleague and second-in-command the man whom he believed to have corrupted his brother for gain.

But the very circumstances which made Disraeli heir to the leadership of the party in the House of Commons also made that leadership into a barren inheritance. For the next thirty or so years England, or rather the classes which controlled English politics, continued to be conservative with a small 'c'. That is to say, they wanted to preserve the Crown, House of Lords, House of Commons, Church of England, Justices of the Peace, rights of property and inheritance, etc., with as little change as was compatible with the new forces transforming society. Yet some changes were inevitable. It was vital to bend rather than break and the events of 1846 convinced powerful elements in those conservative classes for the second time in sixteen years that the Conservative party with a big 'C' was unfitted to cope with the problem. The

[1] Argyll, *op. cit.* I, 279.

first time had been in 1830 when the Tories dug in their toes over parliamentary reform. Peel had managed patiently to overcome that set-back, and, aided by the frivolity and incompetence of the Whigs, to present his party by 1841 as the safer alternative. In 1846 the cleavage over the Corn Laws ruined the Conservative party for twenty-eight years. It was not only the strong economic arguments, and the Irish famine which convinced the upper class that the Corn Laws must go, but fear, irrespective of the merits of the case, that revolution would ensue if they did not. The very fact that almost every man of ability, Whig or Tory, favoured repeal is in itself a fact of the greatest significance, and cannot be laughed off. No one can read the comments of the leading political figures between 1846 and 1852 without realizing how genuinely they feared that a Derby-Disraeli administration would provoke a revolutionary situation by the reactionary nature of its policies.

> The office of leader of the Conservative party in the H. of C. at the present day [wrote Disraeli to Derby in 1848] is to uphold the aristocratic settlement of this country. That is the only question at stake, however manifold may be the forms which it assumes in public discussion and however various the knowledge and labour which it requires.

Peel, Russell, Aberdeen, Palmerston, Graham, even Gladstone at that time, would have concurred in the importance of upholding the aristocratic settlement. They would not have agreed — and here they had the queen and the prince on their side too — that Disraeli and Derby with their totally inexperienced followers were the best people to do it. And in 1852, although there was no serious attempt to reimpose protection, Disraeli's budget which muddled up all the income tax schedules and made flagrantly sectional concessions to the landed interest seemed to confirm that opinion. It was further confirmed when fifteen years later Derby and Disraeli went to the opposite extreme to the Duke of Wellington in 1830 and passed a Reform Bill which apparently upset the aristocratic settlement far more than the Whig measure which they had themselves thrown out the previous year. It was not until 1874 when Gladstone, no longer checked by Palmerston and Russell, had thoroughly disturbed the conservative classes with his reforms that they at last turned to the Conservative party. Disraeli had six years of office with a real majority. But as he pathetically said : 'Power has come to me too late. There were days when on waking I felt I could move dynasties and governments : but that has passed away.'

What has been said so far should not be regarded as implying that Disraeli was other than a most remarkable personality. He was not in general a far-sighted observer or a profound thinker, although he had percipient flashes on occasions. He was a bad administrator and he lacked the sense of detail which makes a legislator ; but he was a consummate politician, a great debater, and a man of immense parliamentary courage. For twenty years he had to face virtually unaided all the great parliamentarians of the day, Palmerston, Russell, Graham, Gladstone, Cobden, Bright. He may have lacked their weight and authority but he stood up to them. He was always in his place, on his own side a professional in an age of amateurs, constantly watching for his chance. He believed, if ever a man did, that the job of the opposition is to oppose. He may almost be said to have invented the notion. He was a man of infinite resource, ingenuity, and tenacity even to the very end of his life when he was worn down by a combination of gout, asthma, bronchitis, and Bright's Disease. 'Disraeli is a man who is never beaten', wrote Gladstone. 'Every reverse, every defeat is to him only an admonition to wait and catch his opportunity of retrieving, and more than retrieving his position.' For courage, determination, and sheer parliamentary skill Disraeli must surely stand as high as anyone in the list of our statesmen.

The fact that the Conservatives were either in opposition or only in office as caretakers for twenty-six out of the thirty-two years during which Disraeli held a key position in the party was not wholly his fault — although there are times when one feels that the case for his being considered the unconscious architect of the Liberal party is almost as strong as the more orthodox view that he was the creator of the modern Conservative party. No one can read the published correspondence between Gladstone and the principal Peelites without realizing what a big part sheer hatred and mistrust of Disraeli played in their crucial decisions in 1852 and again, especially, in 1859 to link their fortunes with the Whigs. Yet if it was not wholly his fault it was also not inappropriate that he should have spent so long in opposition. For despite the remarks of the Duke of Argyll, there was a sense in which Disraeli remained an outsider although not in quite the way in which it has become usual to regard him.

The Victorian governing class can be regarded as composed of two distinct but overlapping circles. There was the traditional landed aristocracy with their country cousins, the county squires. They were rich, grand, but tolerant, sometimes eccentric, not infrequently dissipated. They belonged to monosyllabic clubs; they often kept racehorses, and frequently kept mistresses. The Regency bucks, the dandies of the 1830s, the 'heavy swells' who clustered around the Prince of Wales, form a lineal succession for a certain type among them, though it is right to add that there was also a strong element of conscientiousness and devotion to public duty, often to be found in the very same people. Then there was another circle, the hard-working serious-minded upper *bourgeoisie*, often educated at the same schools and universities as the aristocracy but somehow indefinably different. There were M.P.s and ministers among them, and they furnished the majority of civil servants, divines, judges, academics. Of course there was no hard clear line of division. Many people belonged to both worlds or had a foot in both. Gladstone married into a great Whig family. The Marquis of Salisbury married the daughter of a judge.

Disraeli had nothing in common with this second circle, the one which was perhaps most characteristic and influential in mid-Victorian England. The aristocracy has always been tolerant of individual oddities. It has been prepared to put up with adventurers, entertainers, jesters, buffoons and freaks, as long as they were clever, amusing, and generally gave good value. Actors, writers, artists have never found it difficult to do what Disraeli himself somewhat harshly described the Editor of *The Times* as doing — 'simper in the enervating atmosphere of gilded saloons'. Disraeli's rise was from the very first essentially a social rise, a conquest of London society where he made an impression which for good or ill was seldom forgotten. Moreover — however queer this may seem — he regarded himself as an aristocrat. The Jews were, in his view, a fundamentally aristocratic race, and he believed that he belonged to their most aristocratic branch. Whatever his hosts may have thought Disraeli regarded his reception in the great palaces of the English nobility not as the social triumph of an adventurer but as the belated recognition of an equal.

The moral and intellectual problems which vexed the other and graver portion of the Victorian ruling class were outside Disraeli's comprehension. The religious anxieties of the Tractarians, the issues raised in *Essays and Reviews*, the question of economics and politics which exercised Bagehot or John Stuart Mill constituted a language which he simply did not understand, or if he did, refused to take seriously. He could feel for the wretchedness of the poor. The contrast between the Two Nations appealed to his sense of drama, and within his limited power he did try to do something about it. But he could not feel for the moral anxieties of the prosperous intelligentsia. 'My Lord I am on the side of the Angels.' Thus, in an address to the Oxford dons and undergraduates at the Sheldonian Theatre in 1864, did he dismiss the whole controversy about Darwin's *Origin of Species*. The intellectual world detested him almost to a man. Who but Disraeli could have brought Freeman and Froude on to the same platform?

It is perhaps in his approach to intellectual, especially religious problems that Disraeli most missed the proffered chance of Oxford. Religion dominated politics in the nineteenth century to an extent which historians are only now beginning to appreciate. An agnostic home, an education at a Unitarian establishment, his own highly individual views on Judaism and Christianity,[1] made him singularly ill-equipped to deal with it. Oxford would at least have given him an idea from within of how the Anglican establishment worked, and at lowest have given him some idea of how to exercise patronage. Not that he was in any way against the Church of England. He was all for it. But the arguments that he used in defence of the Establishment, *e.g.* that it was an essential safeguard in local government, or that it would enable the state to check dangerous religious enthusiasm in political issues might well have made the devout mutter, '*non tali auxilio*'. As for patronage he was hopeless. Oxford might have given him at least some acquaintance with clerical personalities. As it was — 'Send me Crockford's Directory', he would cry, adding despondently, 'I must be armed.'

But this is to anticipate. It was to be a long time before Disraeli was in a position to exercise clerical patronage. If we ask what he stood for during and just after 1852, the answer is twofold. He certainly stood — and indeed from his early years always had consistently stood — for what he termed 'the aristocratic settlement'. On that point his letter to Derby had been perfectly sincere. The ordered hierarchy of the county with its landlords and tenant farmers, Justices of the Peace, Lord Lieutenant, and Bishop, was after all the only world which he knew or to which he belonged — apart from London society. It was the world of the Frank Greshams threatened by the Dukes of Omnium, a world, as Disraeli saw it, menaced by the liberalism, cosmopolitanism, free thought of the great Whig magnates, seeking power with the aid of their dubious allies, Scotchmen, Irishmen, dissenters, shopkeepers, and manufacturers. By 1852 Disraeli really was a

[1] The best account of Disraeli's religious opinions is in Cecil Roth, *Benjamin Disraeli, Earl of Beaconsfield* (New York, 1952).

country gentleman, however incongruous the thought may be, and his problems were in part the problems of the minor squirearchy, the possessors of a landed income of over £1,000 a year which was about the figure for the Hughenden estate and which the latest historian of the subject sets as the lower limit for the landed gentry of the day.[1] At the end of his life he wrote to Salisbury. 'I have been profoundly convinced that the greatness and character of our country depended on our landed tenure. All the rest I look upon, and have ever looked upon as "leather and prunella".[2]

By the time he wrote those words it could truly be said that the Liberals had become the enemies of the landed interest, and that its prosperity was bound up with the fortunes of the Conservative party. But, as we saw earlier, that was by no means obvious in the 1850s, and it brings us to the second part of the answer to the question what Disraeli stood for. He was a party politician who believed, or anyway acted as if he believed, that his party alone could protect and preserve the landed interest and hence the greatness of England. The object of politics was power and he was ready to do anything within constitutional limits to secure it. Here he was in sharp contrast with Derby. Early in 1853 Derby's son wrote to Disraeli: 'The truth is — I have always told you so and I see it now more clearly than ever — the Captain does not care for office but wishes to keep things as they are and impede "progress"'.[3] Disraeli could never accept this, to him, defeatist view. He had longed for office, enjoyed every moment of it when he at last got in, and had been ready to engage in the most unpromising manœuvres in order to avoid going out. The history of Conservatism during the next

[1] F. M. L. Thompson, *English Landed Society in the Nineteenth Century* (1963), p. 112. Of course the combined income of Disraeli and his wife was a great deal more but much of her income came from sources other than land.

[2] Monypenny and Buckle, *op. cit.* VI, 596.

[3] Hughenden Papers, Box 111, B/X/S/585: Stanley to Disraeli, 20 January 1853.

fifteen years could be written in terms of the polite but none the less real dispute between the two men over the correct rôle of the party. Was it to oppose the Whigs in order to turn them out or in order to modify their policy while they were in? No doubt it was bound to be a bit of both. The question was one of emphasis and neither of them could push their case to extremes. Disraeli knew that there were some limits to the principle of the union of opposites. Derby appreciated a point which Stanley referred to later in the letter quoted above — 'the impossibility of keeping together the party in opposition, unless they see before them a fair prospect of getting into Downing Street'.[1] But it was Derby who was leader and who had the confidence of his supporters. On the whole his views prevailed.

Disraeli was an opportunist, but all politicians are so in some degree. If they do not adapt themselves to changing times they soon become antediluvian survivals, incapable of affecting events. It cannot be said that any consistent ideology ran through his life, apart from his determination to uphold by however varying means the aristocratic settlement and the territorial constitution. Of course he had ideas, some of them curiously prescient, some of them surprisingly silly, and many of them contradictory. He said so many different things that judicious selection can present him in almost any light. His ideas may have been wild and eccentric but at least the mere fact of his leadership dispelled the notion so prevalent in the 1850s and 1860s that the Conservatives were the stupid party. His personality repelled some people but fascinated others, and many of them very intelligent men too. A glance at his Cabinet of 1874 compared with Derby's in 1852 or 1858 shows how much talent and ability had moved into the party during the interval.

Disraeli contributed something else to politics — an element of sheer fun. More than any single individual he made political and parliamentary life gay, amusing, exciting, and dramatic.

[1] *Ibid.*

Buckle shrewdly observes that he saw his own life as a highly tinted romance. The era in which he lived was one of moral earnestness. Disraeli was the obverse of all that, and his success reminds us of what we easily forget — that the Victorians had to have some relief. They could not take Gladstone all the time. Disraeli's champagne-like sparkle is to be found often in his speeches and everywhere in his novels which, for all their absurdities of character and plot, remain supremely readable. It is this quality which invests so many of his observations with a sort of timeless wit and humour — like that of Sydney Smith and Oscar Wilde. Of all statesmen in our history he occupies most space in the *Oxford Dictionary of Quotations* ; and no wonder. But on the whole Englishmen mistrust the wits and cynics, and are uneasy when they encounter either fancy or irony — at all events in politics. In general — and this is far from confined to the Victorian era — we prefer our public men to be serious figures bearing the load of responsibility on their shoulders with a conscious air and sedate demeanour. As Disraeli himself put it, 'The British People, being subject to fogs and possessing a powerful Middle Class, require grave statesmen'. Perhaps, when all is said and done, that is the real explanation why he spent so many years in opposition. He was never a grave statesman.

9

C. H. Stuart

THE PRINCE CONSORT AND MINISTERIAL POLITICS 1856–9

THIS subject arises from the nature and balance of the printed sources on the life of the Prince Consort. Between 1875 and 1880 Sir Theodore Martin produced his voluminous official biography, which has been the foundation of all subsequent study;[1] but he did not set out with the idea of writing on this generous scale. When in 1876 he published his second volume taking the Prince's life up to the opening of the Crimean war, he expressed the hope that he would complete his work in one further volume.[2] He took three. More recently there have been two serious studies of the Prince Consort and his times, both making use of the royal archives at Windsor, one by Mr. Roger Fulford and the other by Mr. Frank Eyck.[3] Each of these, at least in the political sphere, concentrated heavily on the years before 1854 in complete contrast to Martin. Eyck indeed allotted only one-tenth of his book to the years after 1854, while Fulford, though concluding that 'the attainment of full political power by the Prince' should be dated from the Crimean war,[4] scarcely did more than notice the political changes which followed it. In justice to both these distinguished scholars it

[1] Theodore Martin, *Life of the Prince Consort*, 5 vols. (1875–80). This work was widely read in its day; in 1892 it was published in Calcutta 'condensed and translated into Bengali' with the sub-title 'Father of the future Emperors of India'.

[2] Martin, *op. cit.* II, v.

[3] Roger Fulford, *The Prince Consort* (1949); and Frank Eyck, *The Prince Consort* (1959).

[4] Fulford, *op. cit.* p. 180.

is only fair to add that neither aimed primarily to discuss the Prince's past in ministerial politics. Eyck sought 'to do justice to his essentially Anglo-German and inter-European personality' and not to deal at length with parts of his life 'which are already well known';[1] and Fulford not only attempted to complete the story of the Prince's political activity over the whole of his life but also most successfully treated his personal character, his family relationships, and his influence in the realm of the arts.

The contrast between the extensive and detailed narrative of Martin for the years after 1854 and the comparative silence of modern biographers for the same period, suggests that there is a case for considering anew the part played by the Prince in the politics of the late 1850s. A start was made in this direction by the late G. B. Henderson who published in 1936 an article on 'The Influence of the Crown, 1854–56';[2] this scholarly paper revealed for the first time the important part played by the court in launching Palmerston's first government in 1855, but it did not take ministerial politics beyond that point. It seems reasonable, therefore, to take up this story where Henderson left it and to consider the period of Prince Albert's 'full political power' in more detail than Fulford granted it, relying for this purpose on the considerable material which is available in print.

This material soon began to accumulate after the completion of Martin's biography which had opened the door to public discussion of the Prince's part in politics. Within ten years it had been followed by the publication of two sets of memoirs, each of which in its own way contributed to further understanding of the Prince's political activity. First in importance were the *Greville Memoirs* of which the last two volumes covered the years 1852–60;[3] next were the memoirs of the Saxon minister in London, Count Vitzthum,

[1] Eyck, *op. cit.* pp. 9-10.
[2] Reprinted in G. B. Henderson, *Crimean War Diplomacy* (1947), pp. 68-97.
[3] *The Greville Memoirs* (*Third Part*), 2 vols. (1887), ed. H. Reeve.

covering much the same period.[1] This valuable political material, together with some personal details appearing in the memoirs of the Prince's brother, Ernest II of Saxe-Coburg-Gotha, published about the same time, was used by Charlotte M. Yonge to produce in 1890 a short, fair, and modest book on the Prince which has since been totally forgotten, although it might well be claimed to have more intellectual merit, even if perhaps somewhat less moral fervour, than her better-known works of fiction. Subsequently, as each of the leading statesmen of the Prince's time was commemorated in substantial biographies, more evidence became available, and in 1907 this was greatly extended with the publication of the first three volumes of the *Letters of Queen Victoria*.[2]

Such was the printed evidence when in 1921 Lytton Strachey published his famous life of Queen Victoria more than half of which was devoted to the years before the death of the Prince in 1861. Strachey's importance in relation to the Prince was double. On the political side he recognized, in parts exaggerated, the significance of his career, skilfully extracting from Martin's evidence the conclusions which that cautious courtier had tended to leave implicit in his copious narrative. On the personal side he tore away the shrouding veils of pietistic reverence which for sixty years had concealed the Prince's character. Unfortunately he did not stop there. Not content with this useful, necessary but destructive process, he sought also to offer a positive interpretation of the Prince which would be modern in idiom, comprehensible in form, and acceptable in Bloomsbury. Martin had shown clearly how hard and continuously the Prince had worked.[3] At the same time his interpretation of Albert's existence as one of selfless devotion to duty inevitably left an impression of resignation and disappointment. Charlotte Yonge had

[1] C. F. Vitzthum von Eckstaedt, *St. Petersburg and London, 1852–64*, 2 vols. (1887).

[2] *The Letters of Queen Victoria, 1837–61*, 3 vols. (pocket ed., 1908), ed. A. C. Benson and Viscount Esher.

[3] Martin, *op. cit.* II, 474–6, III, 66, and V, 273–5.

accepted this when she wrote of his life as 'worn and disappointed'.[1] Strachey related these two points and argued that Albert's willingness to undergo long hours of work was to be attributed to his personal loneliness and unhappiness. 'His work,' he wrote, 'for which at last he came to crave with an almost morbid appetite, was a solace and not a cure ; the dragon of his dissatisfaction devoured with dark relish that ever-growing tribute of laborious days and nights.' [2] From this ingenious conclusion he moved with rapid Freudian steps to the suggestion that Albert's unhappiness was caused by sexual abnormality.[3] Clever, internally consistent, and elegantly phrased, this interpretation of Albert's character has one major disadvantage ; it is demonstrably false, and it has since been so demonstrated by Fulford.[4]

Strachey, then, was important as an interpreter rather than as a source of new materials, except in so far as he had incorporated in his work passages from Greville's *Memoirs* which had been suppressed in the 1880s. Since he wrote, two valuable additions have been made to the printed sources in the publication of selections from the Prince's German correspondence, one by Hector Bolitho [5] and the other by Kurt Jagow.[6] These are the chief printed authorities on which any assessment of the Prince's political influence between 1856 and 1859 must be made.

When the Treaty of Paris ending the Crimean war was signed in March 1856 Palmerston's government had been in office for a little over a year. By this time his Cabinet was almost wholly Whig in composition. Although he had originally taken on Aberdeen's coalition Cabinet unchanged

[1] C. M. Yonge, *The Prince Consort* (1890), p. 222.

[2] Lytton Strachey, *Queen Victoria* (Phoenix Library edition, 1933), p. 181.

[3] *Ibid.* pp. 86 ; 90-1 ; 113-14.

[4] Fulford, *op. cit.* pp. 44-45 ; 104 ; 250-3.

[5] H. Bolitho, *The Prince Consort and his brother, 200 new letters* (1933). Bolitho also wrote a life of the Prince Consort which he called *Albert the Good* (1931) but he went out of his way to avoid political history and aimed at 'a new kind of biography . . . with much of the novelist's technique'.

[6] Kurt Jagow, *Letters of the Prince Consort, 1831–61* (1938).

except for the retirement of Aberdeen himself, Russell, and Newcastle, within a fortnight he had lost the majority of its so-called Peelite members, the powerful triumvirate of Graham, Gladstone, and Herbert. Of the Peelite connection Argyll and Canning alone remained and of these Canning soon departed on his appointment as Governor-General of India. Lord John Russell, it is true, had been brought back when the Peelites left, but he also had resigned within a few months.[1] These complex changes meant that from July 1855 Palmerston and his Whig colleagues faced the triple opposition of the Conservatives led by Derby and Disraeli, the small rump of Peelite leaders, and the 'Manchester men' led by Cobden and Bright working in alliance with Russell. But this opposition was more formidable in appearance than in reality. Their only source of common action was opposition to the war, and it was this very opposition which alienated men of moderate feeling in the House of Commons and enraged patriotic feeling out of doors. The continuance of the war and the successful capture of Sebastopol thus strengthened Palmerston and weakened his opponents. So by the spring of 1856, as Argyll noted in his autobiography,[2] 'the opposition was completely broken up. It had no name to conjure with. Lord John Russell was entirely discredited. So was Gladstone.'

This was the political situation which faced the court when the war ended and it is of interest to consider what part the Crown, and therefore the Prince,[3] played in bringing it about. At first sight, from the point of view of the Queen and the Prince, the appearance of Palmerston as Prime Minister presents a paradox. One of the leading features of the years between 1846 and 1851 had been the bitter hostility of the

[1] For the details of Lord John Russell's conduct in 1855 see Henderson, *op. cit.* pp. 33–67.

[2] George Douglas, eighth Duke of Argyll, *Autobiography and Memoirs*, 2 vols. (1906), II, 51.

[3] 'To discuss the influence of the Crown is to discuss the influence of the Prince.' Henderson, *op. cit.* p. 69.

court towards Palmerston, their attempts to persuade Russell to remove him from the Foreign Office, and their pleasure at his eventual dismissal. Yet in the ministerial crisis of February 1855 it was, as Henderson showed, the support of the Queen and the Prince which insured the successful launching and initial survival of his government. To resolve this paradox it is necessary to look back at the political developments of the previous ten years.

Peel's action in repealing the Corn Laws had not only split his party but also created a balance in the House of Commons which, even after the general election of 1847, left Russell's ministry precariously placed. In effect Russell depended on Peel's support to stay in power. When Peel died in 1850, his chief followers had come to resent his policy of supporting Russell's government without joining it. Their commotions, and Russell's excitable actions designed to free himself of his dependence on them, further disturbed the balance of parties in the Commons. At the same time the court's conflict with Palmerston over the conduct of foreign policy was sharpened. Here in detestation of Palmerston was a purpose for royal intervention in politics and in the weakness of Russell's parliamentary position the opportunity of effecting it. In August 1852 Graham summed up this situation in one phrase, 'Princes are strong when Ministers are weak'.[1] The outcome of this situation was the coalition government of Aberdeen formed in December 1852 which was greatly to the court's liking.[2]

One aspect of the coalition government which was particularly pleasing to both the Queen and the Prince was the humiliation of Palmerston, who now accepted the Home Office and in so doing took third place in the Cabinet under

[1] British Museum, Add. MSS. 43190, Graham to Aberdeen, 27 Aug. 1852' The copy of this letter among Graham's papers at Netherby (hereafter cited as Netherby. MSS.') was marked by his daughter for the benefit of his biography, C. S. Parker, 'this must be omitted'. Sensibility to royal feelings of this sort limited much that was published before 1914.

[2] See C. H. Stuart, 'The formation of the Coalition cabinet of 1852', *Transactions of the Royal Historical Society*, 5th series, IV (1954), 45–68.

Aberdeen and Russell. For fully twelve months after this Palmerston remained under the weight of royal displeasure. In August 1853 when the Queen visited Ireland she took Granville, not Palmerston, even though his position as a secretary of state gave him superior claims to attend her.[1] The next month he was only accepted as minister in attendance at Balmoral after Aberdeen had spoken with the Prince and made written representations to the Queen on his behalf.[2] At the end of the year when Palmerston made his tactical resignation and swift return the Prince suspected him of hoping that 'Lord Lansdowne . . . would go out with him and that the whole Ministry would be blown into the air'.[3] But the coming of the war and Palmerston's vigorous and patriotic conduct in Cabinet throughout 1854 altered the attitude of the court and by January 1855 Greville recorded Stockmar's opinion that 'the Queen is much softened towards Palmerston'.[4]

Patriotic feeling was predominant in bringing about this change. At the height of the crisis in February 1855, when it appeared as if no alternative prime minister to Aberdeen would be forthcoming, the Queen noted, 'if Lord Lansdowne refuses, there is Lord Palmerston *himself.* I know this would be objectionable in many respects, and personally not agreeable to me, but *I* think of *nothing* but the country.'[5] The Prince made the same point when he urged on Derby that 'this country was in a crisis . . . which could not be successfully overcome unless political parties would show a little more patriotism than hitherto'.[6] But subordinate to these worthy feelings in drawing the court close to Palmerston in the dark days of February 1855 was the revulsion of feeling in the minds of both Queen and Prince against Russell.

[1] Greville, *op. cit.* I, 82.
[2] *Ibid.* 87 ; *Letters of Queen Victoria*, II, 450–1.
[3] Martin, *op. cit.* II, 534.
[4] Greville, *op. cit.* I, 220.
[5] Henderson, *op. cit.* p. 81.
[6] *Letters of Queen Victoria*, III, 84, printed with slight changes in Martin *op. cit.* III, 204.

The rivalry between Russell and Palmerston for the leadership of the Whig party was the theme of politics throughout the 1850s. This rivalry came into the open in December 1851 when Russell dismissed Palmerston from the Foreign Office. It was taken a step further in February 1852 when Russell's government was forced to resign owing to a defeat in the House of Commons partly engineered by Palmerston, who commented at the time in a memorable phrase, 'I have had my tit-for-tat with John Russell'.[1] But it did not end there, and it is too little remembered that this contest swayed to and fro for another seven years. The immediate consequence of Palmerston's 'tit-for-tat' was that the Queen and the Prince, who in the years before 1851 had consistently supported Russell against Palmerston, were now able to adjudicate between them by subordinating both to Aberdeen. Whereas Palmerston, as we have seen, accepted this unpalatable solution with dignity, notwithstanding the signs of continued royal displeasure, Russell chafed against it from the start. So far as the court was concerned Russell's conduct appeared selfish and unpatriotic. As early as August 1853 the Prince told Stockmar that 'Lord John . . . seems dissatisfied with his position' and he added the fear that Russell would bring down the government and so 'destroy what has cost us so much pains to construct'. At the same time the Prince surmised that Russell's purpose was simply to take on the premiership for himself.[2] The next year he opened a special file which he headed 'Concerning the part which Lord John Russell took in breaking up Lord Aberdeen's Governm^{t}, Nov. 1854–Feby 1855'.[3] As the winter progressed Russell's colleagues came to share this view and they were determined not to serve under him. When eventually the government fell this was made plain and both the Queen and the Prince agreed that in inviting Russell to try to form a government the Queen's

[1] Evelyn Ashley, *Life of Lord Palmerston*, 2 vols. (1879), II, 230.
[2] Martin, *op. cit.* II, 502–3.
[3] Henderson, *op. cit.* p. 34.

purpose was simply 'to have his eyes opened to his own position'.[1]

Political observers at this time saw clearly what was behind Russell's behaviour. So in February 1854 Clarendon told Greville that 'Lord John would break up the Government' and that what was taking place was a 'political duel' between him and Palmerston.[2] As this duel extended, political opinion hardened in favour of Palmerston, and in this respect the Queen and the Prince were in sympathy with it. By the end of the parliamentary session of 1854, although Greville was still prepared to suspend judgment between the two contestants, he foresaw that it was Russell who would soon be making fresh difficulties; within six months he had been proved correct, and in January 1855 he wrote: 'Nothing can, in my opinion, justify Lord John, and his conduct will, if I am not mistaken, be generally condemned'.[3]

This, then, was the background to the court's support of Palmerston in 1855. Whereas in 1851 royal decision had favoured Russell and in 1852 it had subordinated both, in 1855 it supported Palmerston and completed Russell's humiliation. Now it was Russell's turn to cherish his resentment and brood upon his chances of a 'tit-for-tat'. He had some reason for resentment. It had always been his firm understanding when consenting to serve in the coalition government that as soon as the administration had settled down Aberdeen would make way for him to resume as prime minister. Much afterwards Greville recorded that the Duke of Bedford tried to establish by reference to the chief persons concerned whether or not this had been the case, and he noted that, although recollections were not firm, it could safely be concluded that no such engagement was given when the government was formed. Nevertheless he added, 'I did hear some time afterwards that such had been Aberdeen's expressed wish and Lord John's expectation'.[4]

[1] *Letters of Queen Victoria*, III, 92, 95.
[2] Greville, *op. cit.* I, 141.
[3] *Ibid.* 177, 181, 230.
[4] *Ibid.* II, 75.

This is not wholly just to Russell. Certainly Aberdeen had made no written promise when forming his government; but he had been in correspondence with Russell in the previous summer in the course of which Russell had pointedly alluded to his 'pretensions' and the difficulties in face of them.[1] Aberdeen's answer had been clear and encouraging. As for the difficulties in the way of Russell becoming prime minister he wrote, 'I can only regard them as merely temporary', and he added that in his view Russell should 'come to no decision calculated to interfere with your perfect freedom of action'. Russell took this happily and reported it to Graham with the comment, 'This advice I think very good'.[2] It was not unreasonable for him later to build on this exchange the hope of soon succeeding as prime minister. Furthermore, we know on the authority of Aberdeen's son and private secretary at the time that in the summer of 1853 Aberdeen thought 'the time had come when he might retire in Lord John's favour', and that he obtained the reluctant assent of most of his friends to this arrangement.[3] It was the crisis in the Near East which made Aberdeen change his mind and in so doing he goaded Russell into the excitement which the Prince later recorded and deplored. But whatever the rights and wrongs of Russell's conduct before 1855, his conduct during that year completed his loss of favour at court. As Disraeli put it to Lady Londonderry at the time, 'Johnny [is] in disgrace'.[4]

One fact remains to be explained to understand Palmerston's position in relation to the court at the end of the Crimean war. This is the loss of favour of the Peelite leaders. In one sense, as Gladstone subsequently pointed out, the retirement of Aberdeen from active politics after the fall of his government broke the links between 'Peelism' and the court where hitherto

[1] Spencer Walpole, *Life of Lord John Russell*, 2 vols. (1889), II, 155.

[2] Brit. Mus. Add. MSS. 43066, Aberdeen to Russell, 8 Aug. 1852; and Netherby MSS., Russell to Graham, 22 Sept. 1852.

[3] Arthur Gordon (later Lord Stanmore), *The Earl of Aberdeen* (1893), p. 218.

[4] W. F. Moneypenny and G. E. Buckle, *The Life of Benjamin Disraeli*, 6 vols. (1910–20), III, 567.

'it had certainly weighed as an important factor of political opinion'.[1] But it was not this alone. When Graham, Gladstone, and Herbert agreed to join Palmerston's government they did so at Aberdeen's earnest request; Aberdeen in his turn acted in response to a direct appeal from the Prince to achieve this end.[2] Accordingly when, within a fortnight, the three Peelite ministers resigned the Prince felt outraged. 'Things have gone mad here,' he wrote, 'the political world is quite crazy.' Within a few months Gladstone and Graham in the Commons were supporting a motion for peace and the Prince was reduced to the use of exclamation marks when reporting this to Stockmar. Subsequently he even wrote to Aberdeen protesting against 'the line which your former friends and colleagues . . . have taken about the war question'.[3]

Thus many strands were intertwined to produce the paradox of a Palmerstonian government launched and supported by the court. But once the war had been won the political situation was bound to alter and Palmerston's position would then be weakened by several hidden difficulties. First of these was the probability that with the end of the emergency of the war the old differences between Palmerston and the court would reopen. Even while the war was still in progress Granville had noticed, while staying at Balmoral in September 1855, that 'the old mistrust haunts them' and had commented to Clarendon, 'we must do our best to keep both sides quiet'. Clarendon agreed with this diagnosis and the need to accommodate feelings, adding that in his view the Queen and the Prince were 'unfair to Palmerston, and . . . always ready to let their old rancour against him boil up and boil over'.[4] By

[1] W. E. Gladstone, review of Martin, *op. cit.* vol. III, *Church Quarterly Review* (1878).

[2] *Letters of Queen Victoria*, II, 98–101.

[3] Martin, *op. cit.* III, 213, 282, 289–91.

[4] Sir Herbert Maxwell, *The Life and Letters of the Fourth Earl of Clarendon*, 2 vols. (1913), II, 92. This exchange is reversed, abbreviated, and misdated in Lord Edmond Fitzmaurice, *The Life of the Second Earl Granville*, 2 vols. (1905), I, 105, 120.

the end of 1855 Greville considered that thanks to Clarendon's 'constant endeavours' Palmerston 'was on very good terms with the Queen',[1] but a few months later the Prince was complaining to Stockmar of 'the gossiping rumour . . . that the Court is more pacific than Palmerston'.[2]

The second difficulty facing Palmerston in 1856 was the hostility of Russell. Although he had lost confidence at court, in the country, and among most of his former Cabinet colleagues, Russell remained a powerful figure in the House of Commons whose devotion to the cause of parliamentary reform was always liable to provide a rallying point for radical M.P.s satiated by victory and anxious now for signs of legislative progress in the government. Russell in fact, when out of office, was, as Gladstone noted in 1855, 'of necessity a centre and nucleus of discontent'.[3] Fortunately for Palmerston, Russell's character prevented him from taking full advantage of this situation. He was impulsive, easily influenced and flattered by his family connections and often gave the impression of indifference to the views and interests of his natural parliamentary allies. Graham who was in close touch with him in these years confided in his journal in April 1859, 'this little man swells into self-importance and self-confidence, which are boundless, in that little world of Eliots and of Toadies where he lives and has his being'.[4]

Finally, Palmerston was faced with a House of Commons elected in 1852 containing many members who had supported him during the war but who would now view him more critically. Here his greater personal skill in managing people enabled him to outmanœuvre Russell. Besides, as he was in office he could use the power of patronage which this gave him to win support among them.[5] Argyll glanced at this situation in characteristic language.

[1] Greville, *op. cit.* I, 315. [2] Martin, *op. cit.* III, 457.

[3] John Morley, *Life of W. E. Gladstone*, 2 vols. (pocket ed., 1908), I, 392.

[4] Graham's journal for April 1859 in Netherby MSS.

[5] Fitzmaurice, *op. cit.* I, 139, and H. C. F. Bell, *Lord Palmerston*, 2 vols. (1936), II, 137.

One of the many mad suggestions which arose out of the passion of the time was that the Crimean misfortunes were all due to what was called aristocratic government. . . . There was not the smallest reason to believe that there were in the House of Commons, or in the country, neglected men of the middle classes who would have conducted affairs better. But there were undoubtedly at that time in the House of Commons a considerable group of clever and discontented men, who thought very well of themselves, and who had much influence with the press. In attacking what they called the aristocracy, they were in reality blowing their own trumpets, and were perhaps hopeful of forcing an entrance into the highest offices of the State.[1]

Palmerston's skill and good fortune enabled him to overcome these difficulties during 1856. In April the Queen conferred the Garter on him in recognition of the peace, and no signs appeared of the reopening of the old rift between him and the court. Russell did not stir up trouble ; the Commons were quiet. In January 1857 Herbert wrote to Gladstone, 'I must say I look on Palmerston as a fixture'.[2] In February Greville judged that the government was not likely to be shaken in the coming session.[3] Then in March the old Crimean alliance of Conservatives, Cobdenite Radicals, the Peelite triumvirate, and Russell came together to censure the government's conduct in the affair of the lorcha *Arrow* at Canton. They triumphed by 16 votes in a full house. Palmerston advised a dissolution of Parliament to which the Queen, who was expecting her last child, willingly agreed. Even before this had been finally settled the Prince had made it plain to Palmerston that the Queen was physically unable to endure a ministerial crisis and would prefer any other alternative to the government's resignation.[4] In the general election which followed Palmerston and the government were widely successful. On the surface Palmerston was stronger than before.

[1] Argyll, *op. cit.* I, 558-9. This situation is not perhaps peculiar to the 1850s. [2] Lord Stanmore, *Sidney Herbert*, 2 vols. (1906), II, 68.
[3] Greville, *op. cit.* II, 84. [4] *Letters of Queen Victoria*, III, 228-9.

In spite of this, within twelve months Palmerston was defeated and forced to resign. How this came about and what part the court played in it are difficult questions which puzzled men at the time and which have received no very clear answer since. 'The decline and fall of Palmerston and his Government' Greville somewhat forbiddingly observed, 'deserve a narrative which might, if well handled by some well-informed writer, be made very interesting.'[1] Without attempting to fulfil these stringent conditions it is possible to offer a general analysis of the facts behind Palmerston's defeat in 1858. First, there was the revival of the issue of parliamentary reform within the new House of Commons. Intelligent observers had seen this possibility as soon as the election was over. Herbert who, as we have seen, had been defeatist in January 1857, expressed the view in April that 'Palmerston's popularity [is] a bubble' and also that among the liberals this popularity was 'fast becoming secondary to some undefined but not immediate measure of Reform'.[2] What Herbert saw from the point of view of an opponent, Granville confirmed from inside the government. 'Palmerston has had a great triumph,' he told Canning, 'the danger consists in the probable formation of a numerous and respectable Liberal party opposed to the present Government. The game is not an easy one for anybody as regards Reform.'[3] Even before the election, according to Argyll, 'a good number of the Cabinet . . . felt that the name of Palmerston, and the Crimean War, might do very well for the passing moment, but would not do to live upon for the whole duration of a Government'.[4]

Here then was one rock ahead. Strangely the Prince did not see it, and in May he told Stockmar that the delaying answer on reform which Palmerston had contrived at the opening of the new Parliament was right.[5] But a second problem on which the Prince felt deeply was to divide the

[1] Greville, *op. cit.* II, 207.
[2] Stanmore, *op. cit.* II, 92-3.
[3] Fitzmaurice, *op. cit.* I, 227.
[4] Argyll, *op. cit.* II, 76.
[5] Martin, *op. cit.* IV, 42.

court once again from Palmerston. This was the Indian mutiny. When news of this first arrived in June, Palmerston was inclined to treat it lightly and to postpone a decision on whether or not to send military reinforcements. The Queen and the Prince urged vigorous action from the start.[1] Once Palmerston recognized the gravity of the situation he acted energetically and defended himself firmly against the royal criticisms.[2] But he did not thereby recover their confidence. In July the Prince wrote, 'our Ministry is . . . by no means up to the mark;' a week later he added, 'we are constantly digging our spurs into their sides;' and by September he could write, 'Palmerston is once more possessed by all his juvenile levity'.[3]

On this issue, moreover, Palmerston had lost his friend at court in that Clarendon was utterly defeatist. 'Great disasters are still in store for us' he told his wife in September. In the same month he told Cornewall Lewis that Palmerston's 'want of energy, and his system of hoping and believing, instead of acting, have disappointed me woefully'.[4] The effect on Palmerston's position at court was marked. 'Cupid is rather out of favour' was Granville's report to Canning.[5] By November the Queen was feeling the ground with Clarendon to see if he would consent to be the next prime minister in the event of Palmerston's health failing. Clarendon refused to co-operate and urged on a reluctant Queen the claims of Russell in such an eventuality.[6] Thus the shadows of 1859 were already visible with Palmerston out of favour, Russell still in disgrace, and a third candidate required. Nor was India the only problem on which the court differed with Palmerston. For during 1859 the Prince began to entertain suspicions of Napoleon III's intentions in Europe and to

[1] *Letters of Queen Victoria*, III, 234-5, 241. Martin, *op. cit.* IV, 77-82, 90-1.
[2] *Letters of Queen Victoria*, III, 243.
[3] Martin, *op. cit.* IV, 84, 88, 125.
[4] Maxwell, *op. cit.* II, 150, 153.
[5] Fitzmaurice, *op. cit.* I, 261. 'Cupid' was his code-name for Palmerston.
[6] Greville, *op. cit.* II, 134.

question Palmerston's easy confidence in his good-will towards England. This difference was to grow over the next two years.

Meanwhile, although the Indian mutiny had weakened Palmerston at court, it strengthened him, temporarily at least, in the country. In November he made a characteristic fighting speech at the Lord Mayor's banquet. The popular response led him into a serious political error. He decided to use the problem of settling the government of India as an excuse for dodging the question of parliamentary reform at home. His Cabinet colleagues saw his plan and deplored it. Granville wrote to Argyll in October, 'I think with you that Pam's great object in mooting the Indian question is to damp the reform of home institutions'. The next month Argyll wrote to Sir George Grey, 'we shall meet a more formidable opposition than some of us seem to suppose, if we use India to shirk the question of Reform'.[1] By December Clarendon could write to his wife. 'Reform will be the rock on which the government will go to pieces'.[2]

Two accidental circumstances helped to fulfil the fears of the Cabinet. First was the financial crisis of the autumn of 1857. This was brief, but just as Palmerston's jaunty attitude towards the mutiny had separated him from the court so his breezy confidence in face of commercial bankruptcies lost him support in the country. Then early in 1858 he completed his alienation of the Commons by including Lord Clanricarde in his Cabinet. This unfortunate nobleman had recently been the victim of 'some unpleasant disclosures in the Irish courts'. Palmerston's over-confidence had led him into this final error. To have offended the middle classes by showing levity about money was rash ; to complete this by ignoring conventional sexual morality was fatal. In the end, with suitable irony,

[1] Argyll, *op. cit.* II, 94-5 ; see also *ibid.* 97 and 103. In September Granville had warned Canning that Palmerston saw India as a 'counter-irritant to Reform'. See Fitzmaurice, *op. cit.* I, 260.

[2] Maxwell, *op. cit.* II, 158.

Palmerston was defeated in February 1858 by that same alliance which had attacked him a year before for bullying the Chinese and which now censured him for yielding to French demands in introducing the Conspiracy to Murder Bill. The occasion of his defeat is immaterial. As the Prince observed, 'he would have been turned out that same week' over Clanricarde's appointment 'had he not been turned out on the Refugee question'.[1]

In this new situation the court behaved initially with moderation and good sense. Derby was given every chance to form a stable government, but the Prince did not pin great hopes on the Conservatives. 'Our Derby Ministry is now complete,' he wrote in March, 'but whether it can stand, the gods only know.' The next month he openly accepted that 'the decision of Derby's fate will depend purely on whether Lords Palmerston and John Russell are reconciled'.[2] In May, after much consultation, the Queen allowed Derby to know that he would not be refused a dissolution if he asked for one, and in this way enabled him to preserve his position in the Commons. In the course of these consultations Aberdeen's advice was asked as to a successor to Derby if he should resign. The answer was plain, 'The Queen would . . . have no alternative but to send for Lord Palmerston'.[3] When a year later Derby did resign, the Queen and Prince had sufficiently changed their minds to attempt to avoid both Palmerston and Russell by sending for Granville. This strange decision, which invited failure, was the culmination of royal intervention in politics during the Prince's lifetime, and its understanding presents some difficulties.

It seems probable that as a result of their differences with Palmerston during 1857 the Queen and the Prince were not deeply chagrined at his sudden departure. The Prince was certainly puzzled by his loss of popularity which he regarded as a remarkable and curious phenomenon and which he found

[1] Martin, *op. cit.* IV, 195. [2] *Ibid.* 194, 205.
[3] *The Letters of Queen Victoria*, III, 288.

S

difficulty in explaining satisfactorily to himself.[1] Greville, for his part, suspected that the Queen was unwilling 'to see Palmerston made all powerful' and so found it easy to reconcile herself to the Derby government.[2] At the same time the Prince's suspicions of Napoleon III increased — in August he wrote in his journal, 'I am conscious of a change in the Emperor' [3] — so that on several grounds a political settlement without recourse to Palmerston became more attractive. Yet if such a solution was palatable to the court it is still hard to see how they should have convinced themselves by 1859 that it was feasible. Political conditions were markedly different from those of 1852 when last they had adjudicated between the 'Dowager Premiers' [4] and subordinated both to Aberdeen.

Two reasons suggest themselves in explanation. First, there is some evidence to suggest that Prince Albert was losing his capacity to appreciate the political *nuances* of the time. He had given his time and mind for two or three years more to foreign affairs and to administrative questions, such as the reorganization of the Army and of the government of India, than to problems of domestic politics. Indeed by the beginning of 1859 these problems, when mentioned in his letters, were accompanied by such phrases as 'I am weary and out of heart' or 'I am thoroughly disgusted'.[5] Vitzthum, who had a long audience with the Prince in March 1859, observed that 'he has now more than ever the threads of high politics in his hands',[6] but their conservation clearly shows that by this he meant foreign affairs. This decline in the Prince's political awareness at home exposed the Queen to the humiliation of June 1859 when Granville accepted her commission to form a government and failed. The Prince might have prevented this, but he did not.

It is not enough, however, to attribute the Queen's humiliation to her own wishful thinking and to the Prince's loss of

[1] See Martin, *op. cit.* IV, 195, and in particular the Prince's Memorandum of 4 Sept. 1858 in *Letters of Queen Victoria*, III, 300-1.

[2] Greville, *op. cit.* II, 211. [3] Martin, *op. cit.* IV, 275. [4] *Ibid.* 262.

[5] *Ibid.* 362, 410. [6] Vitzthum, *op. cit.* I, 320.

touch. Granville himself is much to blame. If the Prince could have prevented the Queen from sending for him, he, once sent for, could have refused to attempt the task, as Clarendon had indicated he would have done in 1857. But Granville accepted. His decision was the consequence of a mixture of miscalculation and vanity. He had long been a favourite at court. His appointment to the Foreign Office in 1851 on Palmerston's dismissal had been made in deference to the court; before that he had worked with the Prince in the arrangements for the Great Exhibition. In June 1856 he had been sent on the special mission to attend the coronation of the new Tsar, and in 1857 'at the Queen's spontaneous suggestion'[1] he had been given the Garter. But he had begun to entertain political ambitions even before receiving these favours. In February 1856 he wrote to Canning 'I find I have gained ground in the House of Lords this year, and I am treated in the Cabinet as the next leader much more than I was'.[2]

When Palmerston fell, Granville's first inclinations were loyal. 'We mean to stick by Palmerston', he told Canning, while to Argyll he wrote, 'naturally Palmerston is head of the position'. But at the same time he agreed to take on the leadership of the opposition in the House of Lords.[3] And within a few months his loyalty began to evaporate. He disapproved Palmerston's tactics in opposition, thought he had 'lost all influence in the House of Commons', and observed at the same time that 'Johnny has not profited in the least by the descent of his rival'. As for himself he now thought, 'I am accepted as leader, and I never knew our side of the House so cordial and united'.[4]

Early in the session of 1859 the Derby government resolved to introduce a parliamentary reform measure of its own and was soon in trouble. Palmerston and Russell drew together

[1] Fitzmaurice, *op. cit.* I, 227. [2] *Ibid.* 169.
[3] *Ibid.* 294–5, and Argyll, *op. cit.* II, 112.
[4] Fitzmaurice, *op. cit.* I, 300, 310–11.

and the government was defeated. Derby dissolved Parliament and the general election showed that although the Conservatives had gained some seats they had not gained enough. The government was seen to be doomed and it was clear to all who were opposed to it that arrangements would have to be made to ensure the co-operation of Palmerston and Russell in a new ministry.

In May Granville took a hand in this arrangement. Russell had put out feelers to Palmerston and to Herbert, who of the Peelites had always been the most friendly to Palmerston; Granville promptly wrote to Herbert to extend this negotiation, explaining that Palmerston and Russell had agreed to the new government being 'as comprehensive as possible'. He then added, 'they thought it not right to anticipate any decision of the Queen. I have not the slightest idea whom the Queen will send for of the two.'[1] This choice between them was as Herbert saw 'the archdelicate question'. But in his answer to Granville he foolishly opened the door to misunderstanding; 'I am satisfied', he wrote, 'that the two rivals should agree *to serve together as the Queen may direct*'. This language allowed the idea of their being directed to serve together under a third party.[2] Palmerston was too old a hand to be caught by this. He accepted, as he put it to Herbert, that 'we cannot discount the Queen's intentions', but he made it plain to Granville in interview, and confirmed this in writing, that though he would serve under Russell, and Russell under him, 'such an agreement would not apply to the case of any other person being commissioned by the Queen to form an Administration'.[3] The door was closed to reason but Granville's vanity kept it open. The reconciliation of

[1] Stanmore, *op. cit.* II, 188.

[2] *Ibid.* 187, 194 (my italics). That this possibility was intended by Herbert is clear from his language to Gladstone the next day; 'The two leaders must have come to this understanding that both are willing to serve the Queen together, and in such mutual relations as she may herself think best'. *Ibid.* 196. See also Fitzmaurice, *op. cit.* I, 328.

[3] Stanmore, *op. cit.* II, 192. Fitzmaurice, *op. cit.* I, 330.

Palmerston and Russell was greatly to his long-term advantage. As Greville saw, it was likely to lead to his succeeding as Prime Minister 'at some not very distant day'.[1] But he would not wait.

In June, Derby's government was defeated by 13 votes and resigned. The Queen and the Prince were by now positively sad to lose them. In April the Prince had observed, 'we are greatly pleased with our ministry in these trying circumstances [*i.e.* the Franco-Austrian war] . . . . Palmerston on the other hand is out and out *Napoléonide*.'[2] As Palmerston was feared for his foreign policy so Russell was disliked as the apostle of democracy.[3] The way was clear for Granville. Unchecked by the Prince, encouraged by Granville's readiness to make the attempt, the Queen gambled and lost. When it came to the point Palmerston, while expressing readiness to serve under Granville, insisted on the lead in the Commons. Russell was not prepared to take the third place unless Palmerston went to the Lords and he himself led in the Commons. Each repeated that he would serve under the other. The Queen and Granville were neatly trumped. Russell characteristically removed any chance of being chosen himself by rubbing in the Queen's defeat. 'Her Majesty', he wrote cruelly, 'must encounter the difficulty of making a choice.'[4]

Granville now withdrew and the Queen sent for Palmerston, who was able to form a government without difficulty. But Russell claimed the Foreign Office as 'of right' and in this way excluded Clarendon who would have been preferred in that position by the court and by Palmerston himself. The Prince was embittered; 'we have got a Ministry which exactly suits Louis Napoleon', he wrote to the Prince Regent of Prussia. 'Our attempt to keep Granville with Clarendon at the Foreign Office was foiled owing to the personal ambition of Lord John Russell.'[5] But Granville was as much to blame as Russell. Nobody, as Greville pointed out, had

[1] Greville, *op. cit.* II, 248. [2] Martin, *op. cit.* IV, 434. [3] *Ibid.* 414.
[4] Fitzmaurice, *op. cit.* I, 337. [5] Jagow, *op. cit.* p. 336.

thought of any possibility but Palmerston or Russell ; yet when Granville failed he was 'rather disappointed'.[1] His fault was to blind himself to the facts seen clearly by others. Clarendon had written kindly to him in this sense at the time.[2] But a few months later Clarendon was to comment less kindly to the Duchess of Manchester : 'the greatest fault one can commit is not to know oneself and if he [*i.e.* Granville] has deluded himself in that ignorance and has attributed to it the enormous mistake he made it is enough to embitter his life. Vanity and ambition however put a strong coating on a man and are good preservatives against truth entering his soul.'[3]

Although the Prince was mistaken in 1859 his motives were just and his purposes constitutional. Strachey used a flamboyant phrase of Disraeli's, reported by Vitzthum, to erect a theory that the Prince, had he lived, would have brought the Crown into conflict with parliamentary government.[4] This strange doctrine has persisted in spite of Fulford's trenchant criticism,[5] and has recently been improved upon by Mr. Raymond Mortimer who has claimed that 'Prince Albert was determined to increase the power of the Throne, and might have caused a revolution if he had survived'.[6] The reverse is the truth. As Clarendon told Greville in 1857, all Prince Albert's 'views and notions are those of a Constitutional Sovereign'.[7] The Prince was essentially rational and his influence on the Queen was always moderating. The Queen's letters became more emotional, less constitutional, perhaps also more interesting, after his death in 1861.[8] If anti-monarchical feeling made any progress in England it was because the Prince's influence over the Queen had been removed. The death of the Prince meant that, to borrow a phrase of Edmund Gosse, in her mind 'the delicate stream of reason was drowned by the turbid volume of superstition'.

[1] Greville, *op. cit.* II, 252.
[2] Fitzmaurice, *op. cit.* pp. 333-4.
[3] A. L. Kennedy, *My dear Duchess* (1956), p. 67.
[4] Strachey, *op. cit.* II, 192.
[5] Fulford, *op. cit.* pp. 237-9.
[6] *Sunday Times*, 15 March 1964.
[7] Greville, *op. cit.* II, 126.
[8] See Frederick Ponsonby, *Recollections of Three Reigns* (1957), p. 12.

Yet Vitzthum's memoirs can supply a fitting epitaph to the political activity of Prince Albert. In October 1858 Vitzthum met Metternich, then almost at the end of his long life. They discussed English politics. 'What is called the British Constitution', Metternich said, 'is like a whist party *à trois*. The dummy is public opinion. The House of Commons has now for many years been holding this dummy. The Crown and the House of Lords have, therefore, been obliged to play against it. . . . The House of Lords has lost many a trick. I must admit, however, that the Crown's hand has not been played so well for a long time as it has been of late years.' [1]

This was certainly true and that it was so was the achievement of the Prince. His personality did not charm as his son's was later to do : there was in his manner, as Gladstone once observed, 'something that was related to stillness and chillness' ; [2] yet he deserved well of his adopted country. In 1855 he rested his defence of himself against the wild charges that were then being made on 'sincerity and patriotism', [3] and any study of his conduct in this period establishes his claim.

[1] Vitzthum, *op. cit.* I, 253.
[2] H. J. Gladstone, *After Thirty Years* (1928), p. 328.
[3] Martin, *op. cit.* III, 221.

10

Michael Maclagan

THE WHITE MUTINY

THE Indian Mutiny has attracted a vast literature. Many of the British survivors penned their memoirs, and recent Indian historians have sometimes attempted to read the events of 1857,

> That year when the tempest of mutiny broke
> And the empire swayed like a storm-bent oak.

as a premature war of independence. But less attention has been paid to the fact that before the embers of conflict had been stamped out, there was a second outbreak of disloyalty and refusal to obey orders; and, moreover, that it occurred among European troops. This crisis arose in the autumn of 1858, reached a peak in the spring of 1859, and last manifested itself in the summer of 1860.[1]

To understand its nature some examination is required of the various kinds of troops serving in India in 1858–9. They fall into two main divisions, Queen's troops and Company's troops. The Queen's troops were units of the ordinary British army, but serving in India; in May 1857 they comprised four regiments of cavalry and twenty-two of infantry, but at the height of the Mutiny campaign this figure had risen to seventy-five Queen's regiments of all arms. None of them were concerned in the White Mutiny.

The forces of the Honourable East India Company were of a less familiar pattern. To begin with, each of the three

[1] A brief account of these events is given in M. Maclagan, *Clemency Canning* (1962), pp. 242–50, which may also be consulted for the general background.

'Presidencies' — the major provincial governments ruled from Calcutta, Bombay, and Madras — had its own army. It was, for all practical purposes, only the Bengal army which rose in 1857. Within each Presidency there were a large number of native regiments, in which Indian troops and N.C.O.s were commanded by British officers. But in addition each Presidency had three purely European regiments of infantry, and some battalions or batteries of European artillery. These forces were enlisted in the British Isles for permanent service in India (in fact, the number of recruits from both Ireland and Scotland was considerable). Of the nine white infantry regiments in the three armies, the first was in each case of some antiquity, dating back to at least the eighteenth century, the second had been added in 1839, and the third in 1853.

But the Indian Mutiny of 1857–8 created a special problem in the Bengal Presidency, and further white regiments were raised to meet it. There thus came into existence the 4th, 5th, and 6th European infantry and five regiments of European Light Cavalry.[1] To man these formations the other ranks were mainly recruited at home, but the officers were drawn from the large pool of Company's officers in India belonging to corps whose Indian other ranks had mutinied. Thus, for example, the officers of the 4th European Light Cavalry were almost to a man those who had led the 9th and 10th Regiments of (Indian) Light Cavalry, which had both mutinied. It was among these white regiments in the Company's service that the trouble arose in 1858 and 1859, trouble which had its roots not in the campaigns of the Indian Mutiny, but in the field of politics.

The main battles of those crucial years play no part in the story. It is perhaps enough to say that after the capture of Delhi in September 1857, and still more evidently after the final capture of Lucknow in March 1858, there could be no possibility of the failure of British rule. But extensive

[1] For details of these regiments see *East India Register*, 1859 (2nd edn.), pp. 90–111.

operations of mopping up and pacification still remained to be achieved before peace was absolute again ; indeed the restoration of order was not formally proclaimed until 8 July 1859. The events of the Mutiny had, however, focussed attention on the rule of the East India Company, and successive governments at Westminster had resolved that it must be ended. Three different India Bills were laid before the House of Commons. The first had been introduced by Palmerston in February 1858, but his government fell later in the same month. The second was introduced by Disraeli in March, but was largely the brain-child of Lord Ellenborough ; it was more or less laughed out of existence, and probably only the divisions in the Whig party saved the ministry from defeat. In April there was a general debate on certain Resolutions, a form of procedure proposed by Lord John Russell. It was left to Lord Stanley in June to introduce a third Bill which finally received the Queen's assent on 2 August. In the words of *The Times* :

> The most compendious description that we can give of Lord Stanley's Bill is that it is the measure of Lord Ellenborough stripped of its most prominent and startling absurdities. . . . If not a very good Bill, it has ceased to be like its predecessor a very good joke.[1]

In general, control of the possessions, territories, interests, and armies of the East India Company was transferred to a new Secretary of State in London, assisted by a Council of fifteen members. Two of its clauses must be looked at more closely. Clause LVI ran :

> The Military and Naval Forces of the East India Company shall be deemed to be the Indian Military and Naval Forces of Her Majesty, and shall be under the same Obligations to serve Her Majesty as they would have been under to serve the said Company, and shall be liable to serve within the same territorial Limits only, for the same Terms only, and be entitled to the like Pay, Pensions, Allowances and Privileges, and the like Advantages as regards Promotion and otherwise, as if they had continued in the Service of the said Company . . . and the Pay and Expenses of and incident to

[1] *The Times*, 22 June 1858 : leading article.

Her Majesty's Indian Military and Naval Forces shall be defrayed out of the Revenues of India.[1]

And Clause LXX provided that the Act should take effect thirty days after its passing. Accordingly, the rich and varied history of 'John Company' came to an end at the beginning of September 1858, and the troops which it had raised became 'the Indian Military Forces of Her Majesty'. They had not in any way been consulted about this change.

The Governor-General (or Viceroy[2] as he now began to be styled) was required to communicate this great event to the peoples of India. A proclamation from the Queen reached him on 17 October, and it was issued with full pomp and ceremony and in eighteen different languages on 1 November.[3] In the main it is addressed to the natives of India, and it contains no direct reference to the transfer of the armed forces.

While the public controversy over the India Bills had been in progress, the whole military organization of India was also under discussion. Late in 1857 the East India Company had asked the Governor-General, Lord Canning, to appoint a large mixed commission, composed of civil servants, Company's officers, and Queen's officers, to consider the future of the three Indian armies. Lord Canning, who still had the remains of the Mutiny on his hands, and the native Bengal army in ruins around him, replied, almost tartly for him, that he had better uses for the men in question. He decided instead to nominate a single officer who should canvass informed opinion by a series of questionnaires.[4] For this arduous task he chose

[1] The Act may be found in full, and with the various amendments proposed by the Lords, in *Parliamentary Papers* (1857–8), II. Palmerston's Bill is at pp. 261–86 ; Lord Ellenborough's at pp. 287–312 ; and Lord Stanley's Act in its final form at pp. 371–94.

[2] The term 'Viceroy' is nowhere used in the Act for the better Government of India, but is employed in Queen Victoria's Proclamation, and figures in the East India Register from 1859.

[3] For a full text of the Proclamation see Maclagan, *op. cit.* pp. 350–2.

[4] Canning to Vernon Smith, 6 March 1858. All letters from and to Lord Canning are quoted from his MSS. preserved at Harewood, unless other indication is given.

Lt.-Col. H. M. (later Sir Henry) Durand, who carried out his task with conspicuous success; eighty-five officers and officials of various ranks were cross-examined and their answers carefully analysed and collated.[1]

As soon as Lord Stanley's Bill had passed its third reading, the English government also turned to this problem. In July 1858 a Royal Commission was appointed and invited to consider twelve specific questions. It finally made its report in March 1859.[2] The chairman was General Jonathan Peel, a younger brother of Sir Robert and at that time Secretary of State for War, and his colleagues were Lord Stanley himself, the Duke of Cambridge, four senior officers of the Queen's Army, and four retired officers of the East India Company's forces. Among the points which the Commission had to consider were the manner of transferring the forces of the Company to the Crown, how far European troops in India should be troops of the Line doing a tour of duty in India or troops specially raised for permanent service in India, and whether the two kinds of European force could be consolidated. Some English interests, including the Queen,[3] the Duke of Cambridge and the War Office, were soon seen to be against the creation of any large European force not controlled by Whitehall; most informed opinion from India was strongly in favour of such an army. In the event the occurrences of the White Mutiny were to play a significant part in deciding the issue.

As has been mentioned already, the proclamation announcing the end of the East India Company and the beginning of

[1] Durand to Canning, 28 Aug. 1858. The results of Durand's work may be found in *Parliamentary Papers* (1859 : 1), V, 407, 408-13, 419-522.

[2] The report of the Commission was twice issued as a Parliamentary Paper, together with all the minutes of evidence. It can be found in *Parliamentary Papers* (1859 : 1), V, and (1859 : 2), VIII. The latter version contains a long minority report by Major-General H. Hancock (Hon. E. I. C. Service) and also a quantity of material supplied by Durand whom Canning had sent to England to represent his views before the Commission.

[3] See, for example, *Letters of Queen Victoria*, ed. Benson and Esher, III, 404-10.

direct rule by the Queen was promulgated on 1 November 1858. Reaction was swift and unexpected. Brigadier T. Chute, commanding at Lucknow, reported on 2 November that the men of the 4th European Light Cavalry 'consider that they are not bound to serve the Queen until they are re-enlisted for that purpose, and receive a fresh bounty'. He was informed at once by the Viceroy, who was then at Allahabad, that these pretensions were untenable. 'The 56th clause of the new Act for the Government of India shows this to be the case. Pray take immediate measures for disabusing these young soldiers of their error. This should be done kindly and temperately in the first instance, but the mistaken pretension must be put down.' The 4th European Light Cavalry was a new formation, but more serious news was to come. On 8 November Major-General Sir Hope Grant, the commander of the Oude Force which was in the field against the rebels, reported that several men of the 1st Madras Fusiliers were unwilling to serve Her Majesty on the grounds that they were attested solely to serve the Honourable East India Company ; accordingly they asked for their discharge.[1] This was a regiment of great distinction, already well known when Clive began his career, which had fought and marched heroically under General Neill in the summer of 1857. The Queen's Proclamation had thus presented the authorities with an unforeseen problem, which underlined some of the constitutional complexities of India at that date.

The Act had been passed by the British Parliament, sitting in London, and it does not appear that the parliamentary draftsman had envisaged any particular difficulties from Clause LVI. No alteration had been made in it during the debates, although considerable attention had been paid to the preceding clause which dealt with the liability of Indian forces to serve outside India. Indeed Clause LVI of the final Bill

[1] *Parliamentary Papers* (1860), LI, 4-6. This volume is almost entirely concerned with the disturbances among the European troops. *Parliamentary Papers* will be cited henceforth simply as *P.P.* Pages cited as printed.

was identical with Clause XXXVI of Lord Palmerston's Bill in February. No body in India could do more than interpret the wording of a British statute. Within India the Commander-in-Chief was responsible for the immediate control of the military forces, but was also actively engaged in the conduct of a one-sided but intricate campaign. Civil authority and ultimate military authority rested with the Governor-General in Council, but at this moment Lord Canning had positioned himself at Allahabad, while the other members of his Council (except for Lord Clyde, the Commander-in-Chief) were at Calcutta. And the historian of this period has always to remember that it took at least four weeks under the best conditions to send a message or despatch from Calcutta to London or vice versa; to state a case, have it discussed, and receive a reasoned answer often consumed a quarter of a year.

On 4 November Lord Clyde, perhaps better known through his long career as Sir Colin Campbell, had written his first private thoughts to the Viceroy:

This is a very ticklish question, as the idea will probably run through all the Company's European regiments. Enlistment is a personal matter, and I suspect that the men consider the law as on their side, although the Acts may have been so worded as to leave a loophole for such a contingency as that which has actually occurred, but was very certainly never anticipated. Anyhow it is very important that the men should know how they stand. I am surprised that the point should have escaped attention at home. I am not aware that allusion has ever been made to it. There would be great awkwardness, if not indeed calamity, if any serious misunderstanding should arise. I would earnestly recommend that a telegraphic message be sent to Mr. Ritchie [The Advocate-General] for his opinion and advice, in case of the law not being sufficiently clear to the comprehension of the private soldier. If it be not quite clear, the men should, I think, be liberally dealt with, and we must be prepared for many discharges. I am sorry to say that I cannot get in camp a copy of an attestation belonging to one of the Company's soldiers.[1]

[1] Clyde to Canning, 4 Nov. 1858.

A few days later this want had been supplied and the Commander-in-Chief again set forth his views in an official despatch.

4. You will observe in question 8 of that document that the soldier is asked the question whether he is willing to serve the East India Company. There is no doubt in the question; he is asked whether he will serve the East India Company 'only', and in the form of that attestation no alternative of serving the Crown is apparent.

5. At the bottom of the first page of the attestation, the soldier is sworn to be 'faithful' and bear 'true allegiance to Her Majesty' etc. But it would appear that this is in his capacity of serving the Company and of a British subject. It is an 'oath of allegiance' and in so far, as it seems to the Commander-in-Chief, distinct from the attestation which prescribes the particular service to which the soldier shall be hereafter bound.

6. Lord Clyde would beg leave to call to the recollection of the Governor General, with the greatest deference to his Excellency, a fact unknown except to military men, viz., that in the old regiments of the Crown a man cannot be transferred from one to another without his free consent, he having enlisted to serve in a particular regiment. Thus it happens that although the conditions of service are precisely the same in the various regiments . . . volunteers are called for the purpose who receive a bounty in consideration.[1]

A 'bounty' was a small capital sum of a few pounds, paid to the private soldier on first enlisting. The sum varied; at the time of the Crimea it had gone up to £6; in 1858 it was raised from £2 to £3, in both cases with a free issue of kit.[2]

Both the Advocate General and the Judge Advocate General of the Army gave as their opinion that the Act was unequivocal and that the soldiers of the East India Company were bound to serve the Crown without re-enlistment (and in consequence without a fresh bounty).[3] There can be no doubt that they were correct in this interpretation; but there can

[1] Major-General Mansfield (Chief of Staff to Clyde) to Major-General Birch (Military Secretary to the Government of India), Letter No. 147 of 10 Nov. 1858. *P.P.* pp. 5-6.

[2] See Report of Commissioners on Recruiting, *P.P.* (1861), XV, 26 and 327.

[3] *P.P.* pp. 8-9.

also be no doubt that a large number of unlettered men thought that they had only enlisted to serve the Company and that they resented being arbitrarily transferred to the service of the Crown as if they were so many head of livestock.

Lord Canning wrote back to Clyde stating that he was not prepared to give the discontented men of the 1st Madras Fusiliers their discharge and emphasizing the clarity of Clause LVI which was confirmed by his Law Officers. He also argued that, even if the law were not clear, the effect of discharging some and re-enlisting others of the European troops must have a bad effect on the native soldiery. He added that he would be prepared to consider any representations which the troops made and to transmit them to the Queen's government.[1]

The Governor-General now reported to the Home government. In a long and formal despatch he rehearsed what had happened so far, and described his difference of opinion with Lord Clyde.

The law is plain and positive in its words ; I have not heard that any man has a doubt of its intention.

But it is objected that, by the extinction of the Company's Government, which this same law enacts, the soldier has acquired or considers that he has acquired, a right, of which the law would deprive him, and that it would be difficult, if not impossible, to make him understand any legal argument which should set aside this right. Therefore it is proposed that re-enlistment of the Company's soldiers should take place ; and this of necessity implies the discharge of all those who for any reason should decline to be re-enlisted.

Were the Government of India so to act, it would set up its own authority above that of the law and Parliament. It would do so the more pointedly in that it has never had the power to discharge English soldiers from the Indian army.

I consider that I should not be justified in surrendering the law to these objections.[2]

[1] Canning to Clyde, 14 Nov. 1858. See also Birch's official answer to Mansfield, *P.P.* pp. 6-8.

[2] Military Despatch of 18 Nov. 1858. *P.P.* pp. 1-4.

In private he wrote to Lord Stanley more frankly:

I could scarcely exaggerate the apprehension with which I should see any ground laid for a suspicion amongst the Sikhs (there are plenty in Oude) that misunderstanding had arisen between us and our English troops. . . . It might seem that the way to avoid an appearance of misunderstanding with these soldiers is to let them have their way. This is not so. English soldiers could not take their discharge from the Commander-in-Chief's camp, which is now in the presence of the enemy, without producing the worst effect upon our Native Troops.

And after soliciting the view of the Secretary of State and of the British law officers, he continued:

If the claim of right is denied, I would still recommend that something of favour be yielded. The Government of India might be authorized to give discharges to such, or to a certain portion of such, as desire them:—and to the rest, who would be willing to continue in the ranks, a concession of a year, or two, or more of service might be awarded.[1]

Over Christmas Lord Stanley was 'fairly floored by influenza' [2] but wrote briefly:

You will receive by this mail a short despatch [3] entirely approving the view you have taken of the claim of the late Company's European troops to be discharged. It is a question which may require a little more consideration, whether, as a matter of policy, some concession should not be made in the matter of bounty or otherwise, but on the demand for discharge there is, I think, no room for doubt.[4]

In a later letter he wrote that the Council of India [5] agreed with him, and that though he was taking legal advice he

[1] Canning to Stanley, 17 Nov. 1858.

[2] Talbot (Stanley's Secretary) to Canning, 23 Dec. 1858.

[3] Military Despatch to India, No. 110 of 31 Dec. 1858. See *P.P.* pp. 9-10.

[4] Stanley to Canning, 24 Dec. 1858.

[5] The Council of India was an advisory body, set up in London by the Act of 1858 to assist the new Secretary of State. It should be distinguished from the Council of the Viceroy or Governor-General which sat in Calcutta. The London Council was partly composed of directors of the East India Company but also included men like Sir John Lawrence and, later, Colonel Durand who were fresh from India.

had little doubt what the answer would be. He added that when Lord Palmerston had brought in his India Bill (*i.e.* in February 1858) he

used language to the effect that those who disliked the change ought to be free to leave the service. I think (to speak frankly) that considering the state of India a year ago, the pledge thus given was rather rash ; it may fairly be held as suspended by the subsequent and opposite decision of Parliament ; still, coming from the then First Minister, such words must have had their effect upon the malcontents.[1]

Since Palmerston's words came to be widely known in India, it may be as well to see exactly what that ebullient minister had stated. Speaking in the House of Commons on February 1858, he had observed :

The Army in India will consist, as heretofore, of Queen's troops forming part of the regular army of this country, and local corps enlisted in India. With regard to the Queen's troops no change will be made. With regard to the others, they will be transferred to the Crown from the service of the Company, subject to the same conditions of service as those under which they were enlisted, *and if they dislike that change, I think in common justice they will be entitled to their discharge.*[2]

This utterance was printed in the *Overland Mail* of 17 February and thus began to circulate among troops in India towards the end of March. It must be emphasized that the words were used about a Bill which did not become law and by a minister who forthwith fell from power.

Consultations continued in both India and England. In India Canning found himself obliged to reject a General Order drafted by Lord Clyde which he considered to be too lenient and to beg the question involved. Clyde was now against compromise :

If the men are wrong in their demands they must abide by the law and there should be no semblance of concession. If they should be

[1] Stanley to Canning, 3 Jan. 1859.
[2] Hansard, vol. CXLVIII, column 1287. Author's italics.

deemed to be right, they should have the benefit of the mistake which they may have made according to the custom of the service.[1]

Canning's action seemed to Stanley to be 'entirely judicious' and he was authorized by his father, the Prime Minister, to say that he (Derby) took the same view.[2] Lord Stanley proceeded to consult the English law officers, the Duke of Cambridge, General Peel (the Secretary of State for War), and other members of the Cabinet. Gradually opinion in London hardened against making any concession to the men.

Are we then to give reality and importance to their demand by admitting its validity to any extent? I see, no doubt, reasons in favour of concessions. Lord Palmerston's perhaps hastily given pledge of last year — which however he did not repeat; the possibility of future discussions in Parliament; the avowed sympathy of Lord Clyde with the men; and, above all, your opinion, though expressed when the state of things appeared more alarming than it does now, all plead for such a course. It is after much hesitation that I have come to the conclusion that neither the granting of bounty, nor of discharges, nor of a year's service, would be expedient.[3]

Formal instructions were then sent to Canning containing the written opinions of the English law officers (3 February) and a request to make this known to the troops (24 February).[4] Accordingly General Order No. 480 was drawn up on 8 April and circulated later that month to the various stations of India. It ran thus:

Upon the recent transfer of the forces of the late East India Company to immediate service of Her Majesty, under the provisions of the Act of the 21 and 22 Vict. c. 106, certain European soldiers of the East India Company's forces having claimed their discharge, or their enlistment anew into the Queen's service with fresh bounty,

[1] Clyde to Canning, 23 Nov. 1858, enclosed in Canning to Stanley, 3 Dec. 1858.

[2] Stanley to Canning, 8 Jan. 1859.

[3] Stanley to Canning, 28 Jan. 1859.

[4] Military Letters to India No. 40 of 3 Feb. and No. 67 of 24 Feb. 1859, *P.P.* p. 10.

the subject was brought under the consideration of Her Majesty's Government and referred to the Law Officers of the Crown.

His Excellency the Governor General of India in Council has now to announce to the European soldiers of Her Majesty's Indian forces in the three Presidencies, who were formerly in the service of the East India Company, that Her Majesty's Government have finally decided that the claim made to discharge, or re-enlistment with bounty, is inadmissible.[1]

It had been on 10 May 1857, and at Meerut, that the Indian Mutiny had broken out. Now, two years later, and from the same station, came once more the tidings of disquiet. Major-General J. F. Bradford, commanding the Meerut division, telegraphed on 2 May that men of the Bengal artillery and cavalry had shown a very bad spirit and were holding mutinous meetings. The discontent was particularly evident in the 2nd European Cavalry. The lull which had existed since November was over.

General Bradford continued to express anxiety. The spirit was bad in the cavalry: there had been threats of burning the barracks. News (which proved to be false) had been received of mutiny at Lucknow. What General Bradford described as highly inflammatory writings were discovered on the walls of the rear and the wash-houses, 'Stick up for discharge or bounty; if refused, immediately for Delhi'. 'Unity is strength.' 'I sincerely hope no one will volunteer for a fresh bounty. John Company is dead; we will not soldier for the Queen.' Such scribblings at least showed variation from those more normally to be found. On 5 May the Lieutenant-Governor of the Punjab reported that letters from Meerut to the artillery at Lahore had been inspected and gave evidence of a conspiracy to mutiny; the writers affirmed that the Queen's troops in India would not act against them. On the 7th came news from Allahabad that the 1st European Cavalry and 4th European Infantry were restive, intoxicated, and protesting in an excited manner against being handed over

[1] *Ibid.* p. 11.

'like bullocks' to the Crown. Indeed the state of the cavalry grew so bad that Major-General Sir John Inglis (commanding the Cawnpore division) proposed to disarm them. This he was forbidden to do by orders of the Governor-General, in order to avoid any open collision.

The Commander-in-Chief was at Simla, where something was temporarily wrong with the telegraph system, but moved at once to Kasauli in order to keep in touch. Canning wired to him at 1.30 P.M. on 5 May :

I think it of great importance that you should go at once to Meerut. My opinion is, that no concession whatever, as regards re-enlistment and bounty is possible. But that if collision can be warded off by giving discharges to some of the least guilty, this may be done. A simple discharge given at Meerut is in itself a punishment. This is the only relaxation I can suggest, although a collision will be full of danger. But do not consider yourself tied by this opinion. Whatever your own judgement recommends, rely upon being supported.

The Governor-General also held back two Queen's regiments (14th Light Dragoons and one infantry regiment) which were due to go home, and delayed the departure of a third. Courts of Inquiry were set up at Meerut and at Mianmir (the cantonment of Lahore) and a little later at Agra. Minor signs of discontent were reported from Berhampore, among the 5th Infantry, and at Gwalior. All these symptoms were embodied by Canning in a despatch to Stanley which rehearsed also the measures taken to relieve them. He ended by pointing out that he had felt obliged to offer some measure of discharges.

If the men who avail themselves of this opening should be only those who honestly desire to quit the service, the number will probably not be inconveniently large. But if from temper, or fellowship, or by the influence of bad advisers, whom a simple discharge will not satisfy, the example of these men should be followed by many of their comrades the Government of India will be greatly embarrassed.[1]

[1] Military Despatch No. 66 of 14 May 1859. Printed in *P.P.*, with the supporting letters and telegrams, pp. 14-34.

It seems clear that discussion and some measure of discontent had continued among the Company's white troops all through the winter, even if there had been almost no overt symptoms. Palmerston's speech had been circulating, and letters had been passing from station to station spreading the sense of injustice at being treated 'like bullocks'. In this the men of the Bengal Artillery seem to have been forward, and morale was certainly worse in the new regiments raised during the Mutiny than in the longer established corps. Gunner McDougall of the 1st Brigade, Bengal Horse Artillery, at Meerut, wrote to a friend in the 2nd Brigade at Mianmir :

I have got something very new to tell you about my troop and the 4th company [*i.e.* of the 4th battalion of Foot Artillery] and the light Calaverry was at a stand last night about the Queen and the Company. So now to be cup dark we made up all our minds to send a letter from one to an (? other) on or about the 5th instant, so you may be on the alert for it, for we all meet tonight at the Munkey Tank for to apint the day of strike for good or for the worse. . . . Exquse this bad riting as this is the 10th letter that I have sent away today so must exquse me And belave me etc.

A postscript indicates an intention to march to Delhi at a future date : why is not made clear, unless because this was the path which the mutineers had taken from Meerut two years before.[1]

Lord Clyde's immediate remedy was to issue a soothing order in which he announced the setting up of a Court of Inquiry. Every man was invited to come before it and say whether he had a grievance and, if so, what that grievance was. And he assured the troops that their sentiments would be carefully recorded and conveyed to the highest authorities. The court at Meerut was under Brigadier Richard Horsford, and began its sittings on 9 May. If the Government of India had done nothing else, it had at least acted rapidly. Other

[1] *Ibid.* pp. 28–9. Gunner McDougall was a groom, born at Inverness, who enlisted at Lambeth in April 1857, then aged 23. Proceedings against him were contemplated in July 1859, but it was considered unlikely that they would be successful ; after reference to the Governor-General the case was dropped.

courts were soon sitting at stations as widely dispersed as Dagshai (near Simla), Mianmir, Jubbulpore, Allahabad, Gwalior, Lucknow, Ambala, and Hazirabagh. The court at Meerut, to examine one instance in detail, sat for twenty-eight days and interviewed 773 witnesses. Most of their replies exhibited a remarkable similarity. Let Private W. Richardson, the last called at Meerut, serve as a sample. He had been attested at Liverpool on 2 June 1858, and had been posted to the 2nd Light European Cavalry. Like the majority of the deponents, he had not got his attestation paper. When asked what was his complaint, he answered : 'I listed for the East India Company for 12 years, or 14 if required ; and now the Company's done away with, I consider myself done away with. I'd take a free discharge, and consider afterwards what I'd do.' Pte. Richardson could not read but declared he had taken an oath to the Company, 'but there was nothing about Her Majesty'.

Occasionally more curious views were expressed. Bombardier Hamilton, a farrier of 2 Troop, 1st Brigade, Bengal Horse Artillery, presented a petition with his claim to be a free man. When asked if he had heard of the Act of Parliament, he said he had not ; when asked if he knew what an Act of Parliament was, he replied : 'Yes, a company of Lords sitting together'. He added : 'I don't wish to be turned over like a slave or dead stock'. Bombardier John Roddy, enlisted at Dublin and posted to the Third Battalion, Bengal Artillery, was asked about his oath and answered :

> Yes, as long as the East India Company existed, I considered myself their servant, and that I took the oath of allegiance to the Queen to bind myself, should the Company in whose service I had enlisted turn against Her Majesty and take the country, that I would not join or assist them in so doing. I knew that the East India Company had a larger army than Her Majesty, and I thought it possible such a thing might occur.[1]

[1] Full accounts of the Courts of Inquiry can be found in *P.P. passim*. The evidence of Pte. Richardson is at p. 522, of Bombardier Hamilton at p. 147, of Bombardier Roddy at p. 297.

Similar views were held elsewhere. Lieut.-General Marcus Beresford, a Queen's officer commanding the Mysore division, had long debates, which he reported in a demi-official letter, with an intelligent Scottish fusilier called Baird. This man thought that his oath to the Queen was 'only to defend her against aggressors, and those aggressors may have been the East Indian Company itself. They may have tried to create a power independent of the Crown.' Later on he said: 'When the feudal times ceased, man ceased to be a slave, to be transferred over as his masters pleased', but he also revealed that there had been conversations between the Madras Artillery and the 1st Madras Fusiliers, his own regiment.[1] It is pleasant to recall that before they parted the General gave the fusilier a tumbler of pale sherry and water: their whole interview rather recalls an Oxford tutor wrestling with a difficult undergraduate.

Ample evidence came to light of correspondence and discussions during the winter of 1858–9, but little of active urging to mutiny. At one station, Hazirabagh, the activities of a Roman Catholic priest, Father Josaphat, caused some anxiety; but his own colleague, the Catholic chaplain, regarded him as 'weak in his intellect' and thought that Josaphat should be removed to a secure place, where his failing could cause no trouble.[2] One regiment, the 3rd Bengal European Infantry, drew up a joint petition to the House of Commons, setting out their grievances. The soldiers of this unit were well aware of Palmerston's February speech.[3]

Faced with the growing and indubitable evidence of widespread dissatisfaction, the Government of India had to think again. By the middle of June 1859 Lord Canning and his advisers came to the conclusion that they must offer a free discharge to all. They duly reported their decision to Lord

[1] D.O. letter from General Beresford, 20 May 1859, to Lord Clyde, *P.P.* pp. 391–3.

[2] *P.P.* pp. 113 *et al.*

[3] Their petition is printed in the Calcutta *Phoenix*, 3 June 1859. *Cf. P.P.* p. 111.

Stanley in an official despatch which summed up the position very clearly and fairly and set out the course which they proposed to follow :

The men consider themselves to have been treated without due consideration in not having been allowed to volunteer to serve Her Majesty on the terms on which they had engaged to serve the Company, and in having been transferred by Act of Parliament to the immediate service of the Crown without having any option given to them in the matter. Some of the men claim their discharge, and have expressed their desire to return to England ; but the greater portion seem to aim at a grant of a bounty, and are desirous, or, at least, willing to be enlisted to serve Her Majesty, provided that boon be granted. The men argue for the most part that they did not take the first part of the oath 'to obey Her Majesty's orders, and the orders of the generals and other officers set over them' ; but only the latter part of the oath 'to be faithful to the Company and obey their orders, and the orders of their generals and other officers'. That this is a mistake is proved by the fact, that, in the original attestation certificates deposited in the Town Major's office, the oath in both its parts is entered *in extenso*, and the original signature of each man (and the mark of those who cannot write) is affixed immediately below the oath. But the mistake has been certainly impressed most forcibly on the minds of the men by the incompleteness of the copy of the attestation certificate with which each of them is furnished. The copy is deficient, indeed incorrect, in that it states with reference to their attestation, nothing more than this ; that after having replied to the questions put to him, and which are given at length, the recruit 'took the oath of allegiance and fidelity', the oath itself not being recited or otherwise subscribed. . . .

The Viceroy goes on to allude to the speech made by Lord Palmerston and comments :

We have found that knowledge of his Lordship's declared opinion is very general among the troops, and that they place great reliance on it in support of their claims.

It is certain also that the combination to persevere in these demands has been much more widely spread than we had in the first instance reason to believe.

Having very anxiously considered all the circumstances and probabilities of the serious discontent among the European soldiery, and having weighed well the effect, immediate and prospective, which any one of the several measures which have suggested themselves to our minds is likely to have on the discipline of the European troops, on that of the Native troops in the several Presidencies, and on the minds of the ever-observant and easily-aroused native population, we have determined to exercise the discretion which Her Majesty's Government have entrusted to us.[1]

The Governor-General in Council proceeded to give an analysis of the General Order which they were promulgating and which included an offer of discharge ; they anticipated that this offer would be taken up widely.

There will be those, who, for one reason or another, honestly desire to leave the army in India, and to be at home ; there will be some who have no such desire, but who, believing themselves aggrieved, have joined with the first in putting forward their objections to the mode of their transfer, and who will feel themselves bound to act in fellowship with their comrades ; and there will probably be many whose real object is a bounty, and who with the present prospect of easy re-enlistment in England, will be ready enough to return thither in search of it.

After discussing how their vacancies are to be filled (particularly in the artillery) the despatch ends :

We beg your Lordship to understand that we have no wish whatever to see a relaxation of the decision of Her Majesty's Government in the matter of re-enlistment and bounty, though we have taken it upon ourselves to relax it as regards discharge.[2]

This despatch was addressed to Lord Stanley (indeed the Government of India was still addressing him as late as

[1] Discretion was so given in a Secret Despatch from Lord Stanley on 24 Feb. 1859. This channel of communication was a legacy of the Court of Directors of the Company, and implied that the Despatch in question had been seen only by the Secretary of State, the Vice-President, and one other member of the newly constituted Council of India. (Cf. Clause XXVII of the Act of 1858.) Stanley actually wrote : 'But in this, as in all other important matters, I would leave your discretion unfettered, should unforeseen circumstances arise, to take such measures as in your judgment may seem best suited to serve the interests of the State'. (Letters to India, etc., Secret Department I, No. 5, p. 25, in the India Office Library.)

[2] Military Letter 90 (Secret) of 24 June 1859. *P.P.* pp. 229-32. For some reason this despatch did not in fact reach Wood until Aug 11.

16 July), but in fact the Government of Lord Derby had been defeated in the House of Commons on 11 June 1859. Six days later, despite various manœuvres on the part of the Queen, Lord Palmerston again took office as Prime Minister. Sir Charles Wood became the second Secretary of State for India; he had been President of the Board of Control in the Aberdeen government, but — at least according to Lord Granville — was not welcome in this one.[1] He proved, from the point of view of India, to be a dilatory and difficult minister and drove the Viceroy to describe him as 'one of the most unsensitive public men I ever came across — as well as one of the most provocative'.[2] His bold and sprawling handwriting, which must be presumed to have engendered his contemporary nickname of 'The Spider', straggles across many pages of Canning's correspondence.

Wood confirmed the actions of the Government of India. Writing on 26 June about the proposed discharges, he stated:

> I entirely approve of the course which you propose to take, and should approve of anything which you determine upon, which will not be dangerous to the discipline of the army. I should not in the first instance have made any objection to a small bounty, as on transfer from one regiment to another. The cases are not parallel, but like enough to warrant the same course if it was expedient.

(But the previous government had set its face against that course.) And, adverting to the original order (No. 480 of 8 April), he added in a postscript:

> I think the short dry announcement to the troops was not judicious. It would have been better to have wrapped the substance up with complimentary language and conciliatory language.[3]

But, even before Sir Charles Wood had penned these words in London, Lord Canning had published in India on 20 June General Order No. 883. It is an elaborate and cautious

[1] Granville to Canning, 27 June 1859. Granville papers in P.R.O., but printed in Fitzmaurice, *Granville*, I, 345.

[2] Canning to Sir Bartle Frere, 8 Jan. 1861.

[3] Wood to Canning, 26 June 1859.

document, designed as far as possible to make all clear to the ordinary soldier in the ranks. Initially, recruitment is described, and the process of attestation to the Company's service. Each recruit was in fact sworn in before a Justice of the Peace, who was obliged to put to him a number of questions. The eighth asked if he was willing to be attested to serve in the East India Company's infantry (*or* artillery *or* cavalry) for a term of years, plus two more years if required. Later the recruit took an oath which perhaps should be recorded in full, since it is already clear that it had been widely misunderstood.

I, ——, do make oath that I will be faithful and bear true allegiance to Her Majesty, Her heirs and successors, and that I will, as in duty bound, honestly and faithfully defend Her Majesty, Her heirs and successors in person, crown, and dignity, against all enemies, and will obey all orders of Her Majesty, Her heirs and successors, and of the generals and officers set over me.

And also that I will be true to the said Company, and will duly observe and obey all their orders, and the orders of the generals and officers set over me. So help me God.

(The second paragraph was of course omitted *after* the passing of the Act of 1858.) The first part of this oath, expounds the General Order, 'is not a mere oath of allegiance, but an oath both of allegiance and military service'. It is precisely the same oath under which soldiers of the Queen's regular army are enlisted in England. Every man who took this oath bound himself to serve the Crown as well as the Company, but only to do so in India. The order then goes on to quote and explain Clause LVI of the Act of 1858 ; it emphasizes that the only change is in the designation of the troops.

After describing the present discontents, and paying a warm tribute to the services of all arms in the Mutiny, the order proceeds to recount the setting up of the Courts of Inquiry.

The Government [it states] is now satisfied that the objections of the men are founded, in the case of many of them, on an honest conviction, that their rights have been overlooked. This conviction has been strengthened by the expressions of opinion from high authority in England, which naturally have had a powerful effect on the minds of the men. It has been put forward by the men for the most part in a soldier-like and respectful manner, after the first excitement had passed away, consequently upon the orders and warnings of the Commander-in-Chief.

Therefore, the order concludes, every man who desires it will be allowed to take his discharge: thereafter he will be conveyed to England, but under military discipline. Once arrived at home he will not be allowed to enlist into any regiment in India, whether of the Line or of Her Majesty's Indian Forces. There was no change of policy about a bounty or the possibility of re-enlistment in India.[1]

The ink of the signatories can scarcely have been dry on this document, when they had to issue General Order 884 on the self-same day. This tersely exempted the 5th European Regiment at Berhampore from all concessions. The reason for this was a telegram from General Sir John Hearsey, a hero of the Mutiny and now commanding the Presidency division, revealing that 'the greater part of 5th European Regiment have refused to do any duty and are in a state of positive mutiny'. The strength of this unit at this date was about 440 men. It was unlikely to be a strong corps. Like most of the white regiments it was divided into two wings. The officer in command, Major F. Maitland, and most of the officers of one wing, were drawn from the unemployed officers of the 5th Bengal Native Infantry, which had misbehaved at Ambala in May 1857, and been disarmed. The other wing was commanded by Major J. Gordon, sometime of the Judge Advocate General's department: he and the great majority of his fellow officers came from the 6th Native Infantry, which, after extravagant protestations of loyalty, had mutinied sensationally at Allahabad on 6 June 1857. The other ranks were in the main new recruits, fresh from Britain.

[1] General Order No. 883 is printed in full in *P.P.* pp. 238-9 — followed by General Order No. 884.

The men of the 5th were visited by some deserters from up-country, and on 15 June all those who had enlisted for the Company's service refused to turn out on parade, and continued passively disobedient. On the 17th they made a half-hearted attempt to release prisoners from the guard-house, but were warned off by the guard. They then congregated in one barrack and elected their own officers and adjutant.

The Government of India reacted promptly. An experienced officer, Lt.-Col. K. D. Mackenzie, C.B., was detached from staff duties on 21 June and sent down to Berhampore with 500 men and two guns of the Queen's service. His reports make it clear that the officers of the 5th were incompetent and lax, and that its discipline was bad. Punishments imposed had been absurdly light. For example, Private J. Driscoll had been drunk and fighting in barracks on 29 January : for this he was forgiven. On 10 April he was asleep at his post, and was awarded four extra guards ; on 15 May absence from picket without leave drew a sentence of only four extra pickets.

Mackenzie found that 223 men were actively disaffected, and proceeded to address them. Next day all except 39 paraded, and these were promptly arrested : Lance-Serjeant Best seems to have been the ringleader. Mackenzie added bluntly that the manner of the men was totally changed and that he did not think they had fair play from their officers : he had already assembled a Court of Inquiry. On 28 June all the men confined (except for Best) requested to return to duty. The new commanding officer found it difficult to deal with defaulters since in the past they had gone almost unpunished for quite serious offences. By 6 July the Court of Inquiry had completed its task ; in the main the men wanted discharge, but there were a number of complaints about the circumstances of their enlistment in England, of short rations on the ship coming out, and of short pay in India. Mackenzie was finding the work almost too much for him, and with the consent of the government he was invited to promote a senior captain to command the regiment while he took over the station. He was given two names, but one seemed to him 'quite incompetent to hold the command', so it was entrusted to a younger man, Captain A. B. Fenwick. By 9 July Mackenzie himself was laid low with sunstroke, but by this time some order and discipline had been restored among the 5th European Regiment; as will emerge, the improvement was not lasting.[1]

The sequel to the White Mutiny was a long series of applications for discharges. All over India, at the various stations where the former European troops of the Company were posted, a large majority of the men opted for discharge rather than for service with the Queen. In July the Viceroy and the Commander-in-Chief simultaneously conceived the idea that a delay of thirty days between applying for discharge and receiving it might lead some of the men to change their minds; in fact this interval produced little difference.[2] A minor problem cropped up in Bombay, where the army had contrived to enlist new recruits on the *old* Company's attestation form *after* the transfer to the Crown. Lord Canning resolved that these men must be entitled to their discharge.[3] In the fullness of time approval for these various measures arrived from England. The proposals submitted by Lord Canning on 24 June were approved by Sir Charles Wood in October; he had had them under consideration since their tardy arrival on 11 August, but he was not a quick worker.

The total strength of the European regiments, originally enlisted for the Company, was reckoned at rather more than 15,000 men of all ranks. The final count showed that 10,116 of these men secured their discharge and made their way home.

[1] The course of events at Berhampore can be traced in *P.P.* pp. 253-62, 317-21, 402-7, and 505-6.

[2] Clyde to Canning, 7 July 1859. Canning to Stanley (reporting his approach to Clyde), Military Letter 109 of 16 July. *P.P.* p. 381.

[3] *Ibid.* pp. 510-11.

A further 119 volunteered for service on the expedition to China which it had become necessary to mount. It had been supposed that many of those who went home would enlist forthwith in the British Army, and thus draw a fresh bounty. In fact only 2,809 did so — and those mainly in January 1860. The verdict seems to be that the men in India had not only been wearied of life in India, but also of life in the army. The cost of conveying the men home was just over £250,000.[1] Those men who did not take their discharge were later given the benefits of two years' service.

Unfortunately the disease was not totally eradicated. Odd breaches of discipline continued to crop up, particularly in the young regiments raised during the Mutiny. In June 1860 Sir Colin Campbell, Lord Clyde, resigned as Commander-in-Chief. A veteran of the Peninsular wars, he had wrought prodigies in suppressing the earlier stages of the rising ; but when once the crisis was over he became slower and more cautious, and his final relief of Lucknow was marred by military indecision. But he always retained an overwhelming sympathy with the private soldier. He was succeeded by General Sir Hugh Rose (later Lord Strathnairn). Rose had conducted a brilliant campaign in Central India, which has been sadly neglected by military historians, but he had sterner views on discipline than his antecessor. A short survey convinced him that harsher measures were required :

> I have reflected on the present conduct of the European soldiers of the Bengal Army, maturely, and I do not think that I should do my duty were I [to] allow them to continue their present course of combination, and disobedience of the rules of the service as to military complaints.

Accordingly he proposed to the Viceroy the issue of a General Order making clear that this sort of behaviour would no longer be tolerated and that the next case would be treated seriously.[2]

The order was promulgated and once again was received

[1] *Ibid.* pp. 829–33. [2] Rose to Canning, 9 Sept. 1860.

with levity by the troops. Once again the culprits were the 5th European Infantry, now stationed at Dinapore.

Will you show these reports [scribbled Rose] to His Excellency The Viceroy. I think that the two ringleaders should be tried for Mutiny by a General Court Martial, as they rose against the positive order of the Viceroy, read the day before, and, the same day, to the 5th Regiment. The Company of Bengal Artillery behaved admirably.[1]

One of the two culprits was sentenced to death, but with a recommendation for mercy. Sir Hugh Rose went down to Dinapore, and after a personal examination declined to commute the sentence. To the Viceroy he reported :

The state of the 5th is quite hopeless. All the elements of order and discipline are the wrong way in them ; and there is nothing on which to reconstruct or reform. I have sent to you a letter, the proceedings of the Court of the Inquiry, and my remarks on the Court Martial of Pte. Johnson, which will explain everything. Major Maitland who commanded the Regiment last year is rather 'injured Innocence' at being deprived of the command this year, and at not getting a staff appointment. I sent for the 5th Defaulter book, and found that he had contributed, largely, to the present state of things by pardoning and merely reprimanding the most flagrant military offences. Fancy, the 5th, last year, in May 1859 after the order was read stating that they were not to get their Discharges, giving 'three cheers for the Company, and three groans for the Queen'. Nothing will stop the mutinous and insubordinate conduct of the 5th but capital punishment.[2]

Private Johnson was shot at dawn on 12 November. He made a good end, and warned his fellows of the dangers of the canteen. The regimental chaplain gave Sir Hugh Rose an account of the sad scene, but added in a somewhat secular comment that if the execution had taken place earlier, it would have saved a great deal of trouble.[3] The labours of

[1] Rose to Sir E. Campbell, 24 Sept. 1860. Sir Edward Fitzgerald Campbell, 2nd Bart., was Military Secretary to Lord Canning. His mother was the elder daughter of Lord Edward Fitzgerald and the celebrated Pamela, reputed to be a daughter of Philippe 'Égalité', Duke of Orleans.

[2] Rose to Canning, 7 Nov. 1860.

[3] Account enclosed with last-cited letter.

Col. Mackenzie seem to have been spent to small effect. The 5th European Regiment was disbanded on 12 November 1860. On few formations has military glory shed so scant a lustre. Thus, in the squalid execution at Dinapore, ended the obstructive resistance of the white forces of the Company.

Before analysing the lessons of this unhappy episode, it may be convenient to trace the final fortunes of the white regiments. The Royal Commission under General Jonathan Peel had reported on 7 March 1859, but it had not given a decided verdict on the question of a permanent European army in India and had passed the problem on to the government of the day. As long as Lord Derby was in power, and Lord Stanley at the India Office, it seemed likely that there would be an independent force recruited for India and permanently stationed there, though assisted by regiments of the Queen's army doing a limited tour of duty. The weight of informed Indian opinion was strongly in favour of this solution. Canning supported it; so did Ellenborough and Dalhousie, the only living ex-Governors-General. So did Sir John Lawrence, Sir James Outram, Lord Harris (recently Governor of Madras), Sir Henry Somerset (commanding in Bombay), and the Council of India. Against them were Lord Elphinstone (Governor of Bombay), Sir Charles Trevelyan (now Governor of Madras), and, among the generals, Sir Archdale Wilson and Sir Hugh Rose. Lord Clyde had originally been in favour of a European force but changed his mind:

Whatever may now be done, the recollection of this strike or Mutiny will never die out in the local Indian army. It will very possibly affect Her Majesty's army in a minor degree; but in the former, viz., the Indian local army, it will live for ever, and be a precedent to which the minds of men will always revert, when they are dissatisfied with their work or the regulations affecting them.

I am therefore irresistibly led to the conclusion that henceforth it will be dangerous to the state to maintain a European local army.

I believe that, after this most recent experience, it will be unsafe to have any European forces which do not undergo the regular process of relief, and that this consideration should be held to be paramount.[1]

Just before he fell from power Lord Stanley had written that he was 'satisfied that there must be a large, local European army in India' — and that he hoped to have the question settled soon.[2] But the Derby ministry fell in June 1859. Sir Charles Wood was not able to reach any decision till May 1860; it is only fair to him to record that Stanley perhaps underestimated the opposition from the Court and the Horse Guards, and that Wood himself was bombarded with memoranda and arguments from all sides. Canning continued to press for an independent force and described the actors of the White Mutiny with a larger charity than some critics:

A body of raw lads, strange to each other and to their officers, undrilled, unused to obey, landed in India, and immediately marched to the Central Provinces where, with little hope of sharing in the campaign, they were put to severe regimental training, in the hottest part of the year. Such were very many of the young soldiers, who, in 1858 and 1859, forgot their duty.[3]

It was not until April 1861 that the details were finally published in India. Briefly, the artillery and engineer units surviving in the three Presidencies were amalgamated into the Royal Artillery and the Royal Engineers. The three traditional Bengal regiments became the 101st, 104th, and 107th of the Line; those from Bombay and Madras were translated respectively into the 102nd, 105th, and 108th and the 103rd, 106th, and 109th. The 5th Bengal European Regiment had already been disbanded; the 4th and 6th now joined it in limbo but three of the white cavalry regiments raised during the Mutiny now became the 19th, 20th, and

[1] Clyde to Canning, 18 May 1859.

[2] Stanley to Canning, 8 April and 16 May 1859.

[3] Canning to Wood, Military Letter of 5 May 1860. Printed in *P.P.* (1862), XXXVIII, pp. 189–94. This is perhaps the fullest single expression of the Governor-General's views on the Army question.

21st Light Dragoons of the Line.[1] Many minor problems remained to be ironed out in the following months. But the European formation, raised for service in India alone, vanished. All men transferring to these new regiments received a bounty ranging from Rs. 10 to Rs. 50 (approximately £1 to £5).

Writing some time after the event, Lord Stanley described it as 'a most unlucky business', but added, 'I see no reason to believe we could have done better'.[2] In some senses the whole affair was a tragi-comedy of administration. The parliamentary draftsmen might have foreseen the contingency if they had known more about the circumstances. Lord Palmerston might have been more cautious in his utterances; but such was not his habit. When the crisis arose, the hands of the Government in India were tied. They have been severely criticized for not immediately offering a small bounty of £2 or £3.[3] Such a step might (or might not) have averted the discontents; it would certainly have been to flout an Act of Parliament and the declared intentions of the government at home. Canning had indeed proposed some slight concession; Stanley had been firm against him.

More serious was the lack of information in military circles. It was perhaps symptomatic of one root of the trouble that about half the officers of the luckless 5th came from the 6th Bengal Native Infantry, where authority had failed hopelessly and significantly to gauge the temper of the Indian soldiery in June 1857. The long evidence rolls of the Court of Inquiry furnish ample witness that the standard of recruits from Britain was low in health and not high in intellect. Nor was the association of recruits of this calibre with officers of advancing years who had only handled Indian other ranks

[1] The changes were announced in General Order No. 332, of 10 April, which appeared in the *Gazette* of 22 April 1861. See *P.P.* (1861), XLII, 225-38.

[2] Stanley to Canning, 15 Sept. 1859, in a very charming valedictory letter expressing regret at the severance of their official relations.

[3] *E.g.* by L. J. Trotter, *India under Queen Victoria* (1886), II, 126.

likely to be particularly felicitous. But the shortcomings were not confined to the new units : an opinion of Lord Clyde is worth quoting :

In my own mind I must accuse the old soldiers of the Bengal Artillery of having been the prime movers in all this bad business. I can never forget the utter absence of information, the manner in which the officers have been hoodwinked, and how the non-commissioned officers have held aloof, giving no warning, uttering no hint, which might prepare their officers for what was impending.[1]

In the end 10,000 men took their discharge and their transport home cost a quarter of a million pounds. In the event, and despite the anxieties of the government, their departure does not seem to have had much effect on the native forces, who had of course been transferred in an equally arbitrary manner to the service of a Queen of whom they knew even less. A small bounty to the Europeans would have cost only £30,000 or £45,000 ; but if a similar concession had been demanded by their Indian comrades, who would have witnessed its spending, the expense would have risen very sharply. And on the whole the evidence of the Inquiries, and of what occurred, suggests that the men who ultimately took their discharge were more anxious to be out of the army and get home than to gain a small monetary bonus and remain in India.

On the credit side, the Government of India were successful in handling a highly explosive situation without any instance of 'collision' — at no point did white troops of the Queen's army have to employ force against the recalcitrant Company's men. This might easily have taken place, if, for example, Sir John Inglis had been allowed to disarm the disaffected 6th at Allahabad, or even in the first days at Meerut. Except for Private Johnson there was no loss of life. Lord Clyde's Courts of Inquiry were an efficient safety-valve if a laborious one ; and the final volume of men taking discharge probably in the long run facilitated the eventual amalgamation of the

[1] Clyde to Canning, 7 July 1859. Printed in Verner, *Duke of Cambridge*, I, 235–6.

forces. It is true that in the end Lord Canning was compelled to anticipate the consent of the Secretary of State in granting unlimited discharges. But to have done this, or to have offered a bounty, before any crisis had arisen would have been a defiance of constitutional procedure which was certainly not part of his make-up.

One thing is certain. At a time when the whole concept of a specialized European force in India was under question, these unhappy events placed a potent weapon in the hands of those interests which favoured amalgamation. A powerful, professional European army for India remains a tantalizing might-have-been for the historian. Down to the end of the British raj, defence was in the hands of Privates Learoyd, Mulvaney, Ortheris and their ilk.

A BIBLIOGRAPHY OF THE WRITINGS OF SIR KEITH FEILING

1911

'An Essex Manor in the 14th Century', *English Historical Review*, vol. 26, 333.

1913

Toryism, a Political Dialogue, with an introduction by the Rt. Hon. F. E. Smith, K.C., M.P. London (G. Bell & Sons Ltd.)

1924

A History of the Tory Party 1640–1714. Oxford (Clarendon Press). Reprinted, 1959.

1924/1925

Review of F. M. G. Evans: *The Principal Secretary of State: a Survey of the Office from 1558 to 1680*. *History*, N.S. vol. 9, 243–5.

1925

[with F. R. D. Needham] 'The Journals of Edward Warcup 1676–84', *English Historical Review*, vol. 40, 235.

1925/1926

Review of D. Ogg: *Europe in the Seventeenth Century*. *History*, N.S. vol. 10, 262–3.

Review of *Calendar of State Papers, Domestic Series, of the reign of Anne*. Vol. II, 1703–4, ed. R. P. Mahaffy. *History*, N.S. vol. 10, 344.

1927

England under the Tudors and Stuarts. London (Home Univ. Library). Reprinted, 1949.

'A Letter of Clarendon during the Elections of 1661', *English Historical Review*, vol. 42, 407.

1928

'Two Unprinted Letters of Henrietta Stuart, Duchess of Orleans', *English Historical Review*, vol. 43, 394.

1928/1929

Review of A. Aspinall : *Lord Brougham and the Whig Party. History*, N.S. vol. 13, 169.

Review of E. Halévy : *A History of the English People 1815–1830*, vols. 1 and 2. *History*, N.S. vol. 13, 365.

1929

'Clarendon and the Act of Uniformity', *English Historical Review*, vol. 44, 289.

Foreword to R. L. Hill, *Toryism and the People, 1832–1846* (Constable).

1930

British Foreign Policy 1660–1672. London (Macmillan).

Sketches in 19th century Biography. London (Longmans).

'Two Speeches of Charles II', *English Historical Review*, vol. 45, 291.

What is Conservatism? Criterion Miscellany, 14. London.

1932

'Henrietta Stuart, Duchess of Orleans, and the Origins of the Treaty of Dover', *English Historical Review*, vol. 47, 642.

1938

The Second Tory Party 1714–1832. London (Macmillan).

1939

'The British background', in *Essays in Canadian History presented to George Mackinnon Wrong for his eightieth birthday*, ed. Ralph Flenley, Toronto (Macmillan).

1946

The Life of Neville Chamberlain. London (Macmillan).

1947

'A Study of the Modern History of Great Britain 1862–1946'. Inaugural Lecture as Chichele Professor of Modern History. Oxford (Clarendon Press).

1950

A History of England from the Coming of the English to 1918. London (Macmillan).

1954

Warren Hastings. London (Macmillan).

1960

In Christ Church Hall. Essays. London (Macmillan).

PRINTED BY R. & R. CLARK, LTD., EDINBURGH